Social Change in Rural England

by the same author

The Deferential Worker
Property, Paternalism and Power

Social Change in Rural England

Howard Newby
Department of Sociology, University of Essex

Cartoons by Thelwell

The University of Wisconsin Press

Published in the United States of America by
The University of Wisconsin Press
114 North Murray Street, Madison, Wisconsin 53715

Under the title *Green and Pleasant Land?* published outside the USA by
Hutchinson & Co. (Publishers) Ltd
London, England

Manufactured in Great Britain

Library of Congress Cataloging in Publication Data
Newby, Howard.
   Social change in rural England.
   Includes bibliographies and index.
   1. England – Rural conditions.   2. Social change.
3. Country life.   I. Title
HN398.E5N48   1980   301.24'0942   79–20703

ISBN 0–299–08040–4

Contents

6 *Contents*

Tables

Preface

For more than eight years I have been involved in investigating social change in rural England, first through a study of farm workers, then later by way of research into the changing situation of farmers and landowners. In this book I have attempted to draw together some of the results of this research, but, more importantly, I have written it for an audience beyond the narrow bounds of academic sociology, in whose terms my inquiries were originally formulated. This is therefore a book for the general reader and indeed my academic colleagues will be quite familiar with the general drift of my argument from my work which has been published elsewhere. I have therefore dispensed with the conventional academic etiquette of footnotes and citations, although at the end of the book there is a list (related to each chapter) of relevant references and further reading for those who wish to pursue the details of what, perforce in a book of this kind, must often be subsumed under the gloss of assertion and generalization. A more extended consideration of some aspects of English rural life can be found in my earlier books, notably *The Deferential Worker* (Penguin, 1979), a study of Suffolk farm workers, and *Property, Paternalism and Power* (Hutchinson, 1978), which is concerned with farmers and landowners in East Anglia. The latter book was written with Colin Bell, David Rose and Peter Saunders and I am extremely grateful to them for allowing me to use information obtained from our research project and which in a sense 'belongs' to all of us. The reader with a thirst for more detailed information is advised to consult these two volumes.

Some indication of the boundaries of this book is particularly necessary. I have deliberately confined my account to social change in rural England, rather than Great Britain as a whole. Both Wales and Scotland have their own peculiar rural subcultures and social problems which it would be quite mistaken to conflate with those of the English, despite some obvious similarities. They could only be given a proper treatment in a separate publication. I have also under-emphasized those aspects of English rural life which have been given extensive coverage – too much, in my view – in the many accounts already published. Consequently the reader will find little information here about, for example, the Women's Institute, Best Kept Village competitions, village customs, country cooking, country crafts and many other activities which a flourishing literary genre has established, mistakenly, as the hallmark of authentic rural living. Although I have tried to disguise my own East Anglian perspective on English rural society, I fear that in places this is more than apparent. My familiarity with the agriculture of that region is much greater than with the farming pattern elsewhere and although I have tried to do justice to the pastoral areas of England, ultimately I can only write from my own vantage point and hope that my bias is not too pronounced.

There are a number of people whom I would like to thank for their help in producing this book. It owes a great deal to three extremely pleasant years of cooperation with Colin Bell, David Rose and Peter Saunders on a research project, financed by the Social Science Research Council, which investigated large-scale farming in East Anglia. Many of the ideas which we mulled over have found their way into this book. The need for a book of this kind has also emerged over the years from my teaching experience outside the University of Essex. In particular the Danbury and Little Baddow branch of the WEA will, I hope, not be too disappointed in what follows. Janet Newby, Jocelyn Bell, and Ray Pahl read the whole manuscript before publication and offered invaluable comments and reassurances about its content. I have also benefited considerably from the help and advice of Philip Lowe. And Linda Peachey, as always, typed the complete manuscript with her customary efficiency and tolerance.

'*I should decide quickly. It may be gone by tomorrow.*'

1 Rural England: encroachment and disillusion

'The apparent monotony of rural ways', wrote Lionel Johnson, the Victorian poet and critic, 'viewed by spectators used to streets crowded with strange faces, inclines a writer to people his fields and villages with primitive virtues, or with primitive vices, but hardly with both.' To most inhabitants of urban England such an antithesis remains: to them the countryside supports a serene, idyllic existence, enjoyed by blameless Arcadians happy in their communion with Nature; or alternatively it is a backward and isolated world where boredom vies with boorishness, inducing melancholia and a suspicion of incest. It is not easy to move beyond these images, for most of what is written about rural England is influenced in some way by one or the other of these stereotypes. Perhaps this is because our connection with the mainsprings of English rural life is becoming ever more tenuous. Fewer than three people out of every hundred earn their living directly from agriculture, so that even the much larger proportion who live in the countryside are not of it: most are culturally, if not geographically, urban. The changes which they occasionally observe occurring around them are as much a source of mystery and speculation as they are to the city-dwelling daytripper. It is therefore easy for stereotypes to emerge and become consolidated.

During the 1970s it has been the 'primitive virtues' of rural life which have been most widely celebrated. Rural life has become the Good Life with a vengeance. This has been part of a much broader resurgence of Romantic attitudes and values, despite – or perhaps because of – the economic realities of 1970s England. In contrast to the apparently unending gloomy news about conflict-ridden, strike-prone, double-digit inflation, urban, industrial England there has been created a peaceful, if mythical, rural idyll out beyond the high-rise flats and the Chinese take-aways which, if notquite inhabited by merrie rustics, is at least populated by a race which, it is supposed, is attuned to verities more eternal than the floating pound and the balance-of-payments crisis. Somewhere, it is believed, at the far end of the M4 or the A12, there are 'real' country folk living in the midst of 'real' English countryside in – that most elusive of all rustic utopias – 'real communities'. Readers who subscribe to such notions should be warned: this book will leave them either disbelieving or disillusioned. 'Real' English countryside, in this idyllic sense, is located only in the minds of those engaged in the search for it, on a few calendars and chocolate-box lids – and in the wholly misleading paintings of John Constable.

One purpose of this book is to penetrate beyond this image of rural life which most of us, at one time or another, have shared. The intention is not to challenge the sense of enjoyment and pleasure which the beauty of the English countryside continues to evoke, but to investigate the social and economic changes which are less easily observed by the visitor but upon which that much-acclaimed beauty ultimately rests. In recent years 'truly rural' England has appeared to be increasingly threatened by the forces of urban industrialization and therefore to be increasingly precious. Indeed our delight in the English countryside has become even more firmly established because it expresses in a poignant form our widespread disaffection with the reality of living and working in towns and cities. The temptation to escape from the modern urban world into a peaceful countryside has seldom appeared more attractive and more desirable. So rural England has become a retreat for the urban population, a secluded world where we can nurse our emotional and psychological survival by 'getting away from it all' amid the fresh air and green fields of an apparently idyllic rural fastness. It is our collective escape attempt, however fleeting, from an increasingly unbearable rat race.

Our continuing emphasis on the 'primitive virtues' of rural life can, then, be regarded as part of an occasionally despairing search for authenticity in a modern, meretricious world. It reflects not only our dissatisfaction with life in towns and cities, but also our incapacity to have developed an urban culture which would enable us to come to terms with it. Instead there remains the belief that urban life is a superficial and temporary substitute for the real thing: that it is, in a word, unnatural. Only in rural England can we find our roots. In this oblique way the prevailing attitudes towards social change in rural England reveal the gap which exists between the yearning for authenticity in our lives and the circumstances which we believe would guarantee its fulfilment. Even the recent preference for rustic crafts and organic food, for example, reflects an alienation from the mass-produced uniformity of today's manufactured goods. Such evaluations constitute a judgement on the condition of English society in general which must be respected and taken seriously, but when treated as a literal assessment of contemporary rural life they can be positively unhelpful, for in essence they are not a comment on *rural* life at all. This is why it is always necessary to look beyond the conventional wisdom and examine rural life as it is rather than impose upon it a projection of what we would like it to be.

A picturesque world?

Of course, the tendency of the English to idealize rural life is not new. It is connected with a literary tradition of pastoral poetry and art which has an almost uninterrupted history of over two thousand years in Western European culture. It is rooted in the arcadian ideal of the identity between nature and civilization, but its precondition is, above all, a latent conflict between town and country and an associated critique of contemporary institutions and culture. It reached its apotheosis in the Romantic movement in eighteenth- and nineteenth-century England, to which we owe most of our current notions of landscape and which marks the decisive separation of the idea of a picturesque rural world from that of a profitable and functional agriculture. Subsequently, however, the pastoral and the picturesque have been taken as *literal* descriptions of rural life by the ever-increasing urban majority. Even the evolution of the word 'landscape' itself is significant in this context. It was introduced from the Dutch in the sixteenth century to describe a pictorial representation of the countryside. Later the word also came to mean a piece of countryside considered as a visual phenomenon, as if it were a picture. Then, by the mid-eighteenth century, it came simply to mean 'terrain', so that what originated as a pictorial representation came also to mean a literal, visual apprehension. This elision of meaning accompanied the growing importance attached to the contemplation of landscape – 'pleasing prospects' – as a cultivated pastime. Landscapes which conformed to a set of universal compositional rules were eagerly sought out and admired by the *cognoscenti* and to display a correct taste in landscape became a valuable social accomplishment. Thus to become a 'pleasing prospect' the country-side had to conform to formal patterns of composition which hitherto only a landscape painter would have used on his canvas. Where the countryside obdurately refused to conform, it was to be rearranged until it did so by the numerous landscape architects and landscape gardeners who were hired for precisely this purpose.

The eighteenth-century landowner, through the agency of his hired landscapers, invented what we have now come to accept as pictur-esque natural beauty. Nature was rearranged to comply with pictorial design and this contrivance has henceforth provided a standard by which all landscapes have been judged. The eighteenth century thus provided a decisive break between ideas about nature and beauty on the one hand and a functional countryside on the other – a divergence that has remained until the present day. A working countryside had a picturesque order imposed upon it and fields, hedgerows, trees, even complete villages, were cleared in order to provide the eighteenth-century landowner with a 'pleasing prospect' from his window or terrace. Agriculture became an *intrusion* into this Arcadia and so was banished beyond the park boundary or hidden away behind newly planted belts of trees or artificially constructed mounds and knolls, along with all the other necessary paraphernalia of barns and mills and dairies which were an unwanted reminder of the surrounding estate's economic basis. As Edward Hyams has remarked, there are now hundreds of 'views' embracing thousands of acres each, which are exclaimed over, admired, photographed and generally regarded as the epitome of England's natural beauty, but which are the anti-thesis of works of nature. They are works of art, pioneered by artists like William Kent, Lancelot ('Capability') Brown and Humphrey Repton who changed actual landscapes into pictures instead of painting landscapes on canvas. Henceforward unpleasant agricul-tural necessities have not been allowed to interfere with the idyllic vision of the English countryside which they created.

The landscape artists who were responsible for this separation understood these principles very well. Repton, for example, in his manual *Observations on the Theory and Practice of Landscape Gardening*, was adamant that 'the beauty of pleasure-ground, and the profit of a farm, are incompatible . . . I disclaim all idea of making that which is most beautiful also most profitable: a ploughed field and a field of grass are as distinct objects as a flower-garden and a potato-ground.' Similarly, he was convinced that a farm and a park ought never to be brought together in the same view, for, as he put it, 'The difficulty of uniting a park and a farm arises from this material circumstance, that the one is an object of beauty, the other of profit.' William Gilpin, the eighteenth-century observer of English rural life, expressed the same sentiment more succinctly. 'Land which is merely fertile', he wrote, 'is a barren prospect.' Profitability and beauty were therefore opposed to one another and the facts of agriculture were separated from the idea of the picturesque. Although the eighteenth century was also the period of agricultural improvement and enclosure, the practical aspects of agricultural production were banished, literally, out of sight. A new commercial rural economy was being created but all this was separated and hidden away. Selected aspects were then only readmitted as rustic embellishments to enliven an otherwise sterile scene. Very occasionally a complete farm might be allowed, not as a subject of profit, but as an ornament, such as the *ferme ornée* at Leasowes in Shropshire (to which Repton was opposed) but more often individual pieces of agricultural landscape furniture were used either to enliven the view (animals) or to add a vertical dimension to otherwise undulating horizontal contours (like the smoke rising from the chimney of a farmhouse). Even the 'poor, laborious natives of the place' (to use Crabbe's phrase) might be readmitted – though at a distance – as the 'picturesque labouring classes'. In every case, however, the criteria to be applied were aesthetic rather than functional. Those who actually worked on the land became mere figures in a landscape, granted an aesthetic identity but denied any personal or social existence.

Our aesthetic sense has become so completely dominated by this separation of natural beauty from agricultural necessity that today we often fail completely to 'see' what is there. As a consequence, prevailing notions of what constitutes the English countryside obscure rather than clarify, and it now comes as a considerable jolt to be confronted by the aesthetic judgements of those who actually work the countryside. Farmers and farm workers, for example, regard a 'clean' weed-free field as an object of consummate beauty, are impatient with the disfiguring clutter of useless hedgerows and trees and appreciate the hygienic design of modern farm buildings. They maintain a functional aesthetic which is totally at variance with the prevailing urban view. Perhaps it is no coincidence, then, that areas formally designated as being of 'outstanding natural beauty' are predominantly located in countryside of low agricultural value. Nor is this merely a matter of topography; it is because picturesque landscapes have become, almost by definition, agriculturally marginal and our criteria of English landscape beauty are taken from a standard which is destined to be outdated and which obscures current realities. In this sense 'real' English countryside is rarely the typical countryside of the twentieth century. When we uphold areas like the Lake District or Exmoor as English landscape *par excellence* we direct attention away from the underlying social and economic factors on which modern agriculture is based. For the Lake District and Exmoor, whatever their scenic qualities (and few would wish to deny them), are not representative or even indicative of many of the changes that are now occurring in rural England. This may be regretted or welcomed, but it must be *acknowledged* if the problems faced by the inhabitants of these and other rural areas are to be understood. Otherwise we shall be constantly caught unprepared and surprised by the reality of rural life – like the transformation of parts of the Lake District into rustic 'ghost villages' for peripatetic Mancunians or the nibbling away of Exmoor heathland by the ploughs of profit-conscious farmers.

Rural utopia?

If the idealization of rural England represents in part an attempt to escape from the uncongenial reality of modern life, then it is not difficult to understand why, during a period of economic stagnation and decline, rural England should be so widely celebrated. In the last decade we have thus witnessed the extension of rural Romanticism beyond what was originally a rather narrow cultural base. The strongest adherents have always been a particular stratum of the English middle class – professional rather than entrepreneurial, liberal, possessed of a social conscience, faintly intellectual and artistic in their pursuits, sensitive, knowledgeable about natural history but mostly ignorant about agriculture. They were in the vanguard of the great urban commuter exodus to the countryside in the 1950s and 1960s and they have been responsible for a wide range of peculiarly 1970s artefacts which owe much of their popularity to their predilections – from Friends of the Earth to Laura Ashley fabric designs, from the vogue for wholemeal bread to that for corn dollies, from the enthusiasm for 'self-sufficiency' to that for turning 1960s tourist shops into 1970s craft centres. Their impact upon wider public opinion has ensured that in recent years much attention has been lavished on the English rural way of life, but they have also ensured that this attention has been highly selective. In keeping with their Romantic preconceptions they have concentrated on rural aesthetics rather than rural economics and with ideals believed to have been realized in the past rather than with the reality of the present, which, on the whole, is regarded with anxiety. Through their influence retro-spective regret has threatened to replace contemporary observation.

Ironically, however, as our expectations of rural life have been pushed in one direction, towards an understatement of unpleasant economic realities, so the production of food, upon which rural life ultimately rests, has been pushed in the other, opposite direction, away from an arcadian 'way of life' and more towards a rationally calculated business. 'Real' countryside is consequently being reduced to jealously guarded reservations owned by the National Trust and other amenity associations. Elsewhere the harbingers of encroach-ment are in the ascendancy, in the form of tower silos, asbestos barns, uprooted hedgerows, stubble-burning, pesticides, artificial insemina-tion and ovum transplants – let alone battery feeding, zero grazing and direct drilling. Most of us do not know – and increasingly do not want to know – about the factors like these which are shaping modern farming. To do so would merely increase our sense of disillusion. Instead we prefer to allow the countryside to become the repository of nostalgic remembrance for the heyday of an allegedly more atavistic past.

Recent interest in rural affairs thus contains two major themes, each of which interacts with, and runs parallel to, the other: en-croachment and disillusion. Encroachment is the more familiar – and certainly the more public – concern. It stems from the traditional conflict between Romanticism and Rationalism, represented in this instance by a pristine conception of the English countryside on the one hand and the consequences of both urban industrialism and modern farming practice on the other. In this perception the country-side is first being encroached upon from without by an apparently inexorable urban sprawl while it is also being undermined less tangibly from within by urban 'influences' which threaten to absorb the distinctive aspects of rural life into an amorphous, metropolitan culture. These tendencies are manifested by the disappearance of rustic crafts and skills, the decline of 'community' as rural inhabitants become incorporated into an urban way of life, and the development of a more industrial – and hence less quintessentially 'rural' – agriculture. So accompanying the theme of encroachment is that of disillusion, since rural life as it is can never *quite* measure up to rural life as it should be. This is a more privately expressed emotion, since to air it publicly is to admit a kind of defeat. Yet it helps to explain why so many of us, rather than accepting the countryside as we find it, insist upon trying to mould, shape and conform it to our own mental image.

Since the early 1960s these concerns have been channelled into the growing movement to preserve 'the rural environment' – a term which, as we shall see in Chapter 6, encompasses an extremely diverse range of issues. Such diversity is, perhaps, hardly surprising, since in many ways the various conflicts which have taken place in recent years over the preservation of the rural environment offer a series of morality tales about contemporary trends in English rural society. By its very nature environmentalism challenges many of the motives, aspirations and achievement which support the world in which we find ourselves and this invites us to assess a series of conflicting claims which are made upon that world in the light of our own prejudices and values. This is what makes the recent debate about the defence of the rural environment so fascinating and so focal, for although environmentalism offers no generally accepted solution to the predicaments which it has so capably exposed, it has forced interested parties to articulate their most deeply cherished values and to offer a wide range of blueprints on how to construct the ideal rural society. In addition we can observe that, in a paradoxical and even ironical way, disagreement frequently takes place over something which we all favour – in the abstract. Who can possibly approve of 'the destruction of the environment'? The environment is so self-evidently a Good Thing that we all endorse it; we are all environmentalists now. Nevertheless the disagreements continue, partly because of the gap between ideals and actions, partly because of a clash of utopias, but also because it has become possible to cloak purely sectional interests under an altruistic rhetoric of environmentalism. All of this suggests that there is both more and less to environmentalism than many environmentalists believe.

Concern for the environment did not, of course, begin in the 1960s; but that decade saw an exponential growth in environmental awareness. It is easier to chart the history of this development than it is to explain it. Certain landmarks stand out: the publication of Rachel Carson's *Silent Spring* in 1962 and John Barr's *Derelict Britain* in 1969; Sir Frank Fraser Darling's Reith Lectures, *Wilderness and Plenty*, in 1969; *The Ecologist*'s 'Blueprint for Survival' in 1970. In addition there were the set-piece environmental conflicts – Stansted, Cublington, Drumbuie and the countless motorway inquiries – and the environmental disasters such as Aberfan and the *Torrey Canyon*. All of these helped to focus public attention on the environment and to enable the environmental movement to gather momentum. Yet many of the most important pieces of environmental legislation date back much further – to the Clean Air Act of 1956, the Town and Country Planning Act of 1947 and to various public health Acts stretching back to the nineteenth century. Moreover many organizations with impeccable environmental credentials also have a much longer history, such as the Commons, Open Spaces and Footpaths Preservation Society (founded in 1865), the National Trust (1895) and the Council for the Protection of Rural England (1926). Nevertheless environmentalism did not seem to find a uniquely sympathetic response until the 1960s, whereupon it 'took off' and became a public preoccupation. Why did it do so at this particular time?

It is impossible to offer a definitive answer to this question, since systematic investigations of the history of the environmental lobby have only recently begun. However, a few cautious observations can be made. We may note, for example, the coincidence between the rise of environmentalism and the stagnation and decline of the British economy over the same period. Environmentalism is certainly fuelled by (and in turn provokes) a growing anxiety about the future – a loss of confidence in 'progress' and a pervasive uncertainty about where current developments are leading. Environmentalism may therefore be a semi-conscious attempt to make a virtue out of necessity, using as a springboard the Romantic pessimism which, as we have noted, has become such a prevalent feature of English middle-class culture. But to regard environmentalism as part of the 'politics of decline' in contemporary England does not provide a complete explanation, for environmentalism is an international movement which is not limited to societies undergoing economic retrenchment. What also provoked a growing environmental awareness during the 1960s was a new realization of scarcity, fostered by a rapid increase in our knowledge of the complex ecology of the terrestrial environment (the 1960s was also a decade of growth in higher education and scientific research) and by new techniques of economic and demographic forecasting. The finite nature of the earth's resources was repeatedly emphasized, along with the imminent scarcity of food, energy and other raw materials. Such scarcity also extended to more intangible factors, such as natural beauty, open space and pleasing landscapes, which together were somewhat hazily referred to as 'amenity'. The widespread recognition that something had to be done about these scarcities was not so much part of a 'politics of decline' as of a 'politics of affluence', but in rural England the two combined to lend a peculiar piquancy to the conflicts that were to ensue.

This was partly because the 1960s were also the decade in which the centuries-old pattern of rural-urban migration became reversed for the first time. Increasing affluence and widespread car ownership allowed a growing number of urban dwellers to realize their dream of a house in the country. In some respects this was merely an extension of a much older phenomenon, for ever since the Industrial Revolution those who could afford it have sought to escape from the squalor of the urban industrial world, fearful of the breakdown of social order and lamenting the impersonal and superficial character of the relationships to be found there. By the 1960s the ability to leave behind this unpalatable urban existence had simply passed a little further down the social scale, so that the urban middle class could now aspire to a share of rural England rather more modest than their nineteenth-century *nouveaux riches* predecessors. The result is that today the bulk of the population of most of our rural villages are able to live in the countryside and work in nearby towns and cities. This change has been accommodated by the exodus of many of the former rural working population who, displaced by technological change and attracted by an alternative prospect of 'bright lights' and 'streets paved with gold', have sought to escape from *their* uncongenial existence by migrating in the opposite direction. It is not surprising, however, that the contemporary rural population is also a more environmentally aware population, not only because the newcomers are more articulate and better educated than many of their predecessors, but also because their expectations of rural England are frequently difficult to match with the reality. Many of them believe that modern farming practice has transformed the 'traditional' rural landscape for the worse and has become a source of pollution along with cities and factories. Some of the dubious ecological consequences of modern agriculture have therefore attracted some sharp criticism.

The newcomers have also encountered similar difficulties when confronted with the reality of village life – which may turn out to be something less than a touchstone of authenticity. All too often English villages are projected as ideal communities, where life is more wholesome, more reassuring and more indefinably valid than in, say, a suburban housing estate. Again there is a strong and powerful tradition of cultural Romanticism to support such a view. While cities are believed to have suffered from apparently chaotic social dislocation and disorganization, village life, in contrast, has appeared settled, to have lent the weight of continuity to the daily social round and to be characterized by social harmony and meaningful social intimacy. Ideas about the English countryside as a *visual* phenomenon and ideas about the English countryside as a *social* phenomenon have therefore merged together. A locality which looks right must also, it is assumed, support a desirable way of life. In this way rural aesthetics and ideas about rural society have become closely intertwined. Little wonder, then, that there has been a movement to preserve this apparently fragile social *and* visual creation from the ever-present threat of alien encroachment and eventual destruction – and little wonder, also, that there is so much contemporary concern for the vitality of village life.

In the light of these considerations it becomes easy to understand how conventional portrayals of the English village remain almost unashamedly bucolic, influenced in particular by the evocation of familiar sights and sounds – thatched cottages, village greens, lush meadows, the songs of birds, the ringing of church bells. Even work on the land is commonly supposed to be more morally beneficial, more metaphysically rewarding and hence less tainted by 'mere' monetary considerations than any other form of employment. Yet a failure to comprehend the fact that, historically, the English village was organized around a distinctive agricultural economy is to miss the whole point of its existence. And if we place work at the centre of village life a very different history from that depicted in this convention emerges: poverty, exploitation, and the constraints that stem from dependence on the locally powerful. Behind the façade of a happy 'organic community' this darker image always lurks, but to bring it to the forefront would threaten the idyllic conception of rural life. The rural idyll, as an escape from urban squalor, cannot be allowed to be squalid itself. The homeward ploughman may be poor, but his is, in Gray's words, a 'happy poverty'. Indeed, the 'organic community' often turns out on closer inspection to be either illusory or not particularly rural. The agricultural population has no monopoly on authentic living, expounds no homespun atavistic philosophy of life and is quite oblivious to the pastoral image imposed upon it. It is too busy earning a living to be diverted by such considerations. Only if we understand that the village is not organized around a disembodied 'spirit of community' but around matters like these can the social changes that are occurring in villages across the length and breadth of England be completely appreciated.

The prevailing view of rural life is now so firmly rooted, however, that in order fully to comprehend what is taking place in rural England we must see it in an unconventional manner. The countryside is not just a charming view but a working environment. It is not an 'unspoilt' natural landscape, but a manmade artifice that manifests the ultimately inescapable economic realities that underpin it; not a recreation area with unlimited free access, but a factory yard for the production of food; not a static, immemorial Arcadia but a constantly changing, rationalizing, commercial world. We must, then, train ourselves to see not only the aesthetic prerequisites of a picturesque landscape but its functional qualities, to be aware that small fields and ubiquitous hedgerows are no longer economically viable or that a pretty village is no more than a construction of bricks and mortar (or thatch and timber) which in itself bestows no particular meaning on the lives of its inhabitants. Furthermore, we must realize that we can only come to terms with the changes which are currently occurring in English rural society if we first analyse the economic pressures to which it is subject. Consequently we must begin our analysis of social change in rural England by examining the ownership and control of the primary economic resource to be found there: land.

'The wine should be chilled, Benson. Stand it by the door for a few minutes.'

2 Broad acres

Considering the intrinsic importance of land, not least to agriculture, it is surprising how little information is available about it. What it is used for, who owns it, how much it is worth – these and other questions are surrounded by mystery, confusion and hence controversy. For example, it remains a remarkable fact that there have only been two authoritative and comprehensive surveys of the ownership of land in English history – in 1086 and in 1873. For a contemporary assessment we are reduced to reading the entrails of official statistics, usually collected for other purposes entirely and which often succeed, unwittingly or otherwise, in safeguarding our lack of enlightenment. Such considerations are a reminder that the 'land question', as it was known in nineteenth-century politics, remains a live political issue, but it also reflects the fact that even in a predominantly urban and industrial society like ours land remains a source of wealth, prestige and not a little power and that there are, therefore, important vested interests wishing to maintain us in our state of ignorance. Nowhere is this more apparent than at the traditional aristocratic apex of English society. Politically on the defensive for more than a century and a half the landed estate owner has sought to obscure the benefits that derive from extensive landholding, having long recognized the dangers of ostentation and lucidity and the advantages of discretion and ambiguity.

Although the situation regarding the ownership of land remains unclear, at least the methods of recording the use to which it is put have recently become more accurate, thanks mainly to the demands of planners. However, even this information is only approximate since it must be inferred from the Agricultural Census and other data collected from planning authorities and must, as always, be subject to the vagaries of interpretation. The most recent estimates available (for 1971) suggest that 76·9 per cent of the total land surface of England and Wales is devoted to agriculture with a further 7·5 per cent used for forestry. Although it supports a highly urbanized and densely populated society only 11 per cent of land in England and Wales is in urban use. These figures help to keep in perspective the frequently expressed view that our countryside is rapidly disappearing under a sea of cement. Although it is true that the proportion of land in urban use has doubled since the beginning of this century, the absolute level of urban development continues to be small and the rate of transfer has actually declined since before the war. We should also be careful to avoid the arcadian assumption that what is a loss for agriculture is automatically an irretrievable loss for our national heritage. Any assessment requires a careful calculation of the opportunity costs of development – agricultural, industrial, environmental and social. So far increases in agricultural productivity have ensured that the amount of food produced has easily outpaced the decline in the acreage on which it has been grown, although how long this can continue is a matter of some debate.

Steering a course between alarmism and complacency over the pressure of use on our land resources is not easy. In 1976, for example, the Centre for Agricultural Strategy at Reading University issued a report, *Land for Agriculture*, which suggested that the loss of land from agriculture was approximately 76000 acres each year. By projecting trends in population growth, population densities and agricultural productivity it forecast an imminent decline in agricultural production unless immediate steps were taken to reduce this annual rate of attrition. Predictions like this play upon the conventional wisdom of rampant urban encroachment, referred to in the previous chapter; they also seem eminently plausible in the light of the fact that England is part of a small and densely populated island and that land is in more or less fixed supply; but these claims repay rather closer examination. First of all, of the 76000 acres lost annually to non-agricultural uses, a half goes not to urban development but to forestry. It seems less than pedantic to insist that forestry is no more than a highly specialized and somewhat distinctive type of agriculture; moreover it overwhelmingly takes place on land which is unsuitable for other productive purposes and it makes contributions to rural employment and our balance of payments no less than other kinds of agricultural production. So we are left with less than 40000 acres being transferred annually into non-agricultural uses, which covers a variety of functions – industrial, commercial, residential, and 20 per cent remaining as urban open space. This, it should be noted, is one-third *less* than the rate of transfer in the 1930s. The main impetus for change of use today is not so much population growth (in recent years this has become a decline) but the quite reasonable desire on the part of the majority of the population for more space. Customarily part of this space has been a garden and in England it has been the habit of many householders to put their gardens to productive use by growing vegetables in them. In the mid-1960s (i.e. before the recent rise in food prices and the consequent increase in home-grown vegetables) it was calculated that, taking into account the fact that gardens make no demands on transport or distributive services, there was little if any loss of national resources resulting from the loss of agricultural land to urban use. Indeed it was argued by R. H. Best and J. T. Ward in *The Garden Controversy* that the level of production of the average garden compared well with even the best farmland. So claims for an urban-inspired armageddon may be exaggerated; if agricultural production declines in this country it is more likely to be as a result of falling yields than of urban encroachment.

The desire to live in a house with a garden rather than a high-rise flat or a back-to-back terrace is an aspiration with which even the most ardent rural conservationist would sympathize. Indeed such an aspiration is frequently regarded with pride as a civilizing English characteristic. Yet a strict policy of urban containment would, other things being equal, lead to its denial. This is not because the space is not physically available – there is quite a lot of urban derelict land which could be used – but because it flies in the face of current land-market economics. It remains cheaper to build new residential development on green-field urban-fringe estates than in reconstituted inner-city areas where site values are higher. This merely underlines the fact that land is allocated not according to a rationality of use but according to the rationality of the market, a mechanism that remains largely undisturbed despite three decades of planning legislation and a (moribund) Community Land Act. Land, in other words, not only possesses a use-value: it is *capital*. Thus any attempt to control the allocation of land must first involve control over the market for land. And this, in a predominantly market economy, would be to strike at some of the most fundamental rights concerning the ownership of property.

In England today land is a form of capital but it possesses a number of special qualities which differentiate it from other types of investment. It is (relatively) fixed in supply and it cannot be transferred from one physical location to another. Land cannot, therefore, be manufactured or moved according to the dictates of market conditions. Moreover, even though the quality of land may be improved quite quickly – by the addition of fertilizers, for example – there are limits to how much can be achieved within the constraints of topography and climate. This ensures that land cannot always change its character according to the dictates of the market, nor can it be mobile so that landowners may take the fullest advantage of market opportunities. For these and other reasons, short-term yield from landownership may often be low, but land remains a highly secure long-term investment subject to steady capital growth, whose value – like that of gold, old masters, antiques or rare stamps – may increase while producing no income at all. However, unlike these items land cannot easily be stolen or destroyed. As a safe, long-term investment land has frequently attracted the attention of both personal and institutional owners who have little or no interest in how it is used. Recent high rates of inflation in the British economy have revived this interest, bringing non-agricultural considerations to bear on the market for agricultural land.

The constraints which surround the utilization of land may make the landowner appear insensitive to short-term market factors. But this should not be confused with a complete indifference to the commercial world. The long-term nature of the benefits to be derived from landownership have, as we shall see, been instrumental in shaping the characteristic outlook of the English landowner. Moreover the structure of landownership remains instrumental in determining the organization of agriculture and hence of rural society. In a subsistence or near-subsistence economy this would be a truism, since access to and control over land is such a crucial resource that it is both a cause of and closely follows the structure of power in such societies. Even in an advanced industrial society like England, however, the obvious importance of land as a factor of production in agriculture has ensured that the structure of landholding has remained a decisive factor in the shaping of rural society. Thus property rather than occupation is often the most salient principle of inequality in rural areas: the population can be ranked (and ranks itself) by the size of the holding it owns or farms as much as according to urban-oriented rankings based upon the division of labour. Land is often insignificant as a factor of production in most urban manufacturing employment, but its importance in agriculture means that how land is owned and controlled is fundamental to our understanding of rural society.

Landownership

Such comments would have seemed unremarkable to the nineteenth-century observer of English agriculture. It was taken for granted that landownership not only represented a major source of wealth but was also virtually a *sine qua non* of political power and social prestige. The landowner therefore possessed not only an economic function but a set of political and social responsibilities. These were described by Sir James Caird, the nineteenth-century agriculturalist, as follows:

The landowners are the capitalists to whom the land belongs. Their property comprises the soil and all that is beneath it, and the buildings and other permanent works upon it. . . . In nearly all permanent improvements arising from the progress of agriculture the landowner is also expected to share the cost. And he is necessarily concerned in the general prosperity and good management of his estate, and in the welfare of those who live upon it, with which his own is so closely involved. He takes a lead in the business of his parish and from his class the magistrates who administer the criminal affairs of the country, and superintend its roads, its public buildings and charitable institutions are selected. Nor do his duties end here, for the landowner, from his position, is expected to be the head of all objects of public utility, to subscribe to, and, if so inclined, to ride with the hounds, showing at once an example to the farmers and tradesmen, and meeting them on terms of neighbourly friendship and acquaintance. The same example is carried out in his intercourse with the clergy and school-master, and his influence, where wisely exercised, is felt in the church, the farm and the cottage.

This class in the United Kingdom comprises a body of about 180 000, who possess among them the whole of the agricultural land from ten acres upwards. . . . There is no other body of men who administer so large a capital on their own account, and whose influence is so widely extended and universally present.

Caird was writing in 1878 and his figures are taken from the Return of Owners of Land which had been compiled five years previously, and which is more commonly known as the New Domesday Survey. This survey of landownership – unique in modern times – had a curious history. It had been promoted by Lord Derby who was anxious to rebuff the allegation of Liberal reformists that Britain was in the hands of an élite of only 30000 landowners. Unfortunately for Lord Derby the New Domesday Survey showed that the 'notorious 30000' was an embarrassing understatement of the degree of concentration of landownership. Instead less than 7000 men were revealed to own more than four-fifths of the land. Reformist efforts were redoubled, and no doubt Lord Derby learned the lesson of his momentary indiscretion. However, we are left with an invaluable document which can act as a kind of historical benchmark against which we can assess the changes in the distribution of landownership that have occurred until the present day.

The New Domesday Survey provides a glimpse of rural Britain at a time when mid-Victorian high-farming was at the end of its most 'golden era' of unbroken prosperity, when the classic tripartite rural class system of landowner, tenant farmer and landless labourer appeared as the 'natural order' of rural society and before the half-century or more of agricultural depression, broken only by the First World War, had set in. Despite the fact that the majority of the population had ceased to earn its living from agriculture by 1851, landownership still retained its political influence: landowners remained a majority of the House of Commons until 1885 and of the Cabinet until 1906. They were led by the largest estate-owners, the landed aristocracy, who controlled the agricultural interest in British politics and who had also once ensured that British politics consisted largely of the pursuit of the agricultural interest by their parliamentary representatives. In spite of the inevitable challenge to this power which the rise of an urban, industrial society presented, England, in the words of the historian F. M. L. Thompson, 'remained down to 1914, or more precisely until 1922, not merely an aristocratic country, but a country of a landed aristocracy'.

The aristocracy was not necessarily the nobility. Bateman, who compiled the New Domesday Survey, defined an aristocrat as the owner of an estate of over 10000 acres (producing an income of approximately £10000 per year or more). Of the 363 aristocrats according to this definition 117 were not titled and, conversely, there were many peers (over 350) who were the owners of estates insufficiently large to enable them to qualify for the aristocracy. Some of these estates were very large indeed – forty-four were over 100 000 acres. They were, of course, much more than merely a collection of farms and cottages. A large estate was a functioning centre of political and social influence across the territory which it comprised, often extending into the surrounding area and sometimes across a whole county. This involved a complex set of proprietorial rights, not only over the agriculture of the estate, but over its minerals, its game, its Members of Parliament, its clergy – in short over the entire locality and its inhabitants. At its centre lay the 'big house' with its imposing architectural presence, its parkland and gardens and its extensive retinue of servants and other domestic workers. These great estates occupied nearly one-quarter of the land surface of England, but they were unevenly distributed, with a tendency to be situated in the North and the West. Rutland emerged from the New Domesday Survey as the most aristocratic county with 53 per cent of its surface area covered by great estates, closely followed by Northumberland (50 per cent) and then Nottinghamshire (38 per cent), Dorset, Wiltshire (each 36 per cent) and Cheshire (35 per cent). The least aristocratic counties on this reckoning were Middlesex (4 per cent), Essex (9 per cent) and Surrey (10 per cent). However, there was an aristocratic presence in all of the English counties, so that England, culturally and geographically, represented a patchwork of the great country houses which dominated society in the shires.

Below the aristocracy in the hierarchy of landownership came the gentry, over 3000 strong, and defined by Bateman as owners of estates between 1000 and 10000 acres. If the aristocracy controlled the agricultural interest, then it was the gentry who ran it. They formed a more socially fluid class, but one which was also more provincial and more conservative. Less endogamous than their aristocratic superiors, they ensured that landownership was never beyond the aspirations of those whose wealth was founded elsewhere, given the occasional judicious marriage and the odd shrewd purchase. Bateman divided the gentry into two groups: the greater gentry, with estates of 3000 to 10000 acres, and the squirearchy, who occupied estates of 1000 to 3000 acres. Together they accounted for 30 per cent of the area of England, but in a widely diffused manner which tended not to cramp the territorial imperatives of the aristocracy. The strength of the gentry lay in Eastern England and in the West in Shropshire, Herefordshire and Oxfordshire. Although the balance between gentry and aristocratic forces is something which has on several occasions influenced the course of English history, by the nineteenth century the gentry were regarded as the pillars of county – as opposed to metropolitan – society. However, they were a very varied group, ranging from village squires to landowners verging on aristocratic grandees. In some counties their influence could be decisive.

Below the gentry, the New Domesday Survey listed the yeomen with estates of 100 to 1000 acres, long regarded as the epitome of sturdy independence and practical common sense. They, and the small proprietors who lay below them, fitted uneasily into the hierarchy of landed society. Some were *arriviste* manufacturers and many had little personal interest in the land which they owned for they were full-time tradesmen who also acted as petty rural landlords. Together the yeomen and the small proprietors accounted for 39 per cent of the area of England, but this was distributed among more than 170 000 of them, located in the interstices of the larger holdings. They were of local importance, however, in the Home Counties, in Cumberland and Westmorland, in Worcestershire and in the Fens. For many the use of the term 'estate' might give a misleading impression of opulence – but their day was to come again.

Although it was not necessary for a landowner to be a nobleman, it was (until the very end of the nineteenth century) considered essential for a nobleman to be a landowner. The very fact that newly garnered wealth required a landed estate before it could become socially acceptable was a great source of strength to the landowning class, especially the aristocracy. As long as the ownership of land and a country house were acknowledged as the minimum essential accoutrements of legitimate gentlemanly status then the aristocracy remained in the powerful position of determining the entrance qualifications to their coterie. The admission fee of 1000 acres provided an inconvenient, but not entirely discouraging, economic filter. National heroes who had the misfortune to be born commoners had, necessarily, to be fitted out with an appropriately armigeral estate upon their elevation to the peerage by a grateful monarch (as in the case of Nelson, Wellington and Disraeli), while those blighted by wealth accumulated through trade or manufacture similarly searched for a country seat to set the seal upon their ennoblement, as when, for example, the owner of Crossley's Carpets of Halifax became the infinitely less prosaic Lord Somerleyton. Land, then, possessed a *symbolic* importance that stretched far beyond its economic or political significance, a factor which has always muted the attacks on the privileges which landownership confers. It also enabled a social and political order based upon aristocratic values and landed interests to remain dominant long after the purely economic significance of agriculture had declined.

Considerations such as these lay at the heart of the long political controversy over landownership which continued throughout the nineteenth century. This began as an attack upon political privilege – 'old corruption' – and ended as a demand for wholesale dispossession and redistribution – 'three acres and a cow'. It forced landowners into a defensive political stance as successive inroads were cut into their traditional power with each Reform Act from 1832 onwards; nor did parliamentary reform represent the only attack, for a wide range of legislation from the Poor Law Amendment Act of 1834 to local government reform in 1888 and 1894 attempted to pare away their omnipotence. This legislative process culminated in Lloyd George's famous 1908 Budget with its Increment Value Duty and Undeveloped Lady Duty which aimed at breaking up once and for all the 'land monopoly'. It is plausible to regard Lloyd George's measures as having been decisive. They produced a trickle of land sales between 1910 and 1914 which became a deluge once the First World War was completed. In four years between 1918 and 1922 England, in the words of a famous *Times* leader of the day, 'changed hands'. One-quarter of the area of England was bought and sold in this hectic period of transaction, a disposal of land which was unprecedented since the Dissolution of the Monasteries in the sixteenth century. Many great estates were broken up and this aristocratic diaspora from the land left a new class of owner-occupying farmers behind. A decisive shift in the class structure of rural society had thus occurred. Yet a change of this apparent magnitude was barely comprehended at the time beyond the columns of the farming press and the *Estates Gazette*. If the aristocracy had abdicated it had done so with scarcely a whimper and almost entirely unnoticed. This may be a mark of the indifference with which landowners were regarded in an urban, industrial society, but it hardly suggests that a triumph for democracy was consciously engineered and celebrated. It also suggests that all may not have been what it seemed.

If the breaking up of the great estates occurred in a mood of private sorrow rather than public anger, then perhaps it was because the great estates were no longer worth fighting for. Some landowners, it is true, hoped to re-create their past overseas and literally sought their place in the sun in colonies like Kenya and Rhodesia. But most of those who abdicated did so with as much dignity as they could muster, without a fight and with scarcely a backward glance. In the wake of the First World War there were no doubt many landowners who were physically and emotionally exhausted. The carnage in Flanders had robbed them of their heirs and reduced the attractions of holding on. In some cases, no doubt, the sale acted as an emotional purgative and seemed an apt conclusion to what was widely regarded as the end of an era. The war had also brought more mundane, but scarcely less pressing, changes in life-style: higher income tax and death duties (the latter particularly important when two generations could be killed off in quick succession in France); a shortage of domestic labour that was to prove chronic; rationing; and increasing state intervention in agriculture. In their various ways all these factors undermined the style of life to which the landowner was traditionally accustomed and in turn weakened his will to continue. However, they account more for the timing of the departure than its inevitability. Both the new fiscal penalties on landownership and the holocaust of the First World War provided the appropriate moment and may even have precipitated a headlong rush rather than an ordered withdrawal, but the underlying causes lay much earlier in the nineteenth century and were of a long-term economic nature.

The most obvious candidate to account for the decline of the great estates is the long agricultural depression which began in 1873 and lasted uninterrupted, especially in the arable counties in the South and East, until 1914, with only a slight respite after 1896. The depression began amid a series of disastrous harvests brought about by bad weather and this masked the underlying cause – the importation of cheap grain and meat from Argentina, the North American prairies, Australia and New Zealand. Consequently British agriculture was slow to adapt to the new circumstances of international trade and many farmers and landowners remained mesmerized by the social *cachet* of growing wheat, even after its price had halved. Estates based upon livestock or dairy farming escaped the full impact of depression, but in the major corn-growing counties, and particularly in East Anglia, the effects were catastrophic. Mounting rent arrears, bankrupt and ruined tenants, falling rent rolls and neglected farm buildings and equipment were the order of the day. All landowners, whatever their own circumstances, were eventually to suffer some of the consequences of this.

For example, depression affected the price of land, which fell steeply after 1878, even in those areas relatively unaffected by falling rents. The general despondency over the future of agriculture had spread like a miasma across the countryside. The falling value of his main item of capital hindered the capacity of the landowner to exercise his primary economic function – the provision of fixed capital for his tenants. Yet it was this function which was ultimately the source of the landowner's social and political influence in rural society. In the arable counties matters were even worse: landlords were forced to abdicate from their customary role of buffer against economic distress. They neglected their traditional economic duties towards their tenants and looked on helplessly as the latter proceeded to abandon their tenancies, force down rents or go bankrupt. And as the landowner proved incapable of fulfilling his customary role, so his hitherto dutiful tenants began to abandon him. Tenant farmers mobilized themselves in the final quarter of the nineteenth century and succeeded in asserting 'tenant right' through a number of legislative measures, most notably the Agricultural Holdings Acts, which admitted them for the first time to a 'proprietary interest' in the running of agricultural affairs. This was a prelude to the land sales following the First World War. The 'natural order' of the countryside had been irretrievably disrupted.

Although the agricultural depression decisively altered the character of landownership from that of attractive investment to economic encumbrance, it is possible to trace the decline of the landed estate back further still. We must always be aware of the fact that land was pre-eminently capital and that the fortunes of landownership were therefore tied to the laws of capitalist development. According to these laws (to be specific, Engel's Law) the long-term prospects of investment in land were doomed once the British economy underwent industrialization. For as Britain industrialized so a growing proportion of gross national income was expended not on food (because our consumption of this is limited) but on manufactured goods and, much later, on services. Throughout the nineteenth century therefore there was a persistent tendency for returns to agriculture to decline as a proportion of returns to the economy as a whole and for one pound invested in the more buoyant manufacturing sector to earn more than that same pound invested in agricultural land. Land-owners were facing a problem of capital accumulation.

In this way [writes F. M. L. Thompson] the landowners bore a good part of the cost of the ascendancy of commerce and industry and the secondary position to which agriculture was being relegated. Behind the façade of the 'Golden Age of English Agriculture' which is said to have lasted for the twenty years after the outbreak of the Crimean War, a distinct weakening in the economic position of agricultural landowners can be detected. . . . They were accepting financial sacrifices, in the sense that much greater returns could have been secured by putting their money elsewhere, and were therefore in effect 'paying ransom' long before Chamberlain suggested that they must do so.

Thus events between 1873 and 1918 accelerated this decline, but they did not cause it. The underlying cause was always the declining rate of return. Of course, such strictures did not apply to all land-owners since by no means all of them gained all their income from agriculture. Families like the Norfolks, the Derbys and the Bedfords, who owned the land on which the cities of Sheffield, Liverpool and London expanded and developed, became enormously wealthy rentier capitalists; others participated fully in the new industrial age by tak-ing advantage of their mineral wealth, like the coal-owning Duke of Northumberland. Those landowners who had the geographical for-tune to take advantage of such opportunities found them extremely lucrative, but increasingly some such non-agricultural source of in-come was required in order to ensure the continued upkeep of their country residences and their associated lordly life-styles. Others, whose land was not so well-placed, were being forced to economize on personal expenditure long before the depression set in. There is some evidence to show that by the turn of the century a number of such estate-owners wished to sell at least a proportion of their hold-ings if only someone could be prevailed upon to buy, but in the depressed conditions there were few takers. Lloyd George's fiscal proposals, when they came, were simply the final straw. When the brief, euphoric, but deceiving post-war agricultural boom between

1918 and 1922 tempted buyers on to the market in large numbers for the first time in over forty years land was unloaded, not so much with regret, but with relief. In many ways the more pertinent question to ask is not why such an apparent social and economic revolution proceeded so peacefully so much as why landowners had taken so long to act in accordance with the precepts of economic rationality.

Those who purchased the land were mostly tenants, who were virtually forced to buy if they wished to continue farming. Before the First World War only 10 per cent of farmland in England and Wales had been owner-occupied, but by 1927 this had increased to 36 per cent. Nearly two-thirds of agricultural land therefore remained tenanted, so that the landlord–tenant system, despite the upheavals of the immediate post-war years, remained predominant. However, this should not be allowed to obscure the importance of the changes which had occurred: landowning was to become merged with farming in a combined economic activity which had hitherto remained divided. By 1973 the proportion of land under owner-occupation had risen to 61 per cent and this, for technical reasons concerned with the Agricultural Census and the desire of owner-occupiers to avoid undue taxation, is almost certainly an underestimate. The actual figure is probably nearer 75 per cent. Such, then, is the demise of the old tripartite rural class structure. Instead we now find that those engaged in farming consist mostly of owner-occupying farmers on the one hand and hired agricultural workers on the other. The yeoman farmer, who at times appeared on the verge of extinction in the nineteenth century, has made a startling comeback.

Or has he? It is necessary to introduce this note of doubt, for while the Ministry of Agriculture provides us with official statistics on *how* land is held we do not know (and neither do they) *who* owns it. We can only make a few hazardous inferences. The continuation of the agricultural depression throughout the 1930s and wartime state control ensured that the advance of owner-occupation has taken place most strongly only since 1945. By 1950, for example, the proportion of land owner-occupied had risen by only 2 per cent since 1927 – to 30 per cent. So most of the increase in owner-occupation has occurred during the 1950s and 1960s and our assessment of the balance between continuity and change in agricultural landowning depends upon our judgement of who these owner-farmers are. Undoubtedly agricultural estates have continued to be broken up, but we might also surmise that the rate of this dissolution has slowed down considerably. To begin with the state has intervened – decisively – to save both farmers and landowners from the worst ravages of Engel's Law. Investment in land may still offer a poorer yield than investment elsewhere, but agricultural support policies have halted the slide and there are compensating advantages in increasing capital gains. Moreover, until the introduction of Capital Transfer Tax in 1974 estate duty was a notoriously 'voluntary tax', payable only after an untimely accident, the employment of an incompetent accountant, or both. We should be careful not to confuse the doubtless genuine and certainly widely publicized difficulties which estate-owners have experienced in maintaining the upkeep of their stately homes with the viability of their surrounding agricultural land.

Indeed there are good reasons to believe that since the war estates have become not so much fragmented as consolidated in the hands of their owners. Income from rents is not subject to earned income relief, so there are considerable fiscal penalties involved in letting land as opposed to farming it. Furthermore between 1947 and 1958, and again since 1976, legislation concerning the hereditability of tenancies has granted virtually complete security to tenants, leaving landowners with a further disincentive to let. Both of these factors have encouraged landowners to farm more land themselves, irrespective of the other advantages to be gained such as those from economies of scale and a more rationalized structure of landholding. Consequently landowners have taken more land 'in hand' and this probably accounts for much of the increase in owner-occupation – though how much it is impossible to say. It seems likely, however, that England may not have changed hands to the extent that is sometimes imagined. This supposition is reinforced by the continuing high degree of concentration of landownership – in 1973 58·8 per cent of the land in England and Wales was owned by only 0·4 per cent of the population. Tenacity as much as decline has characterized the situation of the estate-owner through the vicissitudes of the last hundred years. Many have as a consequence remained by adapting to changing circumstances. Just as the farmer has become a land-owner, so the landowner, in order to survive, has become a farmer.

It might be misleading, then, to emphasize the disappearance of the landed estate. Many have indeed been broken up and some of the former stately homes of England are now put to more mundane uses as convalescent homes, trade union headquarters, recreation centres and suchlike. Nor can the landowner expect any longer to conduct a life of leisured gentility surrounded by a vast army of servants. However, many of the estates remain, albeit usually reduced in size with the big house no longer hidden from the gaze of a prurient public willing to pay the cost of admission. The landed aristocracy in particular has survived with remarkably few casualties. The estates surrounding Alnwick Castle, Arundel Castle, Badminton, Belvoir Castle, Berry Pomeroy, Blenheim Palace, Chatsworth, Euston Hall, Goodwood, Longleat, Raby Castle, Wilton and many more are still in the hands of the descendants of their nineteenth-century owners and a non-random, but reasonably representative, sample is shown in Table 1. The decline has been most marked, not among the aristocracy, but among the gentry. More conservative, less adaptable and with fewer resources to fall back upon, only about one-third of their estates survive from a century ago. The gentry were always a more mobile group, both socially and geographically, but the last hundred years, unlike those which preceded them, have seen no rise of a new gentry – only new yeomen.

The twentieth century has, however, witnessed the rise of institutional landownership. Indeed the top ten landowners in Britain now include only one private individual (the Duke of Buccleuch with an estimated 258 000 acres), the remainder being a variety of public or quasi-public institutions. Their holdings have nearly doubled in the last hundred years and they now account for about 8 per cent of farmland in Britain and 15 per cent of the total area. Details of a recent estimate of the distribution of institutional landownership are shown in Table 2. These figures require some qualification, however. Some of the monarchical land might more appropriately be regarded as privately owned, such as the Balmoral and Sandringham estates, which alone account for 47 000 acres. The Forestry Commission is one of the largest landowners in Britain as a whole, with 429 460 acres, due to its very extensive estates in Scotland, but much of its land is otherwise extremely marginal in farming terms, a qualification which must also be applied to 88 per cent of the land owned by conservation bodies. The City institutions, on the other hand, generally own land of top agricultural quality. The recent revival of interest in the purchase of land for investment purposes by the City has made this sector the fastest growing of all the institutional owners. It has also

Table 1   *Ownership of landed estates in England, 1873 and 1967*

Owner	Acreage 1873	1967	Location (1967)
Marquess of Abergavenny	28 000	1 000	Kent
Earl of Aylesford	19 500	5 000	Warwickshire
Marquess of Aylesbury	55 000	6 000	Wiltshire
Lord Brocket		4 500	Hertfordshire
Lord Brassey	4 000	4 000	Northamptonshire
Marquess of Bath	55 000	10 000	Wiltshire
Duke of Beaufort	51 000	52 000	Gloucestershire
Viscount Bolingbroke	3 300	4 000	Hampshire
Lord Bolton	29 200	18 500	Yorkshire
Viscount Blakenham		580	Suffolk
Mr E. Brudenell	15 000	10 000	Leicestershire, Northamptonshire
Lord Brabourne	4 100	3 000	Kent
Sir W. Bromley-Davenport	15 600	5 000	Cheshire
Lord Brownlow	58 300	10 000	Lincolnshire
Marquess of Bristol	32 000	16 000	Suffolk
Earl of Carnarvon	35 500	6 000	Berkshire
Lord Clinton	34 700	26 000	Devon
Viscount Cobham	6 900	400	Worcestershire
Viscount Cowdray		17 500	Sussex
Baron Crathorne	5 600	4 000	Yorkshire
Sir J. Craster	2 800	750	Northumberland
Earl of Durham	30 000	30 000	Durham, Northumberland
Earl of Derby	68 900	5 000	Lancashire
Earl of Devon	53 000	5 000	Devon
Duke of Devonshire	138 500	72 000	Derbyshire, Yorkshire
Lord Egremont	109 900	20 000	Sussex, Cumberland
Marquess of Exeter	28 200	22 000	Lincolnshire
Earl Ferrers	8 600	250	Norfolk
Lord Feversham	39 300	47 000	Yorkshire
Fulford of Fulford	4 000	3 500	Devon
Duke of Grafton	25 000	11 000	Norfolk
Earl of Harewood	29 600	7 000	Yorkshire
Earl of Huntingdon	13 500		
Marquess of Hertford	12 200	8 000	Warwickshire, Worcestershire
Lord Iliffe		10 000	Berkshire

Earl of Iveagh		24000 Norfolk
Mr Charles Legh	5800	2000 Cheshire
Viscount Leverhulme		99000 Cheshire
Earl of Lonsdale	68000	71000 Westmorland, Cumberland
Duke of Marlborough	23500	11500 Oxfordshire
Lord Middleton	99500	13500 Yorkshire
Duke of Newcastle	35500	9000 Dorset
Duke of Northumberland	186300	80000 Northumberland
Earl of Pembroke	44800	16000 Wiltshire
Duke of Portland	64000	17000 Nottinghamshire
Lord Redesdale	26400	1000 Northumberland
Duke of Richmond and Gordon	17000	12000 Sussex
Viscount Scarsdale	9900	6000 Derbyshire
Duke of Somerset	25300	5700 Wiltshire, Devon
Earl Spencer	27100	15000 Northamptonshire, Leicestershire
Earl of Verulam	10100	5200 Hertfordshire, Norfolk
Earl Waldegrave	15400	5000 Somerset
Colonel J. Weld	15500	11000 Dorset
Duke of Westminster	20000	18000 Cheshire, Shropshire

SOURCE: R. Perrott, *The Aristocrats* (Weidenfeld and Nicolson, 1968).

Table 2 *Institutional ownership of farmland, England and Wales, 1971*

Institution	Acreage owned
Monarchy	325055
Forestry Commission	80555
Ministry of Agriculture	28112
Other government departments	121663
Nationalized industries	359233
Local authorities	929559
Universities and colleges	180385
Conservation bodies	201452
Agricultural Research Council	6622
Church land	157814
City institutions	170000 (est.)
Total	2 560 450

SOURCE: R. Gibbs and A. Harrison, *Land Ownership by Public and Semi-Public Bodies in Great Britain* (University of Reading, 1973).

sparked off a great deal of controversy in farming circles about the probity of their activity. This issue will be examined in more detail later in this chapter.

Such institutional landownership is by no means new. The monarchy, the church and the older universities have all been involved since at least medieval times. The recent increase in institutional ownership has, however, raised a number of questions over the future of landownership in this country. Where the institutions are public they have resulted in removing many decisions over land use from the preference of a private individual to the control, at least nominally, of the public at large. In the areas of land-use planning and the provision of recreational amenities this has been by no means an unimportant change. Elsewhere, particularly in the case of the City institutions, the rise of institutional ownership has led to suggestions that the future will see the return to a landlord–tenant system covering the majority of agricultural land, and that the rise of owner-occupation over the last fifty years or more has been but a brief historical interlude to the 'natural' situation. If this should occur then a *farming* interest would once again become separated from a *land-owning* interest. In the meantime the idea of farmers owning the land they farm, although such a recent historical development, remains firmly rooted. The ownership of land may no longer be a key to the political power and social influence that it once was, but land is once again a lucrative investment.

Aristocracy, gentry, squirearchy

Changes in the pattern of landownership have brought about a convergence in the upper echelons of rural society. In the ebb and flow of land sales and agricultural fortune the old pecking order has been disarranged and the fine gradations of title and territory fudged and erased. Many former tenants now own farms considerably larger than their ex-landlords', particularly those who, by virtue of hard work, thrift, innovation and entrepreneurial acumen, were buying land in the 1930s at rock-bottom prices when all around were trying to sell theirs. Consequently the possession of a title has, in itself, become less significant, except in an honorific sense, and certainly less indicative of the acreage owned. Moreover a similar convergence has occurred within the nobility itself where the order of precedence –

duke, marquess, earl, viscount, baron – has lost much of its meaning. This lack of emphasis on title and hereditary hierarchy is one of the chief adjustments that the rural élite has made to the expectations of a more democratic age. Indeed the word 'élite' would undoubtedly make many of them wince for the modern aristocrat has gone out of his way to cultivate an image of quite plebeian ordinariness. Unless they are to be seen in the newspapers riding bicycles or driving tractors they have become a by-word for self-effacement. They assiduously adhere to a cult of inconspicuous consumption.

It was not always thus. Whatever their internal divisions and differences of wealth and style landowners had until the First World War formed a group which, from the point of view of the remainder of rural society, was undeniably a rural ruling class. Their local monopoly over the ownership of land conferred an indisputable and largely undisputed control over the major institutions and facilities of rural life: employment, housing, education, welfare, religion and law and order. This dominance expressed itself at the personal level in a supreme self-confidence, a serene assumption in the right – indeed, the duty – of the landowner to rule. The pursuit of ostentation reflected this, not because conspicuous consumption was cultivated in order to impress the lower orders but because it manifested the social distance between them. An avuncular intimacy was allowed only when the immutability of this class barrier had been mutually recognized.

Throughout the nineteenth century this rural ruling class, in exercising its power, had organized a division of labour. The aristocracy was primarily a metropolitan and nationally oriented group whose business it was to run the nation as well as their estates, the day-to-day administration of the latter usually being left in the hands of an agent. While Parliament was in session and the annual tribal gathering of the London season was in full swing they resided in the metropolis. At least annually, however, the aristocrat and his family retinue would migrate to their country seat to settle the estate's affairs, conduct a tour of inspection, keep the local populace up to scratch by a visible presence – and not least to indulge in a little sporting activity. The purpose of such visits was also to replenish the aristocrat's social and political capital by entertaining the local gentry, administering justice via the local magistracy and attending to territorial affairs involving the estate, the church, local schools and local charities. In this sense rural England could seem little more than a loosely knit federation of great estates, each apparently autonomous, shunning the outside world and with its own omnipotent potentate. Rural society was the source of the aristocracy's strength but the drawstring which held this aristocratic network together was undoubtedly the London season, which in its heyday consisted, according to Thompson, of

the world of politics and high society, of attendance at the House and gaming in the clubs, the place where wagers were laid and race meetings arranged, the source of fashion in dress and taste in art, the place where portraits were painted and galleries visited, as well as being the world of drawing rooms and levées, glittering entertainments and extravaganzas, soirées, balls and operas.

The aristocracy found no difficulty in moving to and fro between this glittering social whirl and the more measured parochialism of rural life.

The gentry meanwhile organized the more modest social round of county society. There they complemented the activities of the aristocracy, assisting in the administration of justice, providing the officer corps for the country's military force and engaging from time to time in political life. They or their wives took a leading part in local village philanthropy and, after 1834, the gentry also administered the Poor Law. Their abiding obsession was, however, sport. In some respects, especially gamekeeping, this threatened to be socially divisive. Tenant farmers took no joy from the restrictions and disturbance attached to game preservation, while for the agricultural worker poaching often took on the countenance of an undercover guerilla class warfare. On the other hand, the gentry's particular delight was foxhunting and this developed into much more than a mere sporting pastime to become a celebration of the hierarchy of county society, cementing the divisions of rural class relationships. It created a following which embraced all social classes while providing the country gentry and squirearchy with a convenient excuse for coming together and sharing the same consuming mystique. In so doing the hunt served a similar function to the London season, even offering a parallel set of rituals and taboos in the intricacies of foxhunting etiquette.

Almost invariably the gentry acted as the loyal subalterns of the landed aristocracy. This gave a coherence and a solidarity to the rural upper class which was expressed in a common code of conduct and morality – the ethic of the gentleman. This notion had originated in the medieval code of chivalry, in which honour had been satisfied by a duel, but such a militaristic code had metamorphosed into the ethic of gentility in a more peaceful Tudor England. By the beginning of the nineteenth century military prowess had been replaced by other attributes: a landed estate, a family tree, a certain degree of wealth, but most of all a set of rules concerning conduct and behaviour, of what was 'done' and 'not done'. The gentlemanly ethic was, however, never entirely rigid; it could, and did, accommodate exceptions to each and all of these criteria and thus ensured that the highest status group in English society was never totally exclusive. The door was always left slightly ajar to those who aspired to become 'real gentlemen', so that a fortunate few might achieve gentility without relying solely upon the narrowly ascriptive criterion of birth.

At times it seemed that nothing so exercised the minds of the mid-Victorian middle class than whether or not they were regarded as 'real gentlemen' among the particular élite group with whom they were so anxious to identify themselves. The major problem was, as scores of writers of manuals on manners and etiquette testified, that admission to the elected and recognition by them depended upon an effortless command of the bewildering and intricate nuances of gentlemanly demeanour and behaviour. These ultimately decisive aspects of the gentlemanly ethic were both unwritten and unspoken, and were often changed or modified, as if by some hidden signal, with ungentlemanly haste whenever the need arose. As countless aspirants found to their chagrin, the taste and fashion of the immediate past was no guide to the correct gentlemanly conduct of the present. Such a device was instinctively operated because the gentlemanly ethic was concerned above all with social acceptance, with the need to control and ration the admission to a highly status-conscious, but never entirely exclusive, 'inner circle'. But within this élite gentility also acted as an agency of social discipline ensuring that attitudes and values conformed to a readily identifiable pattern. The standards of gentlemanly conduct thus enabled a geographically dispersed and economically differentiated aristocracy, landed gentry and squirearchy to retain its stability, its coherence and its cultural control.

The ethic of the gentleman was therefore central to the principle of inherited authority which underpinned rural England until the First World War. By his acceptance as a gentleman in rural society the landowner hoped to ensure the deference of farmers and farm workers which, he believed, was essential to the continuing stability and harmony of class relationships. It also enabled the landowner to retain an unassailable moral superiority over the other inhabitants of the rural world; in this way, it was believed, the farmer and the labourer would instinctively acknowledge the landowner as one of their 'betters'. A gentleman might thus be granted a legitimate right to rule but in return those further down the social scale would expect a paternalistic concern for their own welfare. The gentleman therefore accrued to himself certain rights but also took on certain obligations. In order to obtain the legitimate right to rule the village he was also expected to shoulder the responsibility of being its protector, of generally knowing what was best for its inhabitants and acting as its plenipotentiary to the outside world. The *ideal* rural society was one in which a chain of hierarchical relationships existed, paternalistic in one direction and deferential in the other, with each individual 'knowing his place' and not thinking to question the appropriateness of his position. How often this ideal was actually realized must be a matter of some doubt, although ultimately of conjecture. The notion of 'service' to the community was never much more than a polite means of expressing power over it, just as the superficially harmonious exterior of village life also hid the underlying penumbra of class conflict and petty crime. Victorian paternalism always contained these contradictory elements – it was simultaneously kind *and* cruel, autocratic *and* obliging, oppressive *and* benevolent, exploitative *and* protective. This was the only way in which the privileges attached to gentlemanly status could be combined with an idealized conception of 'community', and how the more exploited sections of rural society could be encouraged to identify with a social order which endorsed their own moral inferiority.

During the nineteenth century such a smoothly functioning social order (where it existed) was always under threat of attack by the meritocratic, utilitarian values of the urban, industrial creed. Considerable effort therefore went into trying to ensure that most rural inhabitants maintained their 'limited horizons' and were not contaminated by such alien attitudes. Whenever possible the estate-owner would resist such potential subversion, particularly its more tangible manifestations – the railways, trade unionism, universal education – and cultivate instead a loyalty to the immediate locality and its 'natural' leader. In the more remote and isolated areas of rural England the encroachment of the outside world could be resisted extremely successfully until well after the First World War. Areas like these – sometimes misleadingly termed 'feudal' – only finally succumbed, and then not always thoroughly, under the influence of the motor car and the television set. However, such changes have been sporadic and uneven in their development; nor can they be separated from the economic changes in the pattern of landownership discussed earlier in this chapter. The great estates often formed their own closely-bounded and self-supporting social world. When they disappeared that world irrevocably changed, too.

The gentlemanly ethic has survived until today only in a highly attenuated form. It remains as a code of etiquette and a certain gentlemanly demeanour or 'bearing', but many of the self-confident assumptions of moral superiority are no longer as widely shared and unquestioningly accepted as once they were. The gentlemanly ethic, like the habit of traditional authority generally in Britain, has declined. Growing industrialization, with its continuous techno-logical innovation, has led to a much greater complexity that has permeated all spheres of society. This growth in complexity has perforce been accompanied by a trend towards specialization with the result that an ever-increasing premium has been placed upon the possession of specialized knowledge and technical expertise. Tradi-tion and the cult of the gentlemanly amateur have been overtaken by efficiency and the rise of the professional. Isolated from the cultural mainstream, English rural society has often seemed slow to adapt to these changes, but in another sense these rationalizing tendencies took root there very early in the commercialization of agriculture, over which the gentlemanly ethic became merely a cul-tural veneer. During this century, especially since the Second World War, as farming has become ever more rationalized, so have the values of professionalism taken an increasing hold. Today's landed aristocrat or squire is a wealthy businessman who, almost inciden-tally, happens to be in the business of producing food.

This may help to explain why many (though by no means all) of the aristocracy now regard some of the trappings of traditional authority as anachronistic and faintly embarrassing in a more democratic era. Their self-effacement represents a defensive reflex against anticipated attacks on privilege and snobbery. However, Roy Perrott, in his book *The Aristocrats* – one of the few post-war accounts of the British nobility – demonstrates that the life of the modern landed gentleman by no means consists only of shy melancholy, though such retiring habits do make our knowledge skimpy and bases our stereotypes upon uncertain assumptions. As Perrott points out:

What is surprising . . . is how far the old pattern of individual noble ownership has survived, and how far the gentlemanly classes still keep some measure of their former country position because of it. Lords and old-established gentry are still easily the biggest individual landowners in every county which is mainly agricultural. . . . The old amateur tradition is rapidly disappearing. In its place there is a readiness to exploit the patrimony on businesslike lines. I doubt that there was ever a great deal of sentiment applied in the running of the big estates. There is certainly little now. . . . But it is not easy to get a very clear picture of how truly prosperous or otherwise the landed classes are. In the great days of 'conspicuous display' it was perfectly simple: through the magnificence of his house, his picture collection, even his expenditure on cigars, the nobleman wanted to impress on the world how rich he was. Now that the nobility is going through a long phase of what might be called 'conspicuous modesty' it is necessary to distinguish between the landowner who is genuinely having trouble finding capital, and the sort who regards being a 'hypothetical millionaire' as a sort of hard-luck story.

It is not easy to do so. Such an assessment of the estate-owner's prosperity is complicated by the fact that the nobility is no longer exclusively, nor even particularly, a landed class. Although land-ownership remains one of the major concentrations of wealth in English society, the possession of land long ago ceased to be an essential qualification for a title. Consequently many of the former institutions of the landed gentleman have been infiltrated by the new plutocracy of industry and commerce, and the strength of these institutions may be only a partial guide to the economic health of land-ownership. The London season, for example, seems to remain as vibrant as ever – Perrott estimated that by the late 1960s it included at least six times as many private events as there had been in the 1930s – and county society continues to thrive around the twin totems of horse and hound. But what sustains such traditional tokens of gentlemanly life-style are large injections of cash and snobbery from middle-class *parvenus*. In such circumstances 'real gentlemen' have a tendency to renounce such pursuits and move on – from the ostentatious to the inconspicuous, from the fashionable to the ordinary; to whatever, in fact, those who aspire to their status are *not* doing. Threatened by new forms of wealth the landowner now wishes to appear in genteel poverty. Moreover it always helps in fending off the predatory taxman and avoiding the envy of the poor and the underprivileged.

In a paradoxical way the modest and self-effacing manner of the gentleman landowner is a symbol of the continuing strength of his social influence rather than its decline. It shows that there is still a madding crowd of vulgar outsiders anxious either to attain the status of gentleman or merely to exercise their sense of curiosity. For as long as there are those who wish to share in his prestige or bathe in its reflection then the total eclipse of gentlemanly values will not be realized. Furthermore the landowner remains a symbol of continuity in rural England – and in what is often perceived as an increasingly uncertain and unpredictable age this may be no disadvantage to him. The landowner has long relied on a traditional sense of deference in rural society and has conferred a sense of identity and 'place' in return. These remain valued assets as long as the snobbery and social insecurity on which they feed continue to be engendered among the rest of the populace and as long as the wealth and privilege which lie behind them remain discreetly veiled. Gentility, then, still owes much to 'ancient riches' and the aristocracy remains, in Perrott's words, 'a grand-scale euphemism built around money, a metaphor of continuity which strives to give the illusion of permanence'. Indeed, the most recent threats to the continued existence of the private landowner have come, not from owning too little wealth, but from having had thrust upon him too much.

The taxation threat

In the early 1930s, to take an extreme case, good arable land in East Anglia could be purchased for as little as £5 per acre. There were virtually no buyers and much of it reverted to 'dog-and-stick' farming in the hands of a penurious owner. By 1977 that same acre of land could have cost as much as £1750. Outside onlookers may no doubt wish that they had problems like these, but most of the owners of agricultural land valued at this kind of price regard it as a problem in many ways no less pressing than was the risk of bankruptcy between the wars. This 'problem' is not only due to inflation but has been brought about by the changes in the pattern of land tenure that have occurred since the breaking up of the great estates. While a landlord–tenant system predominated there was also a division in the benefits that accrued. Farming profits were appropriated first of all by tenant farmers, although over time they would pass a proportion on to their landlords in the form of rents; landowners, on the other hand, received not only rental income but the capital gain of their land (should they wish to realize it) whenever it increased in value. Since 1945, however, the increase in owner-occupation has ensured that the new majority of farmer-landowners have reaped the benefit of both profits and capital gains, while at the same time the market for land (and hence its value) has been determined by influences largely outside their control. Land values are now so high that the threat of penal capital taxation has become a real one. The long-term existence of the farmer has, as a consequence, been placed at risk by his other role as a landowner. Ironically the sons and grandsons of those who stepped in and bought when the estate-owners were forced to sell are now faced with the same taxation threat which precipitated the growth of owner-occupation earlier in this century.

This is the background against which it is necessary to consider the current controversy surrounding capital taxation and its threat to agricultural efficiency. The growth of owner-occupation has made farmers extremely sensitive to those changes in the land market which they consider to be contrary to their interests, particularly any increases in value which do not reflect prevailing conditions in agriculture. The price of land, for example, is now so high that it bears no relationship to the yield which can be gained from farming it, so this inflated value threatens both expansion and the ability of new entrants to the industry to farm in their own right. Yet the cost of land and buildings constitutes, on average, 80 per cent of the asset structure of a farming business. Any fundamental changes in the taxation structure affecting capital gains, capital transfers or wealth thus have potentially far-reaching repercussions for farms, given that the vast majority of farm businesses are *de facto* family proprietorships. Consequently any increase in the value of land simply inflates their wealth and increases their tax liability. For these reasons the owner-occupier has a real interest in promoting a stable market in land in which the price rises only slowly and in a manner commensurate with agricultural profitability. Agricultural owner-occupiers were probably unique among private landowners in actually welcoming the reduction in their wealth that resulted in the dramatic fall in the price of land in 1974–5. Equally there were renewed pronouncements of gloom when prices more than recovered in 1976.

As long as owner-occupation prevails this topsy-turvy ideology among landowners will predominate. Most landowning farmers genuinely believe that to have become paper millionaires through no 'fault' of their own really is, in Perrott's words, 'a kind of hard-luck story'. In the fertile farming areas of south and east England, for example, land prices rose from around £300 per acre to as much as £1400 per acre in the space of twelve months in 1972–3, but only a small proportion of this could be accounted for by any increase in farming profits in that year. Agriculture was therefore being asked to carry a burden of capital which it could not ultimately afford, for although it made borrowing easier, it made for a heavier capital tax liability in the future. To many farmers, no doubt, all of this took on a slightly unreal air, as though British agriculture was being financed by Monopoly money, but it certainly revealed some of the convoluted features of the owner-occupier's psyche. For example, it would have been quite in order, of course, for the newly-wealthy landowner to realize his assets and, pausing only as he passed Go to be relieved of some of his burden by Capital Gains Tax, proceed to Free Parking beyond the reach of the Inland Revenue in the Channel Islands or Bahamas. Most, however, were still sufficiently attached to farming as a way of life to resist such inducements. A more sedentary alternative was to sell property back to the Bank, in the guise of the City institutions, allowing them to take on the capital burden and becoming their tenant. The farmer could farm, but would no longer be a landowner. This suggestion, however, was treated with even greater suspicion. Farmers showed themselves prepared to pay through the nose for what they otherwise alleged to be the dubious privileges of ownership, for they were convinced that to be a tenant was to be second-best. However, those who bought farms at the high prices of 1973 on borrowed money faced bankruptcy when the value of their collateral fell by over one-third in the following year. They did not pass Go, but went directly to jail.

The value of agricultural land in the 1970s has taken on a roller-coaster quality which has led to a great deal of acrimonious debate in the farming press. The much sought-after stability in the price of land, whereby it is tied to the prices obtaining for farm produce, has proved elusive – and so has the simple explanation for the turmoil which many farmers have also been seeking. The most popular scape-goat has been the non-agricultural investor who has been attracted into purchase not by an interest in farming but by anticipated capital growth. Such investment also used to be stimulated by the know-ledge that under the old Estate Duty system anyone owning agri-cultural land could claim a 45 per cent relief on that portion of their estate. Capital growth, however, is often unrelated to purely agri-cultural factors, so the price of land has borne little relationship to agricultural prosperity. Agricultural economists have suggested that instead it is associated with such factors as the level of interest rates in the economy generally and movements in the price of industrial shares. This is because land has become an attractive hedge against inflation and it has attracted investment on that account alone. With inflation in the economy generally proceeding at a high rate during the 1970s the price of land has therefore remained buoyant as invest-ors have sought to protect the value of their savings. However, when successive governments tinker with the economy in order to achieve policies unrelated to agriculture, the effects on farming can be startling.

The ups and downs of the land market between 1972 and 1976 illustrate this convincingly. An analysis by Nicholas Byrne in the journal *Farmland Market* in 1975 showed that the spectacular rise in the price of land in 1972 and 1973 was brought about by the coinci-dence of agricultural prosperity and an accompanying boom in the City. In 1973 the Soviet Union conducted its 'great grain robbery' on the Chicago market, with the result that world prices rocketed. In that same year England's arable farmers had their second successive bonanza harvest, so that they enjoyed a local surplus under condi-tions of world shortage. Moreover, with the profitability of cereal farming assured by entry into the EEC, farmers began to look for more land in order to cash in further on their lucrative returns. In addition, 1972 saw the artificially induced 'Barber boom' of that year's Conservative government. City investors found they had capital to invest and chose to extend their portfolios by buying land

as a hedge against inflation. In addition, the Conservative government had been persuaded to allow landowners who sold land at
development prices for housing and industrial use to avoid the resulting Capital Gains Tax, provided that the money was re-invested in
agriculture within three years. Since development value was (and is)
far in excess of agricultural value, these landowners had large sums
to invest quickly and could afford to pay a premium above the going
rate for agricultural land that was equivalent to the forgone tax. It
was estimated by *Farmers' Weekly* that such 'roll-over relief', as it
was called, had resulted in £1000 million urgently seeking land *in one
year*. Since development value was roughly ten times agricultural
value it was like an area the size of the Isle of Wight being up for
sale but sufficient money from roll-over relief *alone* being available
to buy the whole of Hampshire. The laws of supply and demand did
the rest.

There then followed Edward Heath's 'U-turn' and the coming to
power of a Labour government. The end of the Barber boom
resulted in a severe contraction in investment funds in the economy.
A new Labour government in 1974 also resulted in proposals for new
taxation on wealth (Capital Transfer Tax, Wealth Tax) and on
development value under the Community Land Act. Roll-over relief
was abandoned and tax relief on interest payments, introduced by the
Conservatives, was restricted. The property market collapsed under
this combination. The institutions consequently withdrew from land
until such time as its price picked up again and a capital gain was
once more in prospect. As if to add to the depression, 1974 was also
a bad year agriculturally. Although the price of land fell by an average of £200 per acre in a year, the slump proved to be a brief one.
By late 1975 the price was heading back to its former level and early
in 1976 it was moving beyond the £1500 mark. The reasons were
much as before: a general deterioration of confidence in the value of
money; underinvestment in the industrial sector of the economy;
renewed interest in agricultural land by City investors; and the possibility of higher agricultural profits as a result of adjustment to the
EEC's Common Agricultural Policy. However, as prices surged on
towards £2000 per acre, so the agricultural landowner became once
more alarmed by the prospect. Not only was his wealth making him
more and more liable to punitive rates of taxation, but, with the
abandonment of Estate Duty and its replacement by Capital Transfer

Tax, there was an increasing likelihood that payment would no longer be voluntary.

As we have already seen, the private landowner has, over the years, learned to live with the threat of taxation. Rental income is assessed as unearned and thus subject to a maximum rate of 98 per cent, so he has been encouraged to take land in hand which reduces the top marginal rate to 75 per cent; similarly Estate Duty included the 45 per cent abatement relief on farmland and could be avoided altogether by handing over the estate at least seven years before death. Then, in 1974, Estate Duty was replaced by Capital Transfer Tax (CTT), which was virtually unavoidable since it taxed all sizeable transfers of assets (except those between spouses) whether during the lifetime of the owner or after death. Relief applied only to 'working farmers', defined as those whose farming contributed at least 75 per cent of their income in five of the previous seven years. Owner-occupiers below 1000 acres or £250000 assets were also granted a 50 per cent relief across the board and a 30 per cent business relief above those levels. For private landlords no such relief applied. Moreover taking land in hand, which would otherwise undoubtedly have accelerated further in order to qualify for relief from CTT, was made much more difficult by the clauses in the Agriculture (Miscellaneous Provisions) Act of 1976 which virtually guaranteed the succession of a tenancy to a close relative on the death or retirement of the present incumbent. If this state of affairs remains then it is only a matter of time before private agricultural landlordism dies out. Either land will be sold to the institutions – which, because they do not die, do not pay CTT – in order to meet tax bills or it will be offered directly to the Inland Revenue *in lieu* of tax, leading to a process of creeping land nationalization. If the proposed Wealth Tax is ever implemented then this tax burden will increase, particularly if land values rise at their recent rate. Already it has been estimated by the Select Committee on the Wealth Tax that 30 per cent of all those to whom the tax would apply are owner-occupying farmers.

The organization which is determined that this fate shall not come to pass is the 'landowners' trade union', the Country Landowners Association (CLA). Formed by a small group of Lincolnshire estate-owners in 1907 to combat the Liberal threat of land reform, it represents all *owners* of agricultural and other rural land in England and Wales. Although it began as an élitist gentleman's club it has transformed itself into a successful modern parliamentary pressure group and in so doing adapted itself to the growing convergence between estate-owners and farming owner-occupiers. Its membership is approximately 40000 and, in order to deny the upper-class image which still clings to it, the CLA is at pains to point out that more than half of its members own less than 100 acres. The CLA's duties are to further its members' interests as owners rather than as farmers – the latter function is the task of the National Farmers' Union. Hence, given the political realities of the last hundred years, the CLA is essentially a defensive organization, safeguarding the legitimate position, as the CLA sees it, of the private landowner. It is also an astute recognition of these realities that has led the CLA to be much less public than its companion organization: the NFU President is a national figure, but who has heard of the President of the CLA? Well aware of the ease with which it could provoke political attack if it adopted a confrontationist stance, the CLA prefers a more stealthy pursuit of its cause along the corridors of power, paying great attention to its behind-the-scenes consultations with Whitehall officials. According to its promotional brochure, *Your Land*, 'Its leaders have direct access to Ministers and Head Office permanent staff have a close day-to-day working relationship with Government Departments'. In its skilful handling of these relationships the CLA has sought to guarantee its influence.

Given its primary purpose of defending agricultural property rights, it is perhaps not surprising that the main thrust of the CLA's lobbying activities are directed not so much towards the Ministry of Agriculture but towards the Treasury. In the list of CLA achievements set out in *Your Land* nearly a page is devoted to taxation matters, compared with a paragraph or two on most others, and frequently its proposals to the Chancellor of the Exchequer for the Budget are of the same length and detail as its submission to the MAFF (Ministry of Agriculture, Fisheries and Food) for the Annual Review of Prices and Guarantees. Although such matters by no means exhaust the concerns of the CLA – for example, the recent growth of public interest in the environment has meant an increasing involvement in issues relating to land use and access – it has long recognized that punitive levels of taxation could represent the most potent threat to its members' continued existence and has tailored its activities accordingly. For example, the CLA was responsible for persuading the government of the wisdom of 45 per cent abatement relief on agricultural land in the 1920s. More recently the CLA's successes in the 1971 Budget were so many that it listed them in a separate circular to its members, while the CLA was also instrumental in obtaining the postponement of a Wealth Tax in 1975. Its abilities in this regard are undoubtedly the CLA's major selling-point to its members: not only does it save them, as a group, millions of pounds through its political activity, but it can save them individually many thousands through its taxation advisory service.

There may be a historical irony in the sight of the descendants of the nineteenth-century country gentlemen mobilizing themselves in a manner which at times bears a close resemblance to that of a trade union, but it has been this very adaptability which has been one of the landowner's greatest strengths. Political necessity has overridden considerations of status. As *Your Land* bluntly states: 'The individual landowner needs the collective strength and authority of the CLA to exert political influence on his behalf. He cannot do it alone.' It is organizational capability which is now the key to the CLA's influence (perhaps accounting for the preference for retired military officers among its regional and branch secretaries). The nature of its *modus operandi* enforces a highly centralized system of administration, with an expert headquarters staff and Executive Committee capable of serving the interests of the CLA on the dense network of official and semi-official committees that now characterize modern government. The forty-seven county branches may at times seem left out in the cold, but by electing the Council (the CLA's supreme governing body) they are assured of a watchdog role over matters of policy. They are also not unimportant in influencing the direction of local politics over rural affairs. Where decisive influence is exerted, however, is along an invisible nexus between the CLA's headquarters in Bedford Square and Whitehall and Westminster. The CLA is free from party ties and fastidiously maintains a formal political neutrality, but it can count a fair sprinkling of members along the Conservative benches in the House of Commons, and at times the House of Lords can appear to be its political arm. Although often anxious not to overplay its parliamentary hand (and thereby increase its visibility) it ensures that it can 'move in the right circles' and that the CLA's voice is heard where it matters.

If the private landowner has become adept at avoiding his long-predicted oblivion, this has been due in no small part to the CLA's political guile. However, the introduction of CTT to replace Estate Duty has provided a severe blow to the future of the private landowner. Even if he is an owner-occupier and can claim the 50 per cent working farmer relief on his land value and 30 per cent relief on the value of his working capital, a holding of 1000 acres worth £800 per acre would leave his heirs with a CTT bill for £290750, or 29 per cent of the value of the land. If he decides to transfer during his lifetime a lower rate applies, but the transfer would also attract Capital Gains Tax at a rate of 30 per cent of the increase in the value of the land between the time of purchase and the lifetime transfer. Faced with this unnerving prospect most landowners are holding on, hoping for a change in government and a subsequent change in taxation, but if the current situation remains, then the time for a fiscally induced demise may at last have arrived. The landowner who wishes to remain in farming will be forced to consider the possibility of offering the Inland Revenue some land *in lieu* of tax, so a gradual nationalization of land may ensue. Alternatively he may sell to a buyer who is not subject to CTT – that is, someone who does not die. Apart from the state, the only likely candidates with these intimations of immortality and the necessary financial resources are the City institutions.

The City institutions

No recent development in agricultural landownership has created more controversy and more speculation than the activities of the City institutions. Branded one minute with the image of robber barons elbowing the individual landowner aside from his patrimony in their relentless pursuit of Mammon, they are welcomed the next as the saviour of private landownership from the scourge of CTT. In the last decade intense interest, and not a little fear, has surrounded their operations, and despite the fact that they are given wide coverage in the farming press a discernible air of mystery continues to be associated with them. Consequently mythologies about the City institutions abound. It is clear, however, that their activities represent, potentially at least, one of the most significant developments in landownership in this country in the last fifty years. Collectively they also represent the fastest-growing landowner in Britain, having doubled their holdings to approximately 350000 acres between 1971 and 1976. To some observers this trend heralds the eventual return to the landlord–tenant system, with the City institutions assuming the role of traditional landlord and reaping the rewards of capital gain and competitive rents while their tenants are relieved of much of their taxation burden in order to devote themselves to efficient, profitable farming. Most of the institutions argue strongly, and convincingly, that while CTT remains this is the only sensible course of action for estate owners and large-scale owner-occupiers, but even if the realization of these changes depends upon the fortunes of national party politics, they are still likely to increase their holdings of agricultural land whatever the permanence of CTT. For this and all the other reasons outlined in this paragraph they repay close attention.

The City institutions with interests in agricultural land fall into three main groups. First there are insurance companies who invest a proportion of their life assurance premiums in what they consider to be a safe investment whose long-term capital growth will ensure a retention of real value when their policies mature in twenty or thirty years' time. Far from being newcomers to landownership this is quite old-established practice. Norwich Union, for example, purchased its first estate in Norfolk in 1877 and made further purchases both before and after the Second World War. It now owns approximately 48 000 acres. Eagle Star also possesses a portfolio of agricultural land which has been built up over thirty years or more. It is now the largest of the insurance company owners with 72 000 acres. Others are more recent holders of land, like Commercial Union (13 500 acres) which bought its first estate in Scotland in 1974 and Equitable Life which began buying in 1968 and which by the end of 1976 owned 8000 acres in Lincolnshire, Norfolk and Yorkshire. Many of the insurance companies owning land are noted pillars of the City establishment. Their interest has been stimulated not only because agricultural land has appeared to be inflation-proof in the long term but because land is a politically acceptable form of investment and therefore safe in another, equally important, sense. The combination of these interests has meant that they are more concerned with owning land rather than farming it, with capital growth (rising land prices) rather than yield (farm rent). They are consequently happy to remain landlords only – and with their revered reputations to maintain they are careful not to be seen as being too rapacious. However, one or two companies have taken farms in hand, like the Prudential, which owned 25 000 acres at the end of 1976, including thirty tenanted farms, but which also farmed two holdings in Oxfordshire and Shropshire. Matthews Wrightson Holdings Ltd, a City company with interests in insurance and shipping, also farms land through its subsidiaries Fountain Farming Ltd, and Fountain Forestry Ltd, but this is a complicated case which will be considered in more detail below.

The second major group of City institutional owners are the pension funds of individual companies and nationalized industries. The British Airways Pension Scheme, for example, has recently become very active in land purchase, and by the end of 1976 it owned 4000 acres, of which one farm of 1600 acres was farmed in hand. Like most of the other pension funds its first purchase was very recent – in 1974 – but it is expanding very rapidly (at the beginning of 1977 it added further to its portfolio with a purchase from Matthews Wrightson). Other nationalized industries with interests in agricultural land include the Post Office (12000 acres at the end of 1976) and the Electricity Supply Staff Superannuation Fund (12000 acres; 1600 in hand). Many of the pension schemes of the major British privately owned companies also invest in agricultural land – for example, Boots, Pilkington Glass, Esso, Plessey and Vauxhall. Since neither these companies nor their investment managers have much expertise in agriculture, they are mostly content to act as landlords like the insurance companies, although occasionally they may farm land themselves, too.

Smaller companies which lack the necessary financial resources to invest in agricultural land – and indeed, individual members of the public – may do so indirectly by purchasing shares in property unit trusts. Some of these are pension fund consortia, like the Property Unit Trust Group, which first put money into farmland in 1969 and which by the end of 1976 owned 40000 acres almost entirely let to 150 tenants. The Kleinwort Benson Farm Land Trust owns mostly vacant possession farms which it then lets to a specialist farming company, Hallsworth Ltd, which farms the land under an incentive scheme aimed at ensuring the maximum return and profitability. A similar unit trust attached to a merchant bank is the Hill Samuel Mutual Agricultural Property Fund which commenced operations in April 1976 but by the end of the year had amassed nearly 4000 acres in Bedfordshire, Norfolk, Cambridgeshire and Lincolnshire. The

Abbey Life Property Bond Fund, whose advertisements are often to be seen in the quality newspapers, also owns 16500 acres on behalf of its investors, including one intensive arable and fruit farm of 1225 acres near Clacton-on-Sea, Essex, which is farmed in hand.

One of the most innovatory of the unit trusts is Property Growth Assurance (PGA) which has attempted to find a third way of enhancing its investments by farming in partnership with local established farmers rather than letting to a tenant or farming in hand. Of the 12000 acres which it owned at the end of 1976, approximately 10 per cent was farmed in this way. This involves the former owner-occupier continuing to farm after his land has been bought by PGA, but he pays an annual rent and may also hand over a share of the profit. In return for this modern equivalent of *latifundia* the farmer can call on the financial and managerial expertise of PGA. To this extent PGA represents an interesting combination of City interests, land agents and farmers, and PGA's agricultural committee, which directs the farming policy of the group, includes farmers and landowners among its members. Between 1970 and 1974 PGA bought over 17000 acres covering fifty-two separate holdings and initially there were spectacular yields. A bond purchased for £5 in 1970 was worth £7·51 in the summer of 1974 but with the subsequent decline in land prices the value fell to £4·64 by mid-1975. PGA was forced to sell 5271 tenanted acres at £393 per acre to help it through a cash crisis, but it came back on to the market as a buyer in late 1976, by which time its bonds had risen to £5·54. PGA also farms 680 acres in hand in the East Midlands and Humberside in order to gain direct knowledge of farming and farm problems. This, however, has not prevented most owner-occupiers from regarding PGA, together with the other institutions active in farm purchase, as comprising a group of faceless City moguls out for a quick killing from farming. The collapse of one of the institutional owners, the Lyon Group, in 1974 was the cue for an orgy of self-righteousness in the correspondence columns of the farming press, but there are now signs, as the full implications of CTT begin to filter through, that this hostility may have mellowed.

Why, though, have the City institutions attracted so much acrimonious comment? The innate conservatism of the farmer and a hostility to the 'interference' by any 'outsiders' which has characterized the philosophy of the landowner for centuries have undoubtedly played their part. But the causes run deeper than this. The coincidence of swiftly rising land prices in 1972–3 and a growing awareness through the farming press of the revival of interest by the City in agricultural land neatly allowed many farmers to put two and two together and come up with five. Detailed analysis in specialist journals like *Farmland Market* and *Big Farm Management* concluded that the real villain was roll-over relief rather than the City institutions, which were generally not the pacesetters when it came to buying land but *followed* the market in a cannily cautious manner. Journals like these, however, tended to preach to the converted; the more widely read farming press, like *Farmers' Weekly* and *British Farmer and Stockbreeder*, were peppered with references to 'moguls', 'tycoons', 'barons', 'speculators' and so on. As *Farmers' Weekly* admitted in one feature in 1976, 'The eyes of the world are on the company farmer, waiting for a mistake or an action to criticise'. Many private landowners believed in a vague conspiracy by the City and the government: the City institutions, by forcing up land prices, were imposing a crippling CTT burden on the individual landowner, who was thereby forced to sell out to them. The institutions in turn could be excused for viewing this hostility with a certain amount of perplexity. Mindful of the damage which bad publicity could do to the confidence of their investors they had leant over backwards to be model landlords: attentive to their tenants, sensitive to the environment, generous (by agricultural standards) employers, enlightened investors and even efficient farmers. Their studied moderation and careful attention to rural sensibilities merely seemed to incense farmers further, however.

In their puzzlement the City institutions may have regarded all this as merely the massaging of tired prejudices – and some of their spokesmen have not been unknown to hit back at what they consider to be the hypocritical cant of the uninformed farmer. However, the hostility is more fundamentally based than this because it relates essentially to property relationships in modern agriculture and their likely direction in the future. For this reason the individual landowner has correctly perceived, albeit often unconsciously, that his interests are being threatened – and from a totally unexpected direction. At the root of their reaction is fear – fear of the erosion of their property rights. The City institutions threaten the owner-occupier by gaining an 'unfair' competitive advantage by their exemption from CTT and their ability to call upon huge resources in order to inject new capital into the industry. The average owner-occupier cannot hope to match either of these expediencies. No less galling has been the ability of the institutional farmers to undermine many of the owner-occupiers' claims for selfless efficiency by demonstrating the considerable improvements which can be achieved. However, the most significant aspect of their activities has been to signal a possible return to the division of ownership and control in agriculture. Whatever the situation elsewhere in the economy farmers are convinced that in agriculture, with its preponderance of family proprietorships, such a division would be contrary to their interests even though they could retain control over their farming practice by becoming tenants and could, by negotiating sale-and-lease-back agreements, ensure security of tenure for themselves and their heirs in perpetuity. In part this may be due to a vague fear that institutional ownership may render nationalization easier to accomplish at a later date; but, even allowing for this, the crux of the matter is the fear that loss of ownership involves a loss of independence and that he who pays the piper may eventually, in however far distant the future, wish to call the tune. Farmers become even more alarmed, therefore, when they observe the City institutions not only purchasing land but farming it themselves. Is this, they wonder, the shape of things to come?

For these reasons the spotlight of publicity has been turned particularly strongly on Fountain Farming Ltd, the largest of the City-backed *farming* companies with 24 000 acres at the end of 1976. It may be misleading to regard Fountain Farming as being entirely prototypical of the future of farming in England, but its operations pose some interesting questions about the nature of property rights in these circumstances and are worth considering in detail. Fountain Farming is one of six subsidiaries of Matthews Wrightson Land Ltd (MWL) which is in turn a subsidiary of Matthews Wrightson Holdings. The managing director of Fountain Farming, Anthony Rosen, is firmly committed to the view that the future of farming lies in following other industries in the separation of ownership from control. As he wrote in the 1973 *R H M Hampshire Harvest Review*:

There are many in our industry who have long considered that the separation of land-owning from the business of farming can only be to the benefit of both: there are also, need it be said, others who tend to disagree; not

surprisingly these tend to be the existing owner-occupiers. It is my contention that agriculture should, indeed must, follow the pattern set out in
almost all other industries where the owner of the land and the owner of
the business upon it are seldom one and the same.

Fountain Farming scrupulously follows this philosophy. M W L buys
the land and lets it to Fountain Farming, which becomes the permanent tenant. Fountain Farming then sets about improving the efficiency of the holding, often by the simple expedient of the parent company borrowing up to 90 per cent of the land's value in order to
embark on an ambitious programme of investment. Fountain Farming virtually guarantees to produce a 50 per cent increase in production over two years and to double production over five years. This
enables a rent to be fixed which is sufficiently high to provide an
attractive proposition to potential investors. Once profitability is
assured, M W L sells the land off 'over the head' of Fountain Farming
to investors, usually other City institutions like pension funds, although M W L also promises to repurchase at full vacant possession
value if given due notice. Consequently the landowner (in effect, a
group of shareholders) cannot gain possession but can regain the
value of the farm as if it were owner-occupied. Fountain Farming is
effectively 'rack-rented' in order to ensure a worthwhile rent to its
new landlords *and* a cash contribution to the profits of M W L. It must
therefore farm to the maximum possible profitability. In addition
Fountain Farming bids for agricultural tenancies in the normal way,
especially from institutional owners.

Fountain Farming's operations are spread across the entire country,
from Hampshire to Scotland and from Essex to Wales. M W L
pursues its land purchases in both upland and lowland areas and by
the employment of its other major subsidiaries in recreational
development and forestry management it has adopted a philosophy
of 'total land use'. In practice what this means is that once a tract of
land has been purchased it is disaggregated into blocks which are
allocated to their most efficient use and placed in the hands of the
appropriate subsidiary. It then finds different investors for the different uses and, in order to provide a more attractive investment pack-
age, may even combine areas of land with the same use on different
holdings into one block. The aim is always to find the optimal use of
land in order to provide the highest possible rate of return. This
policy of 'high farming' has paid enormous dividends, not only in

terms of the spectacular increases in productivity (which in 1976 was £22000 per employee), but in terms of increased employment, higher salaries, a career ladder for employees, especially managers, and, not least, high profits. According to Rosen the benefits of these arrangements accrue to all the parties concerned: the investors receive a high rent, profits are increased, employees earn higher wages and better working conditions and the consumer obtains a lower cost for food. All this is achieved because the division of ownership and control enables the farming operation to be adequately financed (Fountain Farming requires upwards of £500000 per year to finance its growth), producing high rates of investment, while the tenancy agreement provides for incentives to achieve maximum profitability.

For Rosen British agriculture will not become properly efficient as long as what he refers to as 'the traditional nepotism of the owner-occupier' remains. Owner-occupation, he believes, is a recipe for indolence because it provides no incentive to maximize profitability but only to achieve the minimum necessary to enjoy an equitable life-style. Owner-occupation thus leads to stagnation. There is, Rosen argues, 'no divine right to farm' and 'the best qualification to be a farmer is not necessarily to be a farmer's son'. It is in sentiments like these that some of the implications of a return to a landlord–tenant system can be appreciated. It is not surprising, then, that owner-occupiers react with hostility to the threat posed by the City institutions, for the very economic rationality of their argument is hard to refute on economic terms alone. In order to compete with the likes of Fountain Farming, however, most owner-occupiers would have to turn themselves into tenants in order to raise the capital for the necessary investment – yet this is precisely what they will not do. Rosen, in an article in *Farmland Market* in 1975, is again scathing about what he regards as the hypocrisy contained in this:

Many owner-occupiers decry any rise in land values because of increasing their personal tax problems, totally forgetting – or conveniently ignoring – that reasonable increases in land values are essential if they are to remain economically sound in terms of collateral for their borrowings . . . 'I am not interested in capital appreciation; all I want is for my heirs to farm this land'. . . . Let the rare owner-occupier who believes this form a limited company, let his farm to the company then sell the land to an investor. . . . He then has capital to spare, his heirs have the tenancy in perpetuity, and everyone is happy.

This quotation illustrates the crux of the argument between the owner-occupiers and the City institutions. For the latter increasing land prices are a boon: they ensure capital growth and for their farming operations provide an increased potential for borrowing that can finance investment and reap higher profits. For the owner-occupier increasing land values bring only tax headaches. The advent of CTT will lead to many owner-occupiers taking Rosen's advice. However, the institutions will be choosy. As the chairman of the Property Unit Trust group stated in *Farmers' Weekly* at the end of 1976:

We and the other institutional investors want good units of about 1000 acres on Grade 1 and 2 land and perhaps the better Grade 3 land. But it will be a long time before we consider moving down to lower Grade 3 types. So the hill farms and other farms on poorer land are likely to remain in private ownership until there is insufficient good land to go round the institutional buyers.

Perhaps, then, a slow bifurcation will ensue. Rosen concurs: 'I believe there will certainly always be a place for the efficient private farm, but less and less for the inefficient, nor any future at all for those who believe in their own immortality.' Since this is precisely what the traditional English landowner *has* believed in, these must strike him as chilling words.

Ownership and stewardship

Shorn of economic arguments to champion the cause of individual landownership, its defenders have fallen back on less material and less tangible considerations. Indeed, by denigrating the exclusive pursuit of economic rewards and championing in its place a notion of personal service to the rural community and a protective atavism for the land itself they echo the gentlemanly values of the nineteenth-century landowner. These sentiments are now expressed by a much broader spectrum of the farming population than they were a hundred years ago, however. For example, the traditional populism of the yeoman farmer now finds expression via this idiom. This is Mr Hew Watt, an Essex owner-occupier on 800 acres, in an article, 'Stop Exploiting the Land', in *Farmland Market* in 1975:

For centuries the countryside has been populated by people who contributed more to life than they extracted, be they landowners, owner-
occupiers, tenant farmers, tradesmen, craftsmen, or the rector.

The rural population . . . rely on each other and help each other. . . .
Most voluntary organisations in the countryside are manned by people
who would never think of taking a salary for their services. Rural people
are always on the look-out for those less fortunate than themselves, from
the grave-digger to the squire they see their occupation as a respectable
and worthy one contributing to the betterment of the community in which
they live.

They need reimbursement, but this is not the main yardstick of their
success as in urban society, for once profit becomes the sole aim and
people become labour units, then the quality of life disappears almost
overnight. . . .

The participating landlord-tenant who earns his living from his estate
should be encouraged by tax law, and so should the owner-occupiers. The
rest, who look upon land as similar to gold or a Canaletto purchased solely
for its growth potential for personal gain, will I hope, be completely dis-
couraged by taxes. . . .

From another vantage point Lord Davidson, representing the CLA,
makes a similar case in his evidence to the Select Committee on the
Wealth Tax:

It is fair to say that we do not consider institutions owning rural land are
a proper substitute for the private landowner who lives on the spot, who
understands what it is all about, who has inherited it no doubt from his
parents and is part and parcel of the whole rural scene and the rural
structure, and who has devoted his life to improving amenities and keeping
rural life viable and working. I do not know politically whether it is
thought the man from The Pru will be a better landlord than the private
landowner, but we certainly do not think so.

A number of themes are discernible in these comments (and they
are typical of those which crop up in the farming press and elsewhere
with consistent regularity). There is an antagonism to the urban outsider – to city ways as well as City money – which remains a potent
force in rural affairs. There is also an attempt to conjure up the image
of the wholesome rural community threatened with disruption by
remote and insensitive bureaucrats. As the institutions moved back
into the land market at the beginning of 1976 this fear was encapsulated by Sir Charles Mott-Radclyffe, as reported in *Farmers' Weekly*:

The insurance company may well succeed in extracting higher rents from the tenants and be rougher, if they so wish, in other directions as well, but the directors of the insurance company, unlike the ordinary landowners, do not live cheek by jowl with their tenants and meet them in the village Post Office on Mondays.

Most important of all, though, is the attitude to money, whether this takes the form of the anti-materialism of Hew Watt or the lofty indifference to 'the man from The Pru' of Lord Davidson. Unable to compete with the institutions on these terms, they prefer to change the rules of the game. To be an authentic landowner, they seem to be saying, means precisely *not* to be as efficient and as profitable as possible.

The centrepiece of this ideology is the concept of stewardship. This was a philosophy of property ownership articulated most influentially by Edmund Burke at the end of the eighteenth century to defend the landed aristocracy against attacks on their privileges by the new industrial bourgeoisie. Were he alive today he could be forgiven a sense of *déjà vu*. For stewardship remains an integral part of the conception of landownership and is, of course, intimately linked to the gentlemanly ethic described earlier in this chapter. It is a self-deprecation which attempts to deflect a recognition of the benefits which derive from ownership towards an emphasis on altruism and service. It implies that land is not so much a factor of production to be used to generate profit, but part of a wider national heritage which the landowner sees it as his duty to protect. Rather than he owning the land, it is as if the land 'owns' him. The landowner thus regards himself – and wishes to be regarded by others – as merely a caretaker, holding the land in trust for the nation before handing it on to the succeeding generation, preferably in a better state than when he received it. He is therefore not 'really' an owner, but a custodian, a protector – a steward. Occasionally the ideology of stewardship may rebound – such as when, as we shall see in Chapter 6, the nation decides it would like a say in how the land which is being looked after on its behalf should be cared for and should be made available to it. Nevertheless the notion that the landowner is in effect merely a life-tenant continues to be constantly invoked in order to defend the existing pattern of landownership against any radical changes.

The concept of stewardship has a peculiar affinity with the ownership of land which is often absent from the ownership of other forms of capital. The benefits which accrue from the land are, as we have seen, frequently of a long-term nature. Even the City institutions recognize that the major value of landownership lies in long-term capital growth rather than in short-term yield. Moreover the production cycle in agriculture is much longer than in most areas of manufacturing industry, and in the case of forestry considerably so. In such a uniquely long-term business, where a crop of trees or a herd of cattle may take several generations to mature and where the fertility of the land can be irreparably harmed by short-sighted gain, stewardship need not be an entirely anachronistic idea. However, these considerations, since they concern all owners of agricultural land irrespective of whoever they may be, apply equally to the City institutions. It is in their interests, too, to be good 'stewards' by being mindful of their investments. In this sense good stewardship and self-interest will coincide, just as they have for the private landowner for centuries.

Not surprisingly the defenders of private landownership do not see it this way. As the CLA put it in its discussion document, *The Future of Landownership*, published in 1976, private ownership

rests upon the benefits which private landowners have given in the past, and will continue to give, if allowed, towards the stewardship of the countryside. . . . Long-term landowners can give rather than take from their land. It is an ongoing life that transcends the generations, and it gives a sense of lifetime stewardship as opposed to personal ownership. . . . The stewardship concept encourages landowners to think and act in the long-term interests of the land and the community it supports. . . . The landowner's vision and his belief in improving his heritage for his heirs encouraged him to subsidise the local community in many practical ways and to improve and maintain the countryside. Despite the economic absurdity of this type of activity many, albeit a steadily reducing number, still carry on.

It would be mistaken to deny that words like these evoke a sympathetic response in the minds of most English people. The appeal to selfless altruism, to the nation's heritage, to continuity and even to 'economic absurdity' seems difficult, if not impossible, to resist. Yet these claims require a closer examination. The public is being asked to support a system of landownership which, it is acknowledged, may be less than economically rational under modern conditions but which entails non-economic compensations. The public, however, is not to be allowed a share in the benefits to be derived from private landownership, for there is also opposition to the introduction of taxation on landownership, such as CTT or a Wealth Tax. Neither is the public to be allowed any proprietorial right of control over the land which is being held, allegedly, with its interests uppermost in mind. This would raise the spectre of land nationalization and there is little need to labour the private landowner's apprehension of *this*. Instead control, benefit and the right of alienation – the three component parts of ownership – are to remain exclusively in private hands. Self-interest and public interest are then assumed to coincide on the basis that the private landowner 'knows what is best' for the public.

Too much emphasis upon the notion of stewardship therefore has its dangers. It acknowledges that the pattern of landownership must rest on public as well as private considerations and that the public has a legitimate right to be interested in the land which it entrusts to its custodians. However, should the public ever attempt to exercise its rights in a manner which conflicts with the interests of the landowner, this is resisted. In recent years the private landowner has been hoisted repeatedly on this petard of his own making – over issues like environmental conservation, landscape preservation, countryside access and, most dangerously of all, over the activities of the City institutions. The institutions have threatened to expose the extent to which the private landowner has failed to carry out the functions entrusted to him by demonstrating the extent to which (for whatever reasons) British farming is, in terms of potential, undercapitalized, poorly structured and inefficient. The landowner, defending himself against the institutions' predatory intentions, appeals to the public on the basis of stewardship. This, however, runs the risk of not only drawing the public's attention to his economic shortcomings but, by insisting on the public's right to be consulted, introduces the prospect of public control. The introduction of CTT has highlighted this dilemma: the private landowner is caught between the devil of land nationalization and the deep blue sea of the City institutions.

His response to this has been twofold. The first has been to keep his head down and hope the problem will go away – perhaps with the help of his political friends. For example, the President of the CLA, Mr John Quicke, appealed to members at a conference on landownership in 1976 to keep their nerve: 'It is when things look blackest that sensible men remember that the pendulum always swings back, that the political wind does not blow for ever in the same direction. . . . We must not lose heart too easily. Private property is not unacceptable to the mass of our fellow countrymen. It is not something of which to be ashamed.' The second response has been to look again at the City institutions as defenders of private, even if corporate, landownership, something infinitely preferable to the ogre of state control. The advent of CTT has provoked this reappraisal, providing the institutions with the hitherto unlikely role of saviours of private landownership. There are even those who feel that the City can be educated into a more gentlemanly style of landlordism, following the example of early experimenters like Norwich Union. Here much will depend upon the influence of the estate agents who act on behalf of the new investors and whose traditional role is that of buffer between owners and tenants. But such a view tends to be offered as much in hope as in expectation. In any case more and more owner-occupiers of large- and medium-sized holdings will be forced to consider some form of arrangement with the institutions of the state as CTT begins to bite. What private landowners will resist bitterly, however, is the prospect of becoming an employed class farming for someone else.

What, then, is the future of agricultural landownership in this country? An increasing involvement of the City institutions seems virtually inevitable whatever the changes in capital taxation. Many pension funds and insurance companies have only recently become aware of the advantages of investment in land and with over £3000 million annually at their disposal, they have ample resources to purchase land, even if they devote only a small fraction to this purpose. Even at their current rate of expansion, however, it would take many decades before they owned even a majority of agricultural land. Nevertheless, the rate of transfer from private ownership will depend largely upon continuing levels of taxation and these are far from predictable, both in regard to their extent and their avoidability. In the past the long-predicted demise of the landowner has been confounded by his ability to minimize his tax burden. Most large farms now have an ownership structure of baroque complexity with the full panoply of trusts, partnerships and privately owned trading companies employed to avoid taxation wherever possible. The increasing value of the land was once merely a nuisance because it forced the owner-occupier to engage in this kind of activity in order to retain the bulk of his income and ensure succession. Now the situation is more serious. No doubt a veritable army of accountants and tax lawyers are combing the relevant legislation in search of loopholes in CTT so that similar measures can be taken. Otherwise there are a multitude of possibilities: farms being broken up in order to pay CTT; an investment 'strike' by owner-occupiers because of the uncertain future; even the thought of farmers breeding large families so that there are sufficient children to reduce taxation on a partible inheritance. The essential decision, however, will be political, as have been all those which have determined the progress of 'the land question' over the past hundred years or more. So the issue is reducible to whether the political will is there to engender the necessary changes. There seems to be considerable doubt on this score – even within the Labour Party. Living on the verge of extinction has become a way of life for the landowner which has continued since the beginning of this century. Reports of his death may yet be exaggerated.

'When they stand with their backs to the wind it means someone's left the door open.'

3 The farming industry

While the land itself may be a symbol of continuity in English rural society, the predominant activity which takes place upon it – agriculture – has exhibited the most profound transformations, encapsulated in the phrase 'from agriculture to agribusiness'. It should be emphasized that the commercialization of agriculture is in itself nothing new. Farming has been organized around the principle of profit since at least the eighteenth century and therefore long ago became disciplined to the exigencies of the market. All that has occurred during the twentieth century, and particularly in the last thirty years, has been the increased application of scientific and technological principles to the pursuit of profit and the production of food. The most visible consequence of this has been the changeover from a mainly horse-and-hand technology to the adoption of the internal combustion engine in the form of the tractor and the combine harvester, but agriculture has also benefited from advances in science in other, less obvious ways. Advances in genetics have produced unprecedented increases in output from both plant and animal breeding, while the application of nutritional science has also resulted in immense benefits from the scientific application of animal feed and fertilizers. In terms of their husbandry management farmers have been lucky: science has served them well.

One consequence of these innovations has been that farming no longer corresponds to the dignified rhythm of the seasons to the extent that it once did. Factory farming, which even a generation ago would have been regarded as a contradiction in terms, is now commonplace and combine harvesters can polish off the harvest in a matter of hours. Agricultural production has thus been revolutionized and any sense of continuity has been shattered within the lifetime of most of today's farmers. Farming, in fact, has become very big business indeed – the largest in the United Kingdom in terms of the value of its output. As a result farm management has followed the precepts of rationalization apparent in other industries and farms have become bigger, more capital-intensive and more streamlined in their production. Farmers in turn have become more professional, more profit-conscious and more aware of the necessity to innovate in order to remain in business. On this basis British agriculture has become not only one of the most efficient, but also one of the most prosperous, in the world.

These economic and technological changes in agriculture have been accompanied by the ascendancy of farmers in English rural society. As long as the landlord–tenant system predominated the farmer was automatically assigned to the second of the three 'natural orders' of the rural class system, but the changes that have occurred in the pattern of land tenure during this century have enabled the farmer to take up a place alongside the landowner at the head of rural affairs. The leadership of rural society is now almost universally in the hands of farmers (who, now, of course, are mostly landowners too) and this has represented an important shift in the class structure of rural England which, when contemplated in a historical perspective, is of considerable significance. The history of the English farmer in the twentieth century is, whatever the vicissitudes, a spectacular success story.

The structure of modern farming

Two characteristics typify the structure of modern farming: complexity and diversity. Almost any generalization is bound to be too sweeping to account for the extreme variations that may take place in the pattern of agriculture from one region, one county and even one parish to the next. In part this is due to the diverse conditions of soil and topography that may be encountered within quite small distances in England, but variability is also prevalent in the more manmade aspects of agriculture – the size of farm, the type of production, the proximity to centres of population, and so on. Moreover, agriculture cannot be realistically regarded as a single industry. There are at least six major systems of food production that are encompassed by the term and between them they can produce a variety of combinations that is almost infinite. When all these factors are added together what we find on the ground is a *mélange* of farms that almost defies description. Consequently farmers themselves do not form a homogeneous group. They range from the smallholders and family farmers whose standard of living may be no higher than that of a manual worker in other industries to landed aristocrats and agri-businessmen who are among the richest men in England.

To begin to make sense of this diverse and complex structure we must first of all turn to the geographers who have documented in great detail what they choose to call 'the personality of Britain' – the differences of climate and topography which continue to place environmental constraints on farming practice. One major distinction to which Caird drew attention in the 1850s but which remains important today is that between the predominantly arable agriculture of southern and eastern England and the pastoral agriculture of the North and West. In general the boundary between the two areas is that between the highland zone of relatively wet and less fertile uplands and the lowland zone of drier, warmer, flatter and more fertile ground to the east of a line from the Tees to the Exe. There are important exceptions to this generalization in each sector but overall the distribution of tillage (that is, ploughed land which is under crops other than grass) is clearly concentrated in the southern and eastern counties while grassland predominates in the North and West. Even the lowlands in the North and West are used for dairying rather than cash crops, with the uplands being reserved for the rearing of sheep and cattle.

The distinction is not merely one of geography, however, for the kind of rural society which each of these systems of agriculture has traditionally supported has also varied considerably. In the pastoral areas farms are smaller, employ less hired labour and are on average less prosperous. As a result class divisions are less apparent, both objectively and subjectively, than elsewhere, although much depends on the pattern of land tenure. In areas where the large estates characteristic of the pastoral areas in the nineteenth century have been retained then the division between small tenant farmers and their landlords can be significant, but the division between farmers and farm workers is blurred by the fact that many of the latter are farmers' sons or other kin awaiting their inheritance. In the arable South and East, by contrast, farms are larger, more mechanized, employ more hired labour and are much more prosperous. There is usually a rigid and insuperable class barrier between farmers and farm workers, for the latter have about the same chance of farming on their own account as of winning the football pools – which is what they would need to do to raise the capital required to purchase and equip even a small farm in these regions.

This geographical and sociological distinction is complicated by the presence of a number of other factors which cut across it. Local soil conditions provide exceptions to the general rule on both sides – for example, sheep rearing in the Norfolk Brecklands and on the Kent and Sussex Downs; or arable farming on the Shropshire and Cheshire plains. Most importantly the proximity of large urban centres may have a considerable influence on the pattern of agriculture by providing a readily accessible market for certain agricultural produce, particularly vegetables, fruit and flowers. Modern methods of transportation, however, are slowly reducing the distorting effects of the conurbations and allowing horticultural production to become concentrated in a few localized districts – flowers in Cornwall and Lincolnshire; fruit in Kent, Worcestershire and Herefordshire; vegetables in the Fens, Bedfordshire, Lancashire, as well as in local urban-fringe areas. Crops grown for the food-processing industry also tend to be sited near freezing or canning factories, although most of these are located in the eastern counties. However, any farming activity which takes place indoors on concrete rather than outside on soil can be located virtually anywhere. Consequently the production of pigs and poultry bears little relation to agricultural land as such, although for reasons of history and geographical inertia they have remained important in Lancashire and Cheshire. All these and many other socio-economic factors have ensured that English farming – and the English countryside – never manifests a complete uniformity. Despite the increasing specialization that has occurred since the war the pattern of agriculture continues to show many of the characteristics of the traditional patchwork quilt.

This diverse geographical structure is exacerbated by the pattern of landholding. As we have seen in the previous chapter this can vary considerably from county to county, not only for reasons of regional agricultural economy but because of historical continuity in the ownership of land. In many areas, for example, the timing and extent of enclosure still exerts a considerable influence over the typical size of farm. Unfortunately any attempt to gauge the size of farms across the country as a whole again has to tangle with the official statistics on the subject. The Ministry of Agriculture conducts an annual agricultural census every 4 June which provides the basis of our knowledge on this and most other aspects of the 'national farm'. However, the census does not count either farmers or farms but 'occupiers' of each 'agricultural holding'. An agricultural holding consists of any piece of land used for agricultural purposes. Many of these do not correspond with a common-sense notion of a 'farm' – for example, a golf course which occasionally allows sheep to graze might qualify; so might a child's pony paddock. The Ministry is constantly engaged in weeding out the agriculturally insignificant holdings and excludes all holdings (except glasshouses) of less than one-quarter of an acre. Nevertheless the distribution continues to be highly skewed towards the lower-size groups, where there are tens of thousands of holdings whose contribution to the agricultural output of the country is minuscule. At the other extreme, however, there are a tiny proportion of extremely large holdings which are responsible for the bulk of agricultural production. This distribution is shown in Table 3.

This skewed distribution means that notions like 'the average farm' must be used with extreme care. If we simply divide the total acreage by the total number of holdings we obtain a figure of 112 acres. This, however, includes all the pony paddocks and golf courses

Table 3 *Number and size distribution of agricultural holdings in England and Wales, 1974*

Crops and grass acreage	'000 holdings			Million acres	(crops and grass)
	No.	%		No.	%
¼ –19¾	56·8	27·3 ⎤		0·49	2·1 ⎤
20 –49¾	39·9	19·1 ⎥		1·32	5·6 ⎥
50 –99¾	41·7	20·0 ⎬ 91·6		3·01	12·7 ⎬ 57·9
100–299¾	52·5	25·2 ⎦		8·90	37·5 ⎦
300–499¾	10·7	5·1 ⎤		4·03	17·0 ⎤
500–999¾	5·5	2·7 ⎬ 8·5		3·70	15·6 ⎬ 42·1
1000 and over	1·5	0·7 ⎦		2·24	9·5 ⎦
Total	208·6	100·0		23·69	100·0

SOURCE: MAFF Annual Agricultural Statistics.

which the Ministry has not yet eliminated from its statistics and it also includes holdings which are only 'farmed' on a part-time basis. Even so, it is three times the average for the EEC as a whole. A much better measurement of a 'farm' is a full-time holding – that is, a holding with sufficient crops and livestock to provide full-time employment for one person on the basis of an average labour requirement, known as a 'standard-man-day'. This immediately eliminates over 40 per cent of all agricultural holdings in England and Wales, leaving (in 1974) 124151 full-time holdings on 21·34 million acres (90·1 per cent of the total), with an average size of 172 acres. This is a better indicator of the average size of farm. Nevertheless even this figure needs to be placed in context. Some types of agriculture – 'factory' farming most notoriously – do not utilize much land, so small acreages do not necessarily imply small businesses; the converse is also true, for the employment of enormous acreages of fell and moorland need not involve a large farming enterprise in any but a geographical sense. These qualifications notwithstanding, the average size of holding is increasing. Below 300 acres there has been a marked decline in numbers over the last thirty years and a complementary increase in the number of holdings above this figure as a result of farm amalgamations. This is reflected in a growing concentration of production: the top 10 per cent of holdings, measured by standard-man-days, now produce more than half of the total output.

With 124151 full-time 'farms' it might be concluded that there are a similar number of 'farmers'. This, however, would be to place a naive faith in both the official statistics and the simplicity of modern agriculture. By no means all 'occupiers' are farmers: many are managers employed by an absentee owner while others may occupy the holding but derive their main employment or source of income from elsewhere. A further complication is that of multiple holdings – separate holdings of land farmed by the same farmer or farming business. Again the Ministry has been engaged in the Sisyphean task of removing the element of double-counting which they introduce, but thousands remain to confuse the statistics (and the researcher). These multiple holdings account for the otherwise mystifying fact that some holdings have no 'occupiers', although they do, of course, have 'farmers'. Until 1970 the Ministry excluded farmers and their wives from the census returns, even though other components of the agricultural labour force were included. Assessments therefore involved risky and complex calculations based upon the number of holdings, with the hope that errors would cancel themselves out. In desperation it was always possible to turn to the decennial population census, but that included under the same heading 'farmers, market gardeners, farm managers, bailiffs and foremen' – and the difference in totals was alarming. Then in 1970 the Ministry began to count 'farmers, partners and directors' – though not in Scotland and without any comparable figures for earlier years so that some assessment could be made of how the new method of counting was responsible for any changes in the labour statistics. Nevertheless we now know that in 1974 there were 166981 'farmers, partners and directors' in England and Wales. This represents nearly 40 per cent of the entire agricultural labour force. The number has been falling steadily since the war with the amalgamation of holdings, though not as rapidly as the decline in hired workers. For most farmers, unlike their workers, leaving the industry would involve a loss of independence and a move down the social scale. This has proved a powerful incentive to stay put.

The occupational immobility of farmers is at the heart of the perennial problem of 'farm adjustment', the ever-changing optimum mixture of land, labour and capital which provides the most efficient enterprise under new technological conditions. In general the impact of new agricultural technology has required larger holdings to take full advantage of the new means of production, so that the size of holding which can be considered economically marginal has slowly increased. The changing structure which this requires can, however, only proceed by farm amalgamation and this, given the tenacity of the small farmer, has proceeded very slowly indeed: in England and Wales the average size of full-time holdings has increased by 46 acres in the last decade (although the EEC average is only 2·4). Unless the small farmer is to be removed by force his ambitious neighbour must wait for him to become bankrupt, run out of heirs or take advantage of the many inducements offered by the government to leave – and even part-time employment elsewhere may be preferable to making a complete break with the land. The nature of land tenure is frequently important here, for on the whole less consolidation has been achieved in areas with small, owner-occupied farms than in areas with larger, tenanted holdings. Nevertheless the onward march of capital accumulation and new technology means that the marginal farmer will always be with us. On average the size of a holding which can be considered full-time nearly doubles every decade.

Economies of scale are not universal in agriculture, however, for they vary according to the type of production and in some cases may even be negative beyond a threshold which is still within the bounds of the family farm. Arable production is one of the most conducive to increasing scale because it is one of the most suitable for mechanization and often – as in the case of cereals-growing – requires little individual attention to the crop. Certain types of livestock production have also proved amenable to production in very large units. In a few cases this has provoked spectacular changes in the structure of the industry within a very short space of time – for example, 90 per cent of output of broiler chickens is now in the hands of five public companies; and pig production seems poised to move in the same direction. In other branches of agriculture, however, such as horticulture, dairying and sheep-farming, the benefits of scale are by no means so apparent. Thus a highly capitalized and large-scale commercial agriculture can be juxtaposed quite happily with a quasi-subsistence pattern of farming on small holdings. The relationship between size and efficiency is consequently a very complicated one, over which there is considerable controversy among agricultural economists. In any case much depends on the measure of efficiency that is used – profitability, relative cost or rates of energy conversion.

The variability in the optimum 'factor mix' between different types of farming leads to a distant association between the type of farm and the size of the enterprise. In general the smaller farms tend to be livestock farms, especially those involved in dairying and cattle and sheep rearing. On the other hand, over half of the farms in the largest-size groups are cropping specialists, either arable farms or large-scale horticultural holdings. Nevertheless there is considerable variability within each type of farming system as well as between them, so it is only possible to talk in terms of generalized tendencies. The link between type of farming and geographical location then returns us to the point at which we began this consideration of farming structure. It is an oversimplification to regard the North and West solely in terms of small, livestock farms and the South and East in terms of large-scale arable agriculture, but as a broad generalization this distinction holds. Within this framework, however, all farms are tending to become larger and increasingly specialized, and production is tending to become increasingly concentrated in fewer hands.

The commodity mix

An alternative way of looking at the structure of farming is in terms of production rather than the type and size of farms – in other words in terms of 'commodity mix' rather than 'factor mix'. The total output of the 'national farm' is now double the pre-war level and productivity per man has increased fourfold. Thus despite a 20 per cent increase in the population over this period, the self-sufficiency of British agriculture has risen from 30 per cent to 55 per cent, and to nearly 70 per cent of temperate products. In terms of the value of the output this production is shared more or less equally between crops (including horticulture), livestock and livestock products (mainly milk, eggs and wool). The single most important commodity is milk which alone accounts for more than one-fifth of the total income of English farmers. Next in order of importance are horticulture, cereals and fat cattle and calves, each representing approximately 12 per cent of total output by value, then pigs (11 per cent), eggs (7 per cent), and poultry (6 per cent). The other major commodities are potatoes, sugar beet and fat sheep and lambs. Because the scale and concentration of production varies between the commodity groups, the distribution of holdings does not correspond to the distribution of output. However, it does provide a reasonably representative picture of the distribution of farmers, and this is shown for England and Wales in Table 4. Compared with the situation before the war, the proportion of mixed holdings has fallen considerably. This is because farmers need no longer spread the risk of farming across a variety of commodities to the extent that was once considered advisable. A degree of risk – associated with both the weather and the market – inevitably remains, but it has been reduced by new technological developments and particularly by the intervention of the state in the determination of prices and guarantees.

Each of these branches of agricultural production varies not only in terms of its utilization of land, labour and capital but over a whole range of other factors including the pace and rhythm of work, the length and timing of the production cycle and the techniques and management of husbandry. In this sense, too, English farming represents a patchwork of farming methods and ways of life. There is perhaps little need to emphasize the radical changes that have occurred in these aspects of agriculture since the Second World War, a period which has often been referred to, with some justice, as the 'second agricultural revolution'. Before its advent agriculture was by no means static and unchanging, but tradition did count for something and change proceeded at what was widely regarded as a more orderly pace. Basic farming axioms like the rotation of crops represented not only methods of production but almost moral principles from which the farmer ventured at his peril. In one sense all agriculture was a rotation since farmers were aware of the necessity to adopt a symmetrical pattern of farming which would automatically replenish the land with whatever nutrients were taken from it. This applied as much to pasture as to tillage, although the most famous rotation – the 'Norfolk four-course' – was developed in the eastern counties to form the basis of the cereals-and-sheep high farming which predominated down to the First World War and beyond. Rotations like this were an integral part of farming lore and many landlords insisted

Table 4   *Distribution of full-time holdings by type of farming, England and Wales, 1974*

Type of farming	No. of holdings	% of holdings
Specialist dairy	29 707	23·9
Mainly dairy	15 869	12·8
Livestock: cattle	9 374	7·6
Livestock: sheep	2 948	2·4
Livestock: cattle and sheep	13 753	11·1
Poultry	2 620	2·1
Pigs and poultry	7 118	5·7
Cropping: cereals	8 114	6·5
General cropping	12 498	10·1
Vegetables	1 211	1·0
Fruit	1 631	1·3
Horticulture	10 110	8·1
Mixed	9 198	7·4
Total	124 151	100·0

SOURCE: MAFF Classification Tables.

upon their use by their tenants. Today, however, they are much less common, for the scientist has intervened to facilitate the pursuit of maximum returns by monoculture. This break with the principles of rotation has enabled agriculture to become more specialized and has in turn allowed each branch of agriculture to become more autonomous, especially in terms of husbandry management. To this extent the 'national farm' represents a misnomer – there are instead a variety of components which are becoming increasingly differentiated from each other.

The most appropriate way in which to describe the structure of modern agriculture is therefore to take each commodity in turn. We can begin with the production of cereal crops, not because of the high social status traditionally associated with growing corn, but because cereals remain the cornerstone of the British agricultural economy.

Most cereals grown in this country are used for animal feed rather than for human consumption so the conditions surrounding arable farming in the South and East have a direct impact upon the fortune of livestock production in the North and West. The two major crops are wheat and barley. Oats remain important in the wetter and colder areas of the North (and especially in Scotland) but elsewhere the acreage has declined drastically with the disappearance of horses; in some areas maize has recently been introduced, although it is mainly grown for cattle feed. Over the last thirty years the area under wheat has remained reasonably stable, but the barley acreage has trebled, transforming areas like Salisbury Plain, once the preserve of sheep farmers and now under the ploughs of 'barley barons'. In addition the yields from new strains of cereals – especially wheats like Maris Huntsman – have increased by leaps and bounds, rising to three or even four tons per acre on the best land. Yields like these, the structure of agricultural subsidies and deficiency payments and entry into the EEC have all combined to make cereal farming more profitable than almost any other. In 1974 an arable farmer on 1000 acres in East Anglia could expect a net income approaching £45000 on average, according to Farm Management Survey data.

Cereal crops require little attention during their growing period and the key to profitability is the possession of suitable flat, well-drained land and the managerial ability to time the major operations of sowing and harvesting in such a manner as to maximize the yield and minimize the costs of production. The prime qualities demanded of the cereals farmer are therefore entrepreneurial rather than agricultural. Much will depend on his ability to utilize the large amounts of capital employed – especially in machinery – and on his shrewdness in marketing his crop. Predicting the fluctuations in the market, buying and selling grain futures accordingly, storing the crop in anticipation of higher prices, releasing it in anticipation of a fall, avoiding cash-flow problems – this is the stuff of cereals production as much as drilling seed, spraying pesticide and operating a combine harvester. Growing the crop is comparatively easy compared with the managerial skill required in selling and marketing it. For this reason the medium- and large-scale cereal farmers only rarely clean the pro-verbial mud from their boots. Though they may keep their hand in by driving the combine harvester during their employees' lunch breaks at harvest time, most of the actual husbandry supervision is delegated to managers hired for this purpose. These arable farmers make most of their money behind their office desks.

In many areas of lowland England late autumn takes on the coun-tenance of spring as the fields become covered in the bright green of what looks to the passer-by like fresh new grass. This is winter wheat, which now comprises the majority of the wheat acreage since the autumn-sown varieties are higher yielding; most barley, by contrast, is sown in the spring. By late July in the South of England (later further north) harvest is usually well under way. This was once not only the agricultural climax of the year but a great social event, and even now it conjures up bucolic images of scythes and smocks, beer from stoneware jars, chasing rabbits for the pot and long summer evenings spent riding back to the farm on top of a perilously unstable cart of straw. It is no longer quite like that. It is not even the sight of stooks of corn stood up in bunches in the fields to finish ripening and to dry in the late summer sun. Nowadays a combine harvester can in a few hours take the harvest from a field which twenty or thirty years ago may have taken a few weeks. Go away for an afternoon and you will have missed it; go away for another afternoon and the straw bales will have been carted away; come back tomorrow and perhaps the field is a blackened and charred mess. This is the reality of the modern harvest. Indeed, for many farmers it is not even their busiest time of the year – this has moved forward to October when the lifting of potatoes and sugar beet coincides with autumn ploughing and the sowing of winter cereals to produce an extremely hectic period. Sowing may even be carried on into the night with the help of the tractor's headlights.

The ubiquity of the combine harvester has, then, fundamentally altered the pattern of the grain harvest. Even the weather is no longer quite so crucial as it once was, for grain can be dried later before storage in the silo, though with rising fuel costs this can be expensive. In other respects, however, the consequences of the combine harvester are visible for all to see. Large pieces of machinery need large fields to operate in. A modern combine harvester is of such a size that it cannot turn on a sixpence, nor go grubbing about in the crannies and corners at the intersection of hedgerows. Hedgerows have therefore been removed – thousands of miles of them. The combine harvester has not been solely responsible for this – other reasons include the rising cost and declining availability of labour to carry out hedging and ditching, the loss of income which hedges represent at today's yields and prices, the banishment of grazing animals from most arable farms and the need for the maximum possible returns to be obtained when the capital cost of land is so high. The ideal environment for modern cereals production is therefore the prairie. Following the combine harvester comes the other essential piece of equipment of modern arable farming practice – the box of matches. In August lowland England looks from a distance as though the marauding hordes of Genghis Khan are approaching as huge black columns of smoke billow across the sky. Burning stubble – and even straw if it cannot be sold – is now established as an essential operation on most types of land. It not only kills weeds and the seeds of many weeds but the ash helps to fertilize the soil.

The abandonment of rotations and the removal of hedgerows has led to a number of scare stories about the desecration of the soil and the reduction of lowland England to a dustbowl, but they are mostly mythical. Fenland 'blows', for example, the nearest English equivalent to a dust storm, have existed since the seventeenth century; a greater danger to soil is the compaction caused by heavy machinery being driven repeatedly over wet fields. Although semi-continuous corn growing is perfectly feasible, many farmers like to give the land a 'break' occasionally by growing other tillage crops – mainly potatoes, sugar beet (in East Anglia), beans and peas. Very recently, rape has also proved to be a profitable break crop and its dazzling yellow flowers have introduced a blaze of colour to the landscape in May and June. Many of these break crops are grown under contract for food-processing companies or cartels. Sugar beet, for example, is grown exclusively for the British Sugar Corporation on farms within a short radius of its factories, most of which are located in the eastern counties. Originally introduced between the wars as virtual outdoor relief for destitute cereal growers, sugar beet is now an integral part of the arable farming pattern. The crop requires more attention than most, however, with precision drilling of monogerm seed, spraying and hoeing to keep down weeds and lifting with large and heavy machines in often appalling weather conditions on heavy land in the late autumn and winter. Because many of these machines are side-loading, fields of sugar beet often have a swathe of barley planted around the edges. This is harvested in plenty of time for the sugar-beet lifting to commence.

The twin processes of mechanization and specialization have left the fields of most arable farms empty of human and animal life for almost the whole year round. Mechanization has virtually eliminated the need for gang labour in the fields apart from remaining instances of sugar-beet hoeing and potato lifting carried out by casual labour. There is even the potential to dispense with further numbers of full-time employees for new methods of cultivation can avoid the necessity of ploughing. Although not yet suitable for all types of land it is now possible to spray the stubble and weeds that remain after harvest with decomposing chemicals and drill directly through the resulting 'trash' with the following crop. Many of the traditional processes of cultivation are thus avoided, although the chemicals that are required are expensive. Nevertheless such 'direct drilling' has been heavily promoted by agro-chemical companies and in areas where labour is particularly expensive and the soil is suitable some farms have not used a plough for years. Specialization has also resulted not only in less labour but also in fewer animals on the fields of arable farms, for the land is too valuable under tillage to give cows and sheep the licence to use it. Only pheasants and partridges are consistently allowed this privilege. But the possibility always remains of bringing animals indoors and using some of what is grown in the fields to feed them. This particularly applies to the production of pigs.

Many arable farmers these days are also pig producers, particularly of heavy hogs, on contract from major food-processing companies such as Walls. The pigs are fattened on home-produced cereals, producing a sizeable return, although the market is a notoriously fluctuating one. Pig production also takes place in specialized units and there may even be further specialization between pig-rearing and pig-fattening. The specialized pig units also tend to use factory-farming methods in the fattening stages with the pigs housed in conditions of high temperature and humidity, often with automatic feeding and cleaning systems. Pigs can, however, be grazed outdoors, particularly dry sows during the period between weaning and the next farrowing (birth). Frequently various combinations of the two systems are used. The greatest danger for factory-farmed pigs is the risk of epidemic disease, most recently swine vesicular disease, a bacterial infection which is usually caught from improperly prepared swill. Improper hygiene can also cause high rates of mortality among piglets – it averages 20 per cent – although increased veterinary care is gradually reducing the rate of attrition. As it is, a sow can expect to produce two litters a year of ten or eleven piglets each, so that on average sixteen pigs are weaned per sow per year. They are sold off at any time between twenty-two and thirty-one weeks according to requirements. On the larger units all stages of production will occur concurrently, so that pigs are constantly being dispatched off the 'assembly line' on a regular basis. Recently the severity of cyclical depression in the industry has allowed only the larger units to survive. Some of the major food-processing firms are also showing an increasing interest in some form of vertical integration in order to safeguard their supplies and to guarantee carcass quality.

The same principles that have brought pigs indoors – a controlled environment, saving on the use of costly land and labour, greater rates of feed conversion – can also apply to cattle, particularly beef cattle. All cattle spend their winter lives indoors and in principle there is no reason why this should not be the case the whole year round. Why should a cow waste its energy roaming round a field looking for food, when it could be placed indoors, fed automatically and use its energy to produce more beef instead? Such methods are known as 'zero-grazing' and how far such an innovation spreads will depend very much upon the cost of erecting and maintaining the necessary buildings compared with the cost and alternative uses of the land outside them. Currently such is the variety of farms, in terms of both the quality of the land and access to capital for investment, that methods of beef production range across the whole spectrum from extensive, low-cost, single-suckling herds to intensive indoor and outdoor fattening systems. Much of our beef is a by-product of the dairy herd, but the search for increasing productivity and quality – the latter demanded by supermarket chains and food-processors – has promoted specialized beef production and the introduction of various exotic breeds like Charolais and Simmenthal in the search for the 'perfect' beef cow. Conditions vary so much between farms with regard to soil and topography that a variety of breeds and crosses will always be required, however. Beef production is also subject to cycles of depression and prosperity, particularly as the production cycle is so long – normally two years.

The apotheosis of intensive livestock production comes, however, with the poultry industry. This *is* an industry in every way, with few characteristics which are distinctively agricultural in the traditional sense and forming a part of British agriculture which is almost entirely separated from the remainder. Once upon a time hens scratched around the farmyard and chicken was a luxury; now they are housed inside long, low, barrack-like buildings and chicken has become the cheapest Sunday joint. Most of us do not like to inquire too deeply into how this transformation has occurred, for to do so raises in the most acute form possible the dilemma between our desire for cheap food on the one hand and our ethical scruples over methods of production on the other. Each time we step into a supermarket to buy our polythene-wrapped, oven-ready, standardized 'spring' chicken we must dismiss from our minds that it has been produced according to the same principles as a bolt or washer in a Birmingham engineering factory. For broiler chicken production is simply intensive livestock production under modern commercial conditions taken to its logical conclusion and Sir Jack Eastwood, perhaps the most famous of the poultry entrepreneurs, is no more than the Adam Smith (or the Richard Arkwright) of twentieth-century agriculture. Like the introduction of the factory system into manufacturing its consequences have been no less than revolutionary in poultry farming.

The hen has been marked out for factory farming because of its awesome food-conversion ratio and its short production cycle – usually eight weeks for the standard $3\frac{1}{2}$ lb bird. After birth in a specialized hatchery a day-old chick is likely to find itself with 20 000 others, automatically fed and watered, vaccinated by a visiting poultryman and then, after its short life-span and before it becomes 'sexually troublesome', crated and despatched to a large and highly automated packing-station. Here it is killed, dressed, packed, blast-frozen and eventually retailed as one of 400000000 others that we consume each year. There is a ten-day break while the broiler house is cleaned out to prevent parasitic infection and then the cycle starts again. As in most cases of intensive livestock production disease is the greatest problem, and attempts are made to curb this by vaccination – and by minimizing contact with the outside world. Other problems remain, however, like the disposal of manure and offal – although the latter can be reprocessed to form a constituent of feed. Profit margins per bird are very narrow, so the rate of turnover is extremely high, and so are the number of birds per worker, between thirty and fifty thousand. The phenomenal growth of the poultry industry once made it the darling of the Stock Exchange, but recently the rate of growth has levelled off as market saturation has been approached. Nevertheless broiler turkeys and ducks are now proving to be increasingly popular. In the future these methods might even be extended to other animals; already broiler veal is a perfectly feasible, though ethically controversial, proposition.

Mass-production techniques also characterize the egg industry. Nearly all laying birds are housed in cages – usually four to a cage – which are in turn packed side by side, and even in tiers, in large battery houses. Like broiler chickens they are automatically fed and watered and their environment is carefully controlled and monitored. Birds are specially bred for their egg-production qualities, not only in terms of quantity, but for size and colour. They begin to lay when they are approximately five months old and will continue for a further year, during which time up to 300 eggs per bird will be produced. The birds are then usually slaughtered and the whole battery house is cleaned out before a new cycle begins. When an egg is laid it will roll on to an egg belt which can be started by remote control. The eggs are then automatically carried away to be cleaned, graded and packed. As with broiler chickens, egg production is highly concentrated in the hands of a few large firms and vertical integration also prevails. Nor is it coincidental that factory farming seems to accompany this form of organization, but this is an issue which will be taken up again in examining 'agribusiness' later in this chapter.

The animal which has proved highly resistant to factory farming techniques is the sheep. They pine if they become too enclosed and they also become more susceptible to parasitic infection and other diseases. Thus, although, for agricultural purposes, a sheep is no more than a 'woolly pig', the fact remains that unlike the case of the pig modern breeding methods have yet to perfect a sheep which does not thrive on space. Perhaps this is just as well, for many sheep farmers in the uplands are already marginal farmers and a move towards the concentration of sheep farming under intensive methods of husbandry would have far-reaching repercussions for the vigour of rural life across large tracts of northern and western England, as well as Wales and Scotland. Sheep farming also depends upon a delicate balance between the upland and lowland rural economy in the pastoral farming areas. Nevertheless the system of production of sheep, compared with that of cows, pigs or hens, remains primitive. The end-product of sheep farming is fat lambs, with wool merely a sideline – traditionally enough to pay the rent on a tenanted sheep farm. Lambing – the sheep farmer's harvest – occurs between February and April and the lambs are sold in the autumn. Not all of them go for slaughter, however; in addition to those kept back to improve the breeding stock, some ewes may be sold to lowland farms, including those, usually four years old, which have been culled from the breeding stock in the uplands. In the less harsh conditions of the lowlands they may be retained for another year or two. Transhumance also occurs, with lowland sheep grazing on the uplands in the summer while the fields lower down are used to grow winter feed. In the autumn the flow may be reversed, with upland sheep being fattened on the lowland farms before going to market.

Dairying provides a compromise between the intensive methods recently introduced into livestock production and the extensive grazing characteristic of sheep farms. It also has a strong claim to be considered the mainstay of British agriculture: a majority of farmers depend upon it for a living and a majority of the land in England and Wales is also occupied by farms where milk production is the major interest. Despite a discernible trend towards larger herds, dairy farming remains mostly in the hands of small family farmers, helped along by the monthly milk cheque and with an average dairy herd of about thirty-five cows. Up to 80 per cent of the total cows in England are the familiar black and white Friesians which combine high milk

ields (approximately 850 gallons a year) with considerable beef
qualities. A cow will normally produce milk for ten months of the
year after which she is dry for two months before calving again and
then beginning her next lactation. A cow will be retained for four or
five years before being slaughtered, although this can vary according
to milk yield. Breeding is carefully controlled and, these days, is
carried out almost entirely by artificial insemination. Milking is also
entirely by machine – the days of dairymaids and buckets have long
gone. A modern milking parlour will consist of a rotating drum on
which the cows stand. As they pass the operator their udders are
cleaned, the milking machine is attached and by the time they have
completed the circuit milking is completed. As they pass the operator
again, the machine is detached, the udders are washed and disinfected
and the cow is chivvied into the yard outside. Assembly-line milking
of this kind means that a single cowman might manage as many as
120 cows, although this is typical of only the very biggest enterprises.
Most herds continue to be grazed outside between March and October
and are kept indoors over winter fed on silage which was cut from the
fields during the summer and stored until needed in silos. Grass is
often supplemented by other feed, however, particularly in the winter
– and all cows are fed concentrates (compounds of grain and other
high protein feed). The herd is usually milked twice a day and the
milk goes by pipeline to a refrigerated bulk tank, later to be collected
by tanker and taken to the dairy. Milk churns standing by the road-
side are now a rare sight.

Finally there is the horticultural industry, a term which covers a
wide variety of crops – approximately fifty in all – grown across the
length and breadth of England. Vegetables of some sort, for example,
are grown in virtually every parish. Allowing for some over-simplifi-
cation, the industry (which is institutionally fairly separate from agriculture *per se*) can be divided into five constituent parts: glasshouse
production, the nursery trade, fruit, market gardening and outdoor
flower production. Glasshouses (*not* greenhouses) are mostly used for
the production of salad crops – lettuces, tomatoes and cucumbers.
There are some notable concentrations of production, such as in the
Lea Valley in Hertfordshire, the Fylde area of Lancashire and along
the south coast, although glasshouses are to be found on the out-
skirts of most urban centres. The production of flowers such as daffodils, tulips, carnations and chrysanthemums often alternates with the

main output of salad crops, but this side of the glasshouse industry also merges into the nursery trade which produces seeds, bulbs, plants, shrubs and trees for the gardening public. A new trend here is towards 'garden centres', although many of these are retail outlets which do not necessarily grow plants for sale on their own premises. The glasshouse industry is also closely connected with the outdoor production of flowers either for cutting or for the dry-bulb trade. There are notable concentrations in Cornwall, Pembroke and the Scilly Islands (mostly daffodils and narcissi), around Spalding in Lincolnshire (tulips), in the East Midlands (roses) and in Norfolk (lavender). There has recently been much speculation on growing lupins in large numbers outdoors, but in this case the object is not commercial flower or seed production but to provide a nitrogen-fixing break crop on arable farms.

Fruit production can be conveniently divided into two: 'top fruit', which consists mostly of apples, pears, plums and cherries, and 'soft fruit', predominantly strawberries, raspberries, gooseberries and blackcurrants. Top fruit is grown primarily for the retail trade rather than processing, and there is more to it than simply picking the fruit off the trees. The year-round cycle involves replanting, pruning, spraying, mowing the grass between the trees and even beekeeping to induce pollination. Although there are experiments with new strains of apples which can be reaped by a machine similar to a combine harvester from fast-growing, fruit-bearing saplings, most of the crop is still grown by the traditional methods and is picked by hand by casual labour. Advances have occurred more rapidly in marketing arrangements, however. Most large-scale growers now have storage facilities so that fruit can be released on to the market in an orderly manner, avoiding the late summer glut and the accompanying low prices. With soft fruit, though, the seasonal glut remains – indeed in many cases the season lasts only a few, short, hectic weeks. Most soft fruit is in any case grown under contract for processing into pie fillings, purées, jams and fruit cordials. Only the harvesting of blackcurrants has been successfully mechanized, so casual labour is still required in large numbers. In recent years difficulties in obtaining sufficient numbers of fruit-pickers have led many farmers to introduce pick-your-own harvesting and this has proved immensely popular both among the public, who enjoy the novelty of venturing on to a farm, and among growers, who can obtain very large profits by selling direct to the consumer, provided that the picking is carefully organized and controlled.

The fifth sector of horticulture is market gardening. At one extreme this merges into large-scale arable production, for although many traditional market gardens continue to flourish on small holdings utilizing very intensive methods of cultivation, many vegetables are now grown as break crops between cereals and are mechanically harvested under contract for the major food-processing firms. In the face of this competition the conventional market garden has declined, but they remain on the urban fringe or wherever a ready market for produce is close at hand. They also remain where the soil is particularly suitable for certain vegetable crops – for example, carrots in Norfolk, brussels sprouts in Bedfordshire, cauliflowers in south Lincolnshire and rhubarb between Leeds and Wakefield. Again large amounts of casual labour are often required to pick, grade and pack the crop. Because, like other branches of horticulture, market gardening lies outside the provisions for state aid to agriculture, it can be particularly sensitive to the economic pressures of the market. In some respects this has made the industry ripe for rationalization, particularly for vertical integration with food-processing companies and/or retail chains. Already the insistence on standardized quality and continuity of supply is pushing horticulture in that direction.

These brief descriptions of the major commodity groupings represent only a very superficial and cursory glance at the structure of farming in this country. It is impossible to go through all the commodities in detail, but already some indication of the extent of the diversity and complexity of the industry should be apparent. This particularly applies if we add to this the variety among farming enterprises in terms of size, location and tenurial status referred to earlier in this chapter. Consequently no single farmer can be completely representative of farmers as a whole and generalizations about farmers become extremely hazardous. Yet it is the outlook of the farmer as he goes about his daily business which has such far-reaching repercussions in shaping rural England both socially and environmentally. Since it is by definition the major economic activity in rural areas, farming has, by changing itself, changed the society which is based upon it. And the major agents in this change have been the farmers themselves, whether smallholders or farming tycoons Before moving on to consider the economic forces to which agriculture is subject we therefore need to look at the attitudes of these farmers.

Farmers in England today

The social and economic diversity of farmers is accompanied by the equally diverse and unconsciously contradictory images of them that are held by the general public. Simultaneously, it often seems, the prevailing view of the farmer is of a solid, reassuring, bluff John Bull and of a feather-bedded, Jaguar-driving moaner. Each of these images, however, represents a distorted stereotype of a different kind of farmer – or perhaps someone who is not primarily a farmer at all. For it is always important to bear in mind that the status-enhancing properties of landownership – to say nothing of the taxation advantages – continue to attract the interest of those whose major money-making activities lie elsewhere. Earlier in this chapter we noted that nearly half of all agricultural holdings are part-time and the great majority of these are indeed occupied by part-time farmers who are not dependent upon agriculture for their living. Although their contribution to the output of the industry is small, they remain a socially significant group, particularly in south-east England. Here, owing to the proximity of London, there are high concentrations of stockbroker-farmers, although by no means all part-time farmers fall into this category and occasionally the situation may be reversed, for many wealthy farmers are not averse to dabbling in the City as Lloyd's underwriters or non-executive directors of public companies. To express this in an idiom familiar to radio listeners over the last thirty years – for each Dan Archer there is a Jack Woolley or a Ralph Bellamy.

In some respects, however, farmers exhibit a remarkable homogeneity. To begin with, a number of studies in various parts of the country have shown that over three-quarters of all full-time farmers are the sons of farmers and have inherited either their farm or the capital with which to purchase a farm. The so-called 'farming ladder' – the mechanism whereby, it is believed, a farm worker may one day become a large landowner through thrift and shrewd business – is virtually a myth perpetuated by the farming press. In the 1960s, for example, it was discovered by an official committee of inquiry that only fifty-five out of 15000 smallholders had progressed to larger holdings since the smallholdings scheme began at the beginning of the century. Those farmers who do succeed in climbing the farming ladder – and they form the basis of frequent features in farming journals – usually turn out on close examination to have been sponsored at a crucial stage by family loans or straightforward cash gifts to set up a farm. This high degree of inter-generational continuity in farming confers on farmers a number of other fairly uniform characteristics. If having a farmer as a father is a virtual *sine qua non* of being a farmer then it is hardly surprising that farmers tend also to be both socially and geographically immobile. This is not to suggest that farmers are entirely sedentary, for many farmers (particularly tenant farmers) move around in search of larger holdings and/or enhanced opportunities, but the geographical limits of these movements tend, for reasons of regional agricultural economy and familiarity with established patterns of farming, to be quite narrow. Exceptions to this rule are the long-range migrations of farmers during periods of depression – such as that of Scottish farmers to East Anglia during the last quarter of the nineteenth century and again in the 1930s. Farmers do, however, tend to remain in farming so that the most likely source of any non-agricultural, non-rural experience which the farmer has had will be a period in the armed services. Farmers, as a group, have very little first-hand knowledge of life in urban industrial England.

The continuity which inheritance confers also manifests itself in other respects. In England there is no comparable custom to that in the west of Ireland where farmers' sons must await their inheritance before they can marry, but the high incidence of inheritance does push up the average age of farmers. According to a survey carried out by the agricultural 'Little Neddy' in 1972 it was 46·3 years; 53 per cent of farmers were over the age of 45, and 9 per cent over 65. Although there were small variations among different types of farmer these were not very marked, ranging from an average of 43·3 years among pigs and poultry farmers to 48·1 years among livestock farmers. Inheriting a farm also avoids the necessity for most farmers of entering the labour market to sell their labour. Consequently there is little need for farmers to undergo formal industrial training or to obtain educational qualifications. The 'Little Neddy' survey showed that 82 per cent of all farmers had no educational qualifications whatsoever, 90 per cent had no formal agricultural qualifications and

76 per cent had received no organized farm training. There were signs, however, that this situation was changing, for younger farmers were found to be more highly qualified than the older generation. There was also a noticeable difference between small and large farmers, the latter being much more highly qualified. Nevertheless, in spite of the enormous advances that have occurred in the complexity of agriculture, only 1 per cent of farmers were found to have received any formal management training and less than one-third of 1 per cent had attended courses to help them with the clerical side of the business. So a well-defined pattern emerges of the English farmer as a middle-aged farmer's son who left school at the minimum leaving age in order to work on the family farm and whose preparation for the job has consisted of the practical experience and demonstration of agricultural techniques gathered during childhood and early adulthood.

Farmers, of course, insist that farming is essentially a practical activity and that 'you can't learn it from books'. For most – though not all – branches of agriculture this is undoubtedly true, although it does overlook the fact that agriculture is now much more than growing crops and rearing animals. However, this rather narrow social and educational base of the majority of farmers is repeated in several other respects. Although it has never been systematically investigated there is some evidence from their backgrounds to show that farmers' wives are themselves farmers' daughters. Moreover, farming is the most common occupation of farmers' brothers and brothers-in-law, too. Even the friends of farmers tend overwhelmingly to be other farmers and their leisure activities are predominantly based upon agriculturally-related pursuits. Adding all this together it becomes possible to obtain a sense in which the farmer belongs to a somewhat enclosed and self-contained social world, largely insulated from any personal encounters with countervailing social values and life-styles. There exists, then, a rather clannish farming fraternity which exaggerates and magnifies the cultural influences of family background. This is not to suggest that farmers ought to spend more time attending football matches, going to theatres, concerts or cinemas, reading books or playing bingo – they have other, equally valid, preoccupations. But the round of NFU meetings, farmers' clubs, agricultural shows, shoots and rural Conservative Party functions creates a tightly interlocking and rather inward-looking social network. The horizon of most farmers is definitely local rather than cosmopolitan. This is at once the farmer's strength and his weakness. It provides a solid social base which enables the farmer to espouse the values he holds dear with supreme self-confidence; on the other hand it also involves the risk that this confidence may degenerate into an imperviousness to change and sheer bloody-mindedness. The twentieth-century history of agriculture has exemplified these strengths and weaknesses rather well.

The close-knit social world of the farmer therefore generates its own ambience. The informal pressures on farmers to conform to certain assumed standards of both social and economic behaviour can be quite intense. Farming is a highly visible activity, particularly to other farmers. The exclusive nature of the farmer's network of friends and kin obviously affects the judgements which govern the allocation of prestige and so what constitutes 'good' farming practice can be quite strictly, though informally, enforced. This also applies to other aspects of farming – for example, methods of hiring labour and in particular the amount of remuneration which farm workers receive. Over matters like these the integration of the individual farmer into a circle of neighbours and peers can often ensure that those who step out of line can be reminded in a myriad of subtle and not-so-subtle ways of their error. Such social cohesion also acts as a bulwark against any threats to the interests of farmers from outside and has provided a social basis for political mobilization against such threats. Occasionally this has become a rather unedifying xenophobia – as though to be an outsider to agriculture was to be stigmatized on that account alone – but overall it has enabled the farmer to retain his self-confidence in the face of an ever-increasing non-agricultural majority. The farmer remains convinced that as a producer of man's most essential commodity the rest of society needs him more than he needs the rest of society. This assumption, taken for granted by all with whom he daily comes into contact, automatically confers upon all other ways of making a living a certain insubstantiality.

The farmer can therefore never quite bring himself to believe that he is the same kind of person as, say, a garage owner or a greengrocer. This air of distinctiveness pervades the life-style of all farmers, despite the fact that in several important respects their values and judgements are little different from those of other small businessmen in this country. Farmers share with them a closely related set of fundamental beliefs concerning the sanctity of private property, the freedom of the individual, the inherent value of hard work and the right to prosper from one's own endeavours without the interference of the state. They also remain one of the last repositories of an almost unadulterated Calvinist work ethic and its associated 'spirit of capitalism'. It is for gut reasons like these, rather than for reasons of calculation and anticipated personal gain, that the majority of farmers are stolid supporters of the Conservative Party (except for tenant farmers in those areas where a landlord–tenant system remains allied to a strong Nonconformist tradition – principally the Celtic highland zone). Farmers vote for and work for the Conservative Party in such large numbers mainly because it symbolizes the core values to which they remain unremittingly morally committed. Such commitment is not, however, an uncomplicated matter, for as small businessmen most farmers find themselves subject to somewhat contradictory pressures. Farmers are fierce defenders of independence and individualism, yet they are dependent upon the state for guaranteeing their livelihood; they are vehemently hostile to trade unions and trade unionism, yet they band together into one of the strongest farmers' unions in the world; they adhere to a firm belief in worldly success through hard work and proven ability, yet most farmers have achieved their position through little more than an accident of birth; they subscribe to the pursuit of profit, yet they resent the consequences of big business doing likewise. Paradoxes like these suffuse the outlook of most farmers and they are largely the product of the somewhat uneasy situation which farmers share with many other small businessmen under modern business conditions.

Few farmers manage to escape from these paradoxes entirely – perhaps only those at the aristocratic pinnacle of the rural class structure. As a consequence most farmers share an uncertainty which accompanies their self-confidence. They know unerringly what is right and proper; but they remain unconvinced that the rest of the world either shares their values or cares very much about them. Farmers regard themselves socially, culturally and economically as a beleaguered minority in an alien, urbanized world and it is the condition verging on a collective paranoia which this induces, allied to a strong commitment to the righteousness of their cause, that engenders the forthright manner and the periodic flirtations with political militancy. Farmers always feel that they must exaggerate their very real problems to cataclysmic proportions in order to 'put their case across' to what they perceive to be a largely ignorant or uncaring public. This not only ignores the fund of goodwill which the farmer, in the abstract, still retains among a predominantly urbanized population, but it runs the risk of overkill. As farmers continually cry wolf so the public regards their apparently perpetual avowals of crisis and poverty with cynicism and ennui. But this, of course, merely increases the insecurity and the paranoia and leads to a redoubling of effort. Historically, farmers have had good reason to fear public indifference to their plight, but after thirty or more years of state support for agriculture enshrined in legislation there are few signs of farmers ceasing to believe in their own alarmist propaganda. The sense of beleaguered adversity remains strong – the 'Maginot mind' is how the agricultural journalist Tristram Beresford has described it – and this has undoubtedly reinforced the solidarity of what is otherwise a very diverse group in terms of regional and agricultural characteristics. If nothing else, the common factor of lying in the shadow of a vast urban majority has concentrated the minds of farmers wonderfully on their shared situation in an overwhelmingly non-agricultural society.

All of this continues to foster the farmer's self-image as a member of a unique and distinctive breed of men. Farming, according to the great majority of farmers, is not, and never can be, just another job – it is an inimitable life's experience. Farming, to repeat the cliché, is a 'way of life', a reference also to the fact that most farmers 'live the job', that they 'work all hours that God sends' and that most farmers cannot separate work from non-work very easily or meaningfully. Because the vast majority of farmers live at their place of work they can never completely escape from their occupation – some would say, vocation – except for the (usually quite rare) occasions on which they go away for a holiday. Farmers therefore find it difficult to estimate the exact time that they spend 'working', recognizing that almost any of their activities could be construed as such. The agricultural 'Little Neddy' study, acknowledging these difficulties, hedged its findings on the number of hours per week that farmers work with numerous qualifications and cautionary interjections. Nevertheless the average was sixty-four hours, with dairy farmers undertaking the longest working week and cropping farmers the shortest. What this work actually consists of could vary considerably, however, across different types and sizes of farms. Indeed, a consideration of work takes us away from the more homogeneous aspects of the modern farmer's life-style and leads back to a consideration of the wide range of individuals who constitute the farming population.

So varied are the combinations of activities which farmers perform that it makes for a better understanding if their work is broken down into a number of component parts and each is assessed separately. This is because the farmer usually combines a number of important functions in the productive process. He may perform manual labour of a kind indistinguishable from that of hired workers but he is also involved in various kinds of managerial, supervisory, administrative and entrepreneurial activity, some or all of which may take place in an office rather than out in the fields. The proportion of time spent on each type of activity will vary according to the type and size of the farm and also according to the time of the year in many cases. In general the bigger the farm the more likely there are to be found the trappings of bureaucracy; consequently on the largest holdings the farmer (who may in fact be a managing director of a farming company) will be a full-time administrator and manager who might almost be working in an office in any other industry. Subjectively, of course, such farmers as these would continue to pride themselves on being very different from industrial executives, but as far as their actual work is concerned they do not 'farm' in the popular sense – that is, they do not drive tractors or milk cows. Except in emergencies they would routinely perform no manual labour on the farm at all. On small farms, however, this situation is almost completely reversed. Here the farmer himself provides the bulk, perhaps the total, of the farm's manual labour. Administrative duties are confined to wet days and other slack periods; the accounts, traditionally, are kept behind the clock on the living-room mantelpiece.

Such indications may suggest that in order to make sense of the social variability among farmers we need only take account of the size of their enterprises. This is undoubtedly an important criterion, but it is not the only one. Consider the traditional landed estate owner and the managing director of a City-backed farming company, which were discussed in the previous chapter. Both are in charge of large-scale agricultural businesses, but each probably has a very different life-style and, more importantly, has a very different out-

look on farming as an occupation. For one farming remains a dignified 'way of life'; for the other agriculture is primarily a means of
making money. Both types of farmer produce for a market and must
in the final analysis be concerned with making a profit, but they vary
in the extent to which they are prepared to subsume all considerations
under the maximization of profit. They also vary according to the
degree to which they are sensitive to changes in the market for various
farming products and will alter their farming patterns accordingly.
We can summarize this distinction by saying that by no means all
farmers are 'market-oriented' to the same degree. Such market orientation need not be a function of the size of the business, for there are
many small farmers who are primarily interested in the rate of return
on capital invested and who, within their financial and organizational
constraints, can be as aggressively commercial as the largest farming
company. A more helpful categorization of farmers is therefore to
combine the degree of market orientation which they exhibit with
the extent to which they are directly – that is, manually – involved in
the husbandry operations on the farm. This categorization is shown
in the table below. It should be emphasized that these four categories
represent typifications: individual farmers will correspond only with
varying degrees of approximation to each of them.

A typology of farmers

	Market orientation		
		Low	*High*
Degree of direct involvement in husbandry	*Low*	1 Gentleman farmer	2 Agribusinessman
	High	3 Family farmer	4 Active managerial farmer

SOURCE: C. Bell and H. Newby, 'Capitalist Farmers in the British Class Structure',
Sociologia Ruralis, 1974.

Cell 1 consists of farmers whose orientation to the market is low
and who take little part in the actual farming operations of their
enterprises. One of their prime concerns is the maintenance of a distinctive life-style which involves many of the traditional gentlemanly

pursuits of hunting, shooting, charitable activity and public affairs. In many cases such gentleman farmers (to follow a familiar colloquialism) represent the residue of the landed estate owners whose changing fortunes were considered in Chapter 2. Many would still consider themselves, and be considered by the villagers, as the local squire and they remain widely acknowledged as leaders of rural society, even though their formal power has undergone a sharp decline. They retain a strong commitment to the notion of stewardship – of both the land and the structure of rural society – and this remains partly a cause and partly a consequence of their relative lack of concern with the maximization of immediate farming profit. This does not mean, as we have seen, that they are unconcerned with the making of money, but most of the details of this will be delegated to managers or agents hired for this purpose, while the gentleman farmer continues to indulge his wider interests. Thus their concern may be as much to provide the conditions for a good shoot as to improve their barley yields.

In Cell 2 there are the farmers who can be termed agribusinessmen – that is, they are primarily businessmen whose expertise lies in financial administration and accounting rather than in any detailed knowledge of agricultural husbandry. They are frequently executives of farming companies, although in England such companies tend not to be the subsidiaries of food-processing and other corporations, as in the American usage of the term 'agribusiness'. However, farming is a hard-headed business of making money to such farmers, and, as we shall see, the contractual links between such agribusinessmen and the major food-processing companies can be quite strong. Agribusinessmen also tend to be quite distinct from the generality of farmers on a number of dimensions. They tend to be more highly educated and trained, to be more mobile geographically and, most importantly, to be expansionist in their outlook. Agribusinessmen also tend to adopt a distinctive managerial style. They prefer a more formal and impersonal relationship with their employees, tending to rely upon a purely contractual involvement limited to pay and other working conditions. They are somewhat disdainful of the more paternalistic style associated with gentleman farmers, regarding it as anachronistic and as an unnecessary and time-consuming encumbrance. For similar reasons agribusinessmen also prefer to avoid any undue involvement in local rural affairs. Unlike the gentleman farmer, who accepts the obligations of traditional authority in the locality almost instinctively, the agribusinessman prefers to renounce any leadership of the local community. Indeed the agribusinessman's whole life-style tends to be less local in orientation; he possesses instead a more cosmopolitan outlook which makes him more familiar with, and attracted towards, the world beyond farming circles. This is commensurate with agribusinessmen's general tendency to regard farming as a business like any other.

Cell 3 consists of farmers who spend most of their time actually working on the land, performing manual labour alongside their (few) employees or frequently relying solely upon the labour of themselves and their families. Such family farmers are numerically preponderant in British agriculture. As we have seen, in certain branches of the industry, such as dairying, they also predominate economically, but in general family farms account for a declining proportion of agricultural production as output becomes slowly concentrated on fewer, larger enterprises. In economic terms, therefore, the family farmer is becoming more and more marginal, though it must be emphasized that this is a slow and by no means uniform trend and that family farms will continue in existence for the foreseeable future, relying upon contractors and casual labour to see them over the peaks of labour demand. Family farmers have also been encouraged to join together into cooperatives as a means of ensuring their salvation under modern commercial conditions, but such cooperation has met with only limited success. This is partly because family considerations are often as important to such farmers as maximizing profits. The major concern of family farmers is usually to maintain an equitable level of profitability – or standard of living – rather than involve themselves in the extra work, increased risk, extended borrowing and greater worry which the pursuit of maximum profits might entail. There is also a strong desire to retain control of the farm within the family, to 'keep the name on the land' and 'not to be beholden to anyone'. Such considerations mean that family farmers are only pushed reluctantly, and often by force of circumstance, into the harsher commercial world of finance, credit, cost-accounting and the other necessities of obtaining the maximum return on capital invested. Family matters – such as feuds between kin, the number and age of children, and marital alliances – are as important in shaping the nature of such farms as purely commercial considerations, although no farmer can entirely ignore the latter. Family farms dominate the pastoral areas of Britain, but even in the arable lowlands, while they do not typify the agriculture of the region, they continue to exist in the interstices between the larger enterprises, or as tenancies on the remaining landed estates.

The fourth category of farmers may be termed active managerials. They are both highly market-oriented *and* directly involved in the husbandry of their farms. As such they form an intermediate category between family farmers and agribusinessmen, but they can be differentiated from both. Although like family farmers they spend a substantial proportion of their time working on the land they tend to be far more innovatory and concerned with the maximization of profits. Indeed their *forte* is their possession of a high degree of technical and agricultural expertise over practical matters concerning plant and animal husbandry. They therefore spend a lot of time out and about on the land, rather than delegating such work to a manager and take pride in being able to 'turn their hand' to any job on the farm. Unlike agribusinessmen, they are not desk-bound administrators – and tend to be scornful of those 'armchair' farmers who are. Such active managerial farmers may, however, be aspiring agribusinessmen in the sense that they are expansionist-minded family farmers but they are often reluctant to expand beyond a size which would remove them entirely from any active role in the husbandry of the farm. Because of their hostility to any form of abstract activity and their devotion to practicalities they are reluctant to engage in any task which is not obviously and demonstrably connected with agricultural husbandry, such as engaging in local affairs or involving themselves in the lives of their employees outside working hours. Indeed in their dealings with their workers such farmers rely more on their ability to keep 'one step ahead' in their knowledge of farming techniques and their ability to apply them.

Farmers themselves, mindful of their own individuality, might resent being 'put into boxes' in this manner. It should be emphasized, however, that it is not so much a question of putting people into boxes as finding some way to make sense of the diversity and variety which exist among the farming population. There is, perhaps, something of each of these typifications in every farmer, but each farmer will also correspond approximately to one or other of these typifications. For farmers are not the homogeneous group which casual observers and occasionally government policy-makers assume. It is mistaken, for example, to believe that all farmers are motivated by calculations of economic rationality to the same degree – and many attempts to persuade or cajole farmers into pursuing desired policy objectives have foundered precisely on this point. Nowhere is this more apparent than in the various attempts by the Ministry of Agriculture to come to terms with the so-called 'small farm problem', where a bureaucratic faith in the effects of economic incentives has produced some unintended consequences of well-meaning policy decision.

Small farms are believed to be a 'problem' because they provide an obstinate hindrance to the further rationalization of agriculture. ('Small', it should be emphasized, refers to the size of the enterprise rather than acreage.) They also represent a social problem: the fabric of rural life in some areas would suffer considerably if small, marginal farmers were allowed to go out of business. Until Britain's entry into the EEC, government aid centred on the Small Farmers' Scheme, introduced in 1958. It was designed to give special assistance to viable small farms struggling to overcome under-capitalization, to aid 'small businesses that are economic, in the sense that they are capable, with reasonable management, of giving remunerative full-time employment to the average occupier'. The assistance took the form of a series of grants for capital and husbandry improvements, made in accordance with a plan approved by the Ministry's Advisory Service; later, in 1965, a further condition of keeping and using proper farm records was added. A glance at the typology on page 103 will show that by no means all small farmers react readily, or even willingly, to incentives and conditions like these – only the active managerial farmers are likely to do so. The rationality of family farmers, on the other hand, may only tangentially be understood in purely utilitarian terms – their behaviour is moulded not so much by economic incentives as by family, social and even religious values. To an agricultural economist they might appear to be irrational or erroneous and undeserving of state support, but to overlook the way in which they create a highly selective response among farmers conflicts with the social aims of such policies. It is not surprising, then, that the Small Farmers' Scheme helped only a little over half of those for whom it was intended before it was wound up in 1973. Ten years earlier a study of the Scheme in part of Devon by J. Bradley had concluded that: 'The composition of the group of farmers with schemes is in many respects untypical of the area as a whole. They tend to be young immigrants to the area, the majority being owner-occupiers.' Rather than providing a prop for the yeoman virtues of solitary self-help, it was allowing 'up-country johnnies' to dabble in uneconomic farming with social consequences for the area which we are left to contemplate.

The experience of the Small Farmers' Scheme illustrates a common assumption that is often held of farmers: that their economic rationality can be taken as 'given' and that only the size of their farms and the type of commodities which they produce account for variations in their behaviour. Yet economic imperatives are still not sufficiently draconian to rule out any freedom of choice on the part of the individual farmer. Thus – to take another example of contemporary public concern – farmers vary according to the extent to which they are sympathetic to environmental considerations when deciding upon their farming practice. Some farmers – agribusinessmen, most notably – have been responsible for perpetrating wholesale and widely deplored changes upon the agricultural landscape; others – for example, gentlemen farmers – are staunch defenders of the environmental lobby and go to great lengths to preserve existing landscape patterns as far as possible. So some such classification as that presented in the table on page 103 is required if we are to understand the nature of the strains and tensions which exist *within* the farming community as well as appreciating the differing economic outlooks and life-styles that are encompassed by the term 'farmer'. We shall have cause to refer to these distinctions on a number of occasions during the remainder of this book.

The political economy of agriculture

Although some farmers are more interested than others in extracting the maximum possible profits from their land, all farmers must make a living and therefore some sort of profit in order to survive. The market for farm produce is not, however, one which the individual farmer can control. Each farmer on his own contributes such a small proportion to the overall market that he is a 'price-taker' rather than a 'price-maker'. It would be mistaken to believe, though, that farmers are subject merely to impersonal market forces, for the principles of *laissez-faire* economics were long ago abandoned in agriculture so that the major parameters of the market are today matters of hard political negotiation, both nationally and internationally. Ultimately the outcome of these negotiations affects not only the prosperity of agriculture but the standard of living of all of us due to their effect on the price of food. Moreover, the way in which the market is organized eventually has a profound effect on social change in the English countryside, as any comparison between the situation in the 1930s and that prevailing today will bear witness.

Why is agriculture so suffused by political considerations? One quick answer to this question is to point to the intrinsic importance of food as the most essential of life's necessities, but the reasons for state intervention in and political control of agriculture run far beyond this. The economic problems which would beset British agriculture if it was left to the vagaries of the free market would be severe, if not catastrophic. First, there would be a persistent low-income problem among farmers, for the reasons outlined in Chapter 2 – the tendency for returns to agriculture to decline as a proportion of returns to the economy as a whole as the standard of living of the population increases. Although this could be rectified if sufficient farmers left the industry to allow equitable incomes for those that remained, this would have to occur on such a massive scale as to be unrealistic, not to mention the social dislocation which would be caused in many rural areas if this were to take place. One major objective of state intervention has therefore been to maintain the income levels of farmers at a sufficient level to regulate the outflow from the industry. This may be carried out on purely social welfare grounds, as in the subsidies paid to hill farmers, or for strategic reasons in order to maintain indigenous food supplies. More recently the need to grow more home-produced food in order to improve the balance of payments situation has also been an important consideration.

The second major objective of state intervention has been to improve the stability and the efficiency (eventually they amount to the same thing) of agriculture in this country. Left to a free market many agricultural commodities are subject to extreme fluctuations in supply and (given virtually inelastic demand) price. This is because fluctuations caused by extraneous factors like the weather become magnified by the activities of the farmers themselves. If, say, poor weather conditions cause the price of a particular crop to rise then other farmers, observing the high prices prevailing, move in and grow more of that crop for the following year. As a result there is a glut when the crop comes on the market, the price slumps and farmers are either driven out of business or move into other crops, producing a shortage and high prices once again. Fluctuations like these can be extremely damaging if the slump is so severe as to render farmers bankrupt, and in commodities involving a high capital investment and/or long production cycles this can be a real possibility. Such violent fluctuations also inhibit investment and technological innovation, so reducing the efficiency of those farmers who survive. They also ultimately raise the price of food to the consumer.

In order to ameliorate the low-income problems of farmers, to stabilize the industry and make it more efficient all British governments since the war have followed a policy of state support for agriculture. From the Agriculture Act of 1947 until entry into the EEC the cornerstone of this policy was a system of 'deficiency payments' whereby the government guaranteed the price of certain key commodities to farmers at a level that would render production profitable. When the market price was above the guaranteed price then the market price prevailed; when it fell below the guaranteed price then the government made up the deficit to the producers while the consumer was allowed to take advantage of low food prices in the shops. The comparatively free importation of cheap food from overseas was also allowed on to the British market. Hence this was familiarly known as a 'cheap food' policy. The guaranteed prices were negotiated each February by the Ministry of Agriculture and the National Farmers' Union, although the government could impose a settlement if it chose to do so. By varying the level of guarantees and tinkering with the precise details of their implementation the government could have a far-reaching effect on the structure and the prosperity of the agricultural industry. In addition the government had a variety of other measures at its disposal which fashioned the conditions prevailing in the industry, ranging from the imposition of selective import quotas and tariffs to the organizing of marketing boards and the payment of direct grants and subsidies for items such as buildings, machinery and fertilizers.

Entry into the EEC has altered the system of state support, although the commitment to maintaining a stable and prosperous agriculture remains. Because of the higher proportion of farmers in the other EEC countries the Common Agricultural Policy is operated by direct intervention in the market rather than by making payments to millions of farmers which a deficiency payments system would involve. Each year in Brussels the agricultural ministers of the Common Market countries decide upon a series of target prices for each of the commodities covered by the CAP. These prices are arrived at after consultations with the member states' farming organizations, their European federation (COPA) and with the EEC Commissioner for Agriculture. The target price is set in theory to give a fair return to the efficient producer, while a support price, slightly lower, is also agreed upon, below which prices are not allowed to fall. If the price on the market falls below the target price the European Guarantee and Guidance Fund may intervene to purchase the relevant commodity and take it off the market – that is, place it in storage – in order to protect the price. If the price rises above the target price it may then release it from store to bring prices down again. When the market price falls below the support price, however, then the Fund *must* purchase everything that is offered to it at that price. Clearly much depends upon the level at which prices are set, especially since the whole system is protected by a high tariff wall which prevents the importing of food from the world market at below the target price. For political reasons (especially in France) these prices have historically been sufficiently high to encourage overproduction and heavy intervention buying. The result has been the formation of the notorious beef and butter 'mountains' and wine 'lakes' and the eventual dumping of surpluses in Eastern Europe at enormous cost to the European taxpayer. Moreover, intervention buying ensures that the consumer is unable to take advantage of cheap food in the shops. For most British farmers, however, entry into the EEC has proved to be a boon since the target prices for most commodities have been substantially above those prevailing under the former deficiency payments system.

Whichever system has prevailed, however, for over thirty years farmers have received a virtually unquestioned commitment on the part of successive governments to support agriculture. The effects of this commitment have been felt at even the most mundane level. Intervention has enabled farmers to expand their output and increase their productivity without suffering a commensurate loss of income and technological innovation has been encouraged without its resulting in depressed prices. Government intervention has thus enabled a wholesale substitution of capital for labour to take place and for farmers' incomes to increase in unison with, rather than in inverse proportion to, their increases in production. For this British farmers can be truly thankful – although state regulation has not been without its troubles. Quite apart from the constant problem of adjusting agricultural policy to prevailing economic conditions, the twin objectives of the policy have always been somewhat contradictory. Securing the low-income problems of farmers meant essentially keeping marginal producers in business, yet the whole logic of the other aim of increasing efficiency was to drive them out of business in order to promote amalgamations and economies of scale. In any case, as long as the deficiency payments system operated the lion's share of any payment was bound to go to the largest (and usually the most efficient) producers – that is, those who arguably required least help from the taxpayer. It was the realization of this which led to charges of 'feather-bedding' and until the early 1960s the 'open-ended' nature of deficiency payments to cereals growers in particular meant that they had virtually possessed a licence to print money. Yet to redirect money to those farmers who most needed it would be to perpetuate the uneconomic and the inefficient. This was, and is, the classic dilemma of state support, and one which again can divide farmers among themselves.

The organization which has successfully held farmers together in order to present a united front in their negotiations is the National Farmers' Union. The political character of modern agriculture has meant that the profitability of many, if not most, farmers has depended to a large extent on the NFU's negotiating ability and its efficiency as a parliamentary lobby in what virtually amounts to the collective bargaining of its members' incomes. In this farmers have been well served, for the NFU is undoubtedly one of the most successful pressure groups in Britain. It was founded in 1908 in response to the threat of unionization among farm workers and although it never publishes any details about its membership informed estimates put it at around 75 per cent of all farmers. This is an extraordinarily high figure when compared with similar organizations in other countries, and also when one considers the wide disparities between different types of farmers in this country, often with conflicting interests. Like the CLA the NFU prefers to work quietly behind the scenes and has a quite remarkable influence within the

Ministry of Agriculture. The NFU is therefore fortunate that the Ministry of Agriculture has been retained as a separate organization from the Department of Trade and Industry, and that the Minister himself has invariably been given a seat in the Cabinet. The NFU always tries to ensure that any matter which impinges on agriculture comes under the aegis of the MAFF rather than, say, the Department of the Environment, for only the former has the special understanding of agriculture that the NFU believes is required. This is not surprising, for on average one civil servant looks after the needs of every ten farmers. Consequently the NFU likes to 'keep farming out of politics', which is to say out of *party* politics and public debate. It prefers instead the more private and often more effective processes of persuasion in Whitehall.

Over the years the NFU and the Ministry have developed an almost symbiotic relationship. The Ministry needs the NFU in order to have a representative organization to negotiate with, one which can 'deliver' its membership on any agreed deal over prices and guarantees. The presence of the NFU also enables the Ministry to sound out farming opinion on any issue before developing a definite policy on the matter. Similarly the NFU needs the Ministry, without which it would lose much of its *raison d'être*. It provides the NFU with a direct channel of influence into even the highest of government circles and the Ministry also confers a degree of legitimacy on the NFU by refusing to negotiate ('consult') with any other organization. This has enabled the NFU to retain its unity and to see off the occasional breakaway movement from within its own ranks, such as that which saw the foundation of the Farmers' Union of Wales in 1964. As a *quid pro quo* the Ministry is often able by skilled manipulation to use the NFU to dampen down any nascent militancy among farmers, for the NFU likes to be seen to be acting 'responsibly'. The result, however, is that farmers remain unified in one major organization and in the long run this has undoubtedly benefited them. Despite the conflicts of interest which exist between small- and large-scale farmers and between different commodity groupings they have been contained sufficiently to allow the NFU to pursue its course with almost unparalleled success.

The NFU's lobbying machine reaches out into any area which in any way affects the agriculture industry. Nationally it may be involved in continuous consultation with the government, but at the local level it is no less effective in its negotiations with local authorities, particularly in the areas of planning and countryside access. The NFU is also a past master at publicity. In 1975, for example, it issued 162 national press notices, held twelve major press conferences, sent out eight hundred press releases to local newspapers, placed two hundred special articles and was involved in one hundred local radio programmes. As a consequence its monitoring service picked up no less than 1200 references to the Union on radio and television involving about thirty-one hours of material on farming *each week*. By utilizing this panoply of publicity the NFU hopes both to influence wider public opinion and to apply pressure on the relevant authorities to implement policies beneficial to farmers. However, recourse to such methods is often as much a sign of weakness as of strength, for it is often an indication that the NFU has failed to achieve its objectives during its less public discussions. Nevertheless the NFU's ability to obtain publicity allows it to act authoritatively as the spokesman for all farmers – indeed it is difficult for those farmers who disagree with the NFU to obtain a hearing. Consequently if we consider the post-war history of agriculture then it is not only the government of the day but the NFU which has been responsible for guiding and shaping the destiny of the majority of British farmers.

Such considerations as these may seem barely relevant to a discussion of *social* change in rural England. In fact it is impossible to understand the changing social pattern of the English countryside without reference to the economic trends in agriculture which have emerged out of the discussions between the government and the farming organizations. Once the weather may have been the major determining factor of farmers' incomes; today, however, the politics of agriculture have assumed substantial, if not equal, importance. In general, as the distribution of subsidy payments amply illustrates, agricultural policy has consisted of encouraging the rationalization and concentration of the industry, while providing relief for those specially disadvantaged by this, such as hill farmers, where important non-economic considerations are seen to apply. Agricultural support has therefore been structured so that farmers have never quite been fully reimbursed for increases in their costs during the subsequent Price Review, thus providing a 'stick' for goading them into greater efficiency, while the availability of a series of grants and subsidies on capital investment has provided the 'carrot' to tempt farmers into greater mechanization and other aspects of capital-intensive agriculture. This has put farmers on a treadmill of capital accumulation and investment which has transformed the character of British farming. However, new technologies require ever-increasing rates of capital accumulation which only the larger farmers can afford. Small, marginal producers have therefore found themselves squeezed out – and have again been encouraged to leave by a series of state-sponsored mobility schemes. It is not merely coincidental, therefore, that the NFU, which has largely acquiesced in this policy, has seen the greatest threat to its authority come from splinter groups consisting of small farmers, mostly in Wales and the West Country.

Government regulation has profoundly altered both the structure of the industry and the day-to-day nature of life and work in the countryside. The encouragement of fewer, larger and more efficient capital-intensive farms has resulted eventually in all of the catalogue of changes which we associate with rural life today: the mechanization of agriculture, the 'drift from the land' of farm workers, rural depopulation, the changing social composition of rural villages and widespread changes in the rural landscape and other environmental aspects of the countryside. These changes have not been the result of some immutable natural law. They are the result of deliberate policy decisions taken in Whitehall or Brussels which have eventually worked themselves through to produce the kind of agriculture, the kind of rural life and the kind of countryside with which we are familiar today. But the transformation of agriculture into a highly capital-intensive and energy-intensive business has had one further effect which deserves serious attention: it has made farmers more and more dependent upon non-farm inputs (machinery, agrochemicals, etc.) and has drawn them into the embrace of a much wider complex of industrial companies involved in food production and processing.

The rise of agribusiness

The growing incorporation of agriculture into sectors of the engineering, chemical and food-processing industries raises the question of how long British farming can remain structured in its traditional form, consisting mostly of small family-run businesses. Viewed cross-nationally, farming in Britain is somewhat unusual in the low degree of vertical integration which it exhibits. With very few exceptions the major food-processing companies have not directly involved themselves in farming and have preferred to deal on a contract basis with formally independent farmers. 'Agribusiness' can therefore seem like an ungainly piece of American jargon which has little relevance to British agriculture, but the rise of agribusiness has in some respects been no less significant here than elsewhere. In this chapter the term has been used on several occasions to refer to agriculture organized around scientific, rational, 'industrial' business principles and likewise those farmers who share this approach to crop and animal husbandry have been described as agribusinessmen. Yet it is precisely those factors that have encouraged the activities of agribusinessmen farmers which have also attracted the interest of agribusiness in the American sense – the large food-producing and processing conglomerates, often multi-national companies, that have moved in on both the provision of farm inputs and on the control of marketing, processing, packaging and distribution.

Governmental control of agriculture, in promoting a highly capitalized farming industry, has therefore, unwittingly or otherwise, promoted the interests of agribusiness companies in British agriculture. The government, in supporting the farmer, is now also supporting large sections of the engineering industry, through the farmers' purchases of farm machinery, the chemical industry (fertilizers, pesticides, etc.) and food processors, packagers and distributors. On the input side a farmer can find himself at the mercy of companies like Ford, Leyland, John Deere, Massey Ferguson and International Harvesters for machinery, and ICI, Shell, Fison and BASF for fertilizers and pesticides. There is little the farmer can do but accept their rising prices. Equally, however, he can find it difficult to bargain on the output side with food processors like Unilever (Bird's Eye, Walls), Imperial Tobacco (Ross Foods), Rank-Hovis-Macdougall and Spillers-French, or with the large supermarket chains who buy perishable produce directly from growers. It will come as no surprise to learn, therefore, that farmers have received a declining proportion of retail food prices since the war.

The rise of agribusiness in Britain has thus proceeded by proxy, with food-processing companies often seeking out agribusinessmen farmers with whom to place contracts. Sufficient numbers of farmers have, indeed, proved sufficiently flexible to the needs of food processors for the latter not to feel the necessity to vertically integrate and take up farming themselves. This has enabled them to avoid both the high cost and the political risk of land purchase in Britain (it is, perhaps, significant that where British companies have vertically integrated into farming it has usually been overseas) and to avoid the cost of purchasing managerial expertise in agriculture. Nevertheless many farmers, and occasionally the NFU, have been conscious of the threats to their independence manifested in these developments. Farming under contract for the food-processing companies has generally speeded up the trend towards the rationalization of agriculture and its concentration among fewer farmers. Food-processing companies naturally prefer to deal with fewer, larger farmers; and farmers are in turn encouraged to specialize further in order to make the maximum possible use of their specialized technology and skills, particularly if the food-processors are willing to extend them credit to purchase the necessary machinery. Agriculture becomes more 'industrialized' as a consequence and smaller farmers, who do not participate in such contractual arrangements, find themselves becoming increasingly marginal.

The impact of agribusiness can extend far beyond this, however. Most food-processors like to retain strict control over the quality of the produce which they purchase and the rate and timing of production. In the case of Bird's Eye peas, for example, the company employs fieldsmen who tell farmers when to sow the crop, who then inspect it, supervise spraying and direct the harvesting operations. Walls also retains considerable control over pig farmers in order to safeguard the quality of their pork pies and sausages. On occasions farmers can be reduced almost to the function of caretakers with most of the major entrepreneurial decisions removed from their hands. To date, farmers in England have not shown themselves to be particularly resentful of these trends, mainly because the contracts offered by most food-processors have ensured them reasonably lucrative returns and the companies themselves, perhaps with an eye to their public relations, have found it prudent to be helpful and sensitive to the requirements of most agribusinessmen farmers. In any case few farmers are as yet totally reliant upon a single food-processing company for the majority of their income. However, many farmers have found it politic to combine themselves into growers' groups and other cooperative groupings in order to negotiate contracts and to pool machinery and labour where appropriate. Moreover, the NFU maintains a constant watching brief.

Wherever agriculture comes into contact with agribusiness, though, it finds itself transformed by the latter's relentless industrial logic. Hence 'factory farming' is often associated with the rise of agri-business: farming simply becomes the transformation of one set of industrial products into another set of industrial products which happen to be edible – and all of this is carried out as far as possible under conditions which approximate to the industrial assembly line. As a result agriculture can become organized around largely non-agricultural criteria, on the assumption that agriculture is merely a disguised form of manufacture. We have already seen the consequence of this in the broiler chicken industry – but a similar logic is working its way through all other branches of farming and in those areas resistant to the logic of agribusiness, research effort is being poured into overcoming the problems. To agribusiness it makes much more sense to produce a tasteless product lacking in any nutritional value under conditions of semi-automated technology and *then* add the colouring, flavouring and vitamins, helpfully provided by the flourishing science of food technology. The public can then be con-vinced of the 'country goodness' of the product by packaging and advertising. Moreover, agribusiness is not going to fade away. On the contrary the trend is to more and more 'industrial' production in agriculture with as a consequence fewer, larger farms. In terms of new methods of production the second agricultural revolution is still far from completed.

The general public is largely unaware of these trends – and, for that matter, rather uncaring. What counts primarily to the consumer is the price of food. Agribusiness companies are therefore not alone in being responsible for the changes currently being wrought in the food-production business and neither are successive governments for encouraging the conditions under which agribusiness expands. Consumer demand for cheap food – and resistance to rising food prices – has also been responsible for the rationalization of agri-culture, since a highly 'industrialized', large-scale farming industry can significantly reduce prices, as we have seen in the case of chicken. Agribusiness companies themselves certainly believe that they are performing a public service. The changing pattern of consumer demand for food is also encouraging the growth of agribusiness. More of the food that we buy is processed food and, given current social trends (such as the increasing proportion of working mothers), the demand for convenience food is likely to increase, even to the point of more meals being prepared outside the home in 'take-aways' and other 'fast food' outlets. These changes will only lead to a further dominance of the provision of food to the consumer by the large food-processing companies. In turn the farmer is likely to see his share of retail prices decline further and to find himself even more vulnerable to the vagaries of these companies' marketing policies.

None of this is to suggest an apocalyptic vision of the future of British farming, for the changes which will occur will largely be the extrapolation of already existing trends. Some farmers may find themselves reduced almost to the status of farm operators, but they will more than likely retain their nominal independence of the companies which in all other respects will continue to dominate the production of food. In general, production will continue to be concentrated on fewer, more specialized farms where the processes of production will in turn become more standardized and more mechanized. However, juxtaposed with the large 'industrialized' farms there will continue to exist the rump of family farms, reduced in number and contributing relatively little to the output of the industry as a whole. Some such farmers may be retained by virtue of policies which emanate from social rather than narrowly economic considerations, but they will also remain as a result of their willingness to engage in specialized forms of production which cannot easily be fitted into the pattern of large-scale agriculture. Many may even be part-time farmers. So the English countryside of the future will contain fewer farms, fewer people occupied in agriculture, a more industrialized system of production – and a landscape which takes account of all of these factors. Those who find this unpalatable should pause before they next step into a supermarket.

. . . buying up property that should be occupied by land workers!'

4 The farm worker

It is easy to forget that the majority of those who work in agriculture are neither landowners nor farmers but farm workers. For despite their numerical majority farm workers are the least considered section of the farming population. Indeed their existence often remains unacknowledged beyond their own circle of friends and workmates. This is not too difficult to understand for the 'second agricultural revolution' has brought about a drastic decline in the number of agricultural workers since the war and has left those who remain more isolated and scattered throughout the countryside as a result. All too often anyone passing through rural England hardly senses the farm worker's presence, for the fields are deceptively still and during the daytime the villages can also be devoid of any human activity. Someone must plough the fields or milk the cows, but much of this endeavour takes place hidden from public view and when a tractor is glimpsed across a field it is often assumed that it is a farmer who is in the cab. The farm worker, in the meantime, receives little attention from those who profess an interest in the changing conditions of rural England. The social invisibility of the farm worker has enabled his plight to be virtually ignored over the years.

The farm worker has become resigned to this public indifference, although he becomes annoyed by the continuing refusal to recognize the importance of his contribution to food production. He still finds it difficult to shake off the smock-and-straw image of the unintelligent country yokel and to convince those outside the industry of his skill and versatility. However, the farm worker rarely achieves what is necessary to bring himself before the attention of the public. There has been no strike in agriculture since 1923 and the instinct of the farm worker is to shun rather than seek the kind of publicity which would be required to engender public support for his cause. Hence, despite the brave attempts of many farm workers' leaders since the days of the Tolpuddle Martyrs, the farm worker has little history beyond poverty, dependence and remorseless labour. His conditions have gradually improved, but his pay and his status remain (when compared with the rest of the population) relatively poor. So much has changed in the life of the farm worker, especially the nature of his work; yet so much, as we shall see, has remained resistant to change. This is the nature of the paradox which often leaves the older farm worker bewildered by the experiences of his lifetime.

The drift from the land

As was noted in the previous chapter, the drive towards increased efficiency has led to the wholesale substitution of capital for labour in agriculture. There has therefore been a steady and persistent 'drift from the land' of agricultural labour, which is either pushed out by continuing mechanization and the adoption of other labour-saving techniques or lured into other industries by the prospect of higher wages and better conditions of employment. In 1948 there were nearly 573000 regular whole-time workers in England and Wales, but by 1975 the number (not exactly comparable because of changes in the basis of the statistics) had fallen to 184000. The recent distribution of the labour force is shown in Tables 5 and 6. The number of workers on the land has been shrinking at the rate of nearly 20000 per year, although this has not occurred in a completely uniform fashion. The rate of decline has owed a great deal to the overall level of employment in the economy, so that year-to-year fluctuations have varied considerably – it has been calculated, for example, that a 1 per cent decline in the national level of unemployment is sufficient to provoke an increase in the outflow of labour from agriculture eight times as large. Much also depends upon local employment conditions, for, with a few exceptions, the greatest decline has taken place where there has been the greatest competition for labour, principally in the South East, in the West Midlands and in South Wales. All types of labour have been affected, but among arable workers, where mechanization has been most extensive, it has been disproportionately rapid. Finally, the decrease has been greatest among full-time male workers. In their search for sources of cheap labour farmers have turned more to female, part-time and casual workers and here the decline in numbers has been nothing like so great. All these

Table 5 *Workers employed on agricultural holdings in England and Wales, June 1975*

			'000	%
Regular whole-time workers				
Hired	Men	Foremen	7·0	6·0
		Dairy cowmen	8·9	7·6
		Other stockmen	13·8	11·9
		Tractor drivers	31·9	27·4
		General farm workers	40·9	35·1
		Horticultural workers	10·1	8·7
		Other farm workers	3·8	3·3
		Total	*116·4*	*100·0*
	Youths		15·2	
	Females		12·7	
	Total hired regular whole-time workers		(144·4)	
Family	Male		30·1	
	Female		9·6	
	Total family regular whole-time workers		(39·7)	
Total regular whole-time workers			184·1	
Regular part-time workers				
Hired	Male		17·3	
	Female		24·1	
	Total hired regular part-time workers		(41·4)	
Family	Male		9·9	
	Female		15·8	
	Total family regular part-time workers		(25·7)	
Total regular part-time workers			67·1	
Seasonal or casual workers				
Male			36·1	
Female			30·2	
Total seasonal or casual workers			66·4	
Total workers			*317·6*	

SOURCE: MAFF Statistics.

Table 6   *Distribution of hired, regular whole-time workers by labour-size groups, England and Wales, June 1975*

Number of hired, regular whole-time workers per holding	'000	%
1	21·2	
2–4	47·0	
5–9	31·8	
10–14	13·2	
15–19	7·4	
20+	22·5	
Total	*143·1*	*100·0*

SOURCE: MAFF Statistics.

general trends are, however, capable of being reversed at the local level where conditions may occasionally fly in the face of the overall pattern.

The decline in the number of farm workers partly accounts for the peculiar age structure of the industry. Farm workers are an ageing labour force as the cohort from the days when they were more numerous gradually works its way through to retirement. The average age is thirty-nine, but in some areas, such as East Anglia, over half of the labour force is over the age of forty-five. This would offer a considerable threat to the future supply of labour were it not for the fact that agriculture also attracts a disproportionate number of school-leavers – more, in fact, than it could possibly cope with if they were all to stay in the industry. Employment opportunities for school-leavers in rural areas are usually highly limited and their choice is often further circumscribed by a lack of personal mobility. A job on the land is therefore regarded as a handy stop-gap until the possession of a driving licence opens up a much wider labour market, both geographically and occupationally. On average, a sixteen-year-old recruit to farming will have moved on by the age of twenty-three – usually to the building and construction or road haulage industries. Increasingly agriculture is regarded as a residual employer, something to turn to when other jobs are unavailable.

In the remoter rural areas, where agriculture has traditionally held a virtual monopoly of employment opportunities, the declining demand for labour in agriculture has historically led to widespread rural depopulation. Former farm workers have felt the need to move out to the towns and cities in search not only of employment, but of higher pay, better working conditions, and increased opportunities for personal advancement; and farmers have felt the need to shed labour as an accompaniment to increasing productivity. This is, of course, no new process: rural depopulation first became identified as a social problem in the middle of the last century. On occasions rural depopulation has aroused considerable public concern and has even been represented as a draining away of the nation's life-blood, to the detriment of the national character and vigour. However, an evaluation of rural depopulation needs to take account of a whole variety of factors. Undoubtedly the people left behind can experience immense dislocation, amounting in extreme cases to complete social and economic dereliction, but with no economic base to support a larger rural population, conditions would have been worse if those who moved to the towns had chosen to remain in the countryside. Many who moved were glad to do so and the economy as a whole has benefited from the release of agricultural labour to take up employment in the expanding manufacturing and service sectors. The conventional wisdom has been that those who left the countryside were the energetic and the intelligent, leaving only a residue of the old and the inert, but we also ought to note that the urban view has often been the exact opposite: that the towns have received the rural dregs – the drifters, the shiftless, the work-shy, the unattached flotsam of agricultural change. There is, in fact, no hard evidence to show that rural depopulation has been *socially* selective either way.

In England, at least, rural depopulation is now regarded as less of a problem than it was up until the 1940s. Since 1961 the proportion of the population living in rural areas has actually undergone a small increase and, if anything, a more frequently voiced problem is one of how to preserve the countryside against increasing population pressure. Nevertheless the social composition of rural areas is now vastly different from that which existed before the drift from the land set in. Any increase is due to the non-agricultural, 'adventitious' rural population, while the number of agricultural workers continues to decline. Indeed there remains sufficient slack in some sections of the labour force and enough new technological innovations on the horizon for there to be no end in sight to the continuing reduction in the number of workers in the industry. It may not be too long before farm workers cease to be a majority of those engaged in farming.

Work on the land

Technological change has not only brought about a drastic decline in the number of farm workers, but has fundamentally altered the nature of the work which they now perform. Most farm workers over the age of forty have witnessed the disappearance of a predominantly horse-and-hand technology and its replacement by one based upon the internal combustion engine. Moreover the pace of technological change has increased steadily during the latter half of the twentieth century so that the farm worker in turn has had to become more adaptable to successive new innovations. Looking back over this period most farm workers view the introduction of the tractor and the combine harvester as representing a decisive break in the hitherto orderly pace of agricultural change – and in many respects this is undoubtedly what has occurred. However, the nature of the change must not be overstated. The internal combustion engine did not destroy an unchanging pattern of work stretching back into immemorial antiquity and neither is rapid technological change in agriculture a purely twentieth-century phenomenon. Not all farm workers have been affected equally by the new technology and certain aspects of working on the land have remained almost untouched by it.

Technological change since the war has undoubtedly altered the pace of work on the farm, but it has barely affected its rhythm. This is because the length of the production cycle and the rhythm of the work in agriculture continue to be governed by the seasons of the year except in those branches of the industry which have been turned over to factory farming methods. The traditional rhythm of work remains because most operations in agriculture, especially where the growing of crops is concerned, must take place sequentially rather than concurrently. In other words, each state in the production process can only be begun once the previous stage has been completed. The land is ploughed and *then* the seed is sown, the crop sprayed, the harvest taken, and so on. It is impossible to perform each stage of production simultaneously. In replacing horses and men by machines, the practice of carrying out agricultural production in sequential steps is not disturbed, as it is in the changeover from handicraft to mechanized manufacture in industry. As a result mechanization in agriculture has wrought a spectacular change in the implements that the workers use to produce the crop and an equally drastic change in the pace at which each step in the productive process is carried out, but in most branches of agriculture the fundamental sequential organization of production remains undisturbed. From this simple, yet significant, starting-point many of the distinctive features of working on the land follow.

On arable farms, traditionally the most labour-intensive section of the industry and now the most capital-intensive, the changes wrought by technological innovation have not only resulted in a reduction in the number of workers, but a dramatic decrease in the division of labour among those that remain. Whereas a horseman might manage to plough an acre a day, a tractor driver might now manage up to forty. A farm employing twenty workers before the war in a complex hierarchy of bailiffs, foremen, charge-hands, horsemen and day-labourers may today make do with less than five. These five workers have been forced to become adept at tackling the complete range of jobs which may arise on the farm over the year. Thus, whereas a horseman's work formerly revolved almost entirely around his horses, his modern counterpart must not only be a tractor driver but a 'general farm worker' – a mechanic, a labourer and perhaps even a part-time stockman, too. His work has therefore become more varied and, because he is no longer subject to close personal supervision while out in the fields, the farm worker has become more autonomous. In both cases this is the opposite of the prevailing trend in manufacturing industry.

The only major division of labour which remains in agriculture relates to those who work with livestock and those who do not. In some respects the stockman has been less affected by mechanization, although this depends upon which type of worker we are considering. For example, the introduction of mechanized milking parlours has reduced milking to a process akin to assembly-line production; on the other hand the life of a shepherd has been only marginally touched by technological change. What has changed for the stockman is more often connected with the intensification of livestock production. There has, in other words, been a quantitative rather than a qualitative change in his work. The number of stock under the supervision of a single worker has increased considerably and this has placed an additional burden on the skill of the stockman to face the new challenges which have resulted. Because intensive livestock production renders the animals more susceptible to disease most stockmen have developed a degree of veterinary skill which can make them a decisive factor in the profitability of any livestock enterprise. Science has also intervened in such matters as breeding, feed-conversion, and the control of the environment to reduce mortality and disease, forcing the stockman to keep accurate records of the necessary information and plan his husbandry strategy accordingly. The modern stockman thus approximates more to a 'farm technician' than the old image of the 'farm labourer'.

While many of the older farm workers nostalgically regret the passing of horses, none regrets the way in which mechanization has removed much of the physical effort and routine drudgery that used to be involved in working on a farm. For the younger workers, in particular, mechanization has become a badge of their modernity which they can show off to otherwise uncomprehending townies in a manner which the latter can understand. To work with a large and complex piece of machinery demonstrates to the rest of the world that the farm worker is both skilled and in the vanguard of scientific progress. Farm workers appreciate the status involved in working with the biggest or newest piece of agricultural equipment in their district and take an almost proprietorial interest in the purchases of their employer. Mechanization has not therefore necessarily involved any decrease in job satisfaction among farm workers. Variety is endemic to working on the land, variety introduced by changes in the weather, the seasons, soil conditions and, as we have seen, by the increasing versatility demanded of the farm workers themselves. Farm workers also gain intrinsic satisfaction from working with living and growing plants and animals and they share a sense of achievement when they are finally brought to maturity, the sequential nature of production allowing workers to be involved in all of the stages through to completion. Compared with most other manual jobs, working on the land offers far more in the way of intrinsic interest, variety, autonomy, challenge, responsibility and control. Of course, working on a farm like any other job contains its boring, repetitive aspects and any worker can become tired of driving up and down large modern fields for weeks on end during ploughing, but in general job satisfaction is extraordinarily high. Few farm workers leave the land because they dislike the job itself; on the contrary many would return were it not for the poor pay and prospects.

For many farm workers the major problem introduced by mechanization has been an increase in the loneliness of the job. Not only are there fewer workers around on each farm than formerly, but the modern farm worker spends much of his time isolated in the noisy interior of his tractor cab. Even if he is working in a field with other workers the sense of isolation can remain, for the noise and the increased pace of work hardly lend themselves to easy conversation between workmates. This is a considerable contrast with the camaraderie of the field which frequently existed before the widespread introduction of tractors. In the past farm workers worked alongside each other in gangs or small groups far more than is customary today and meal breaks would also be taken together out in the fields. On return to the farm in the late afternoon there was likely to be a further round of gossip and conversation while grooming the horses and bedding them down for the night. Today the farm worker often works on his own and drives home for lunch on board his tractor. He is by no means a total social isolate for there are still occasions when work is carried out in groups of two or three, but contact is more desultory and the closely knit relationships developed out of lengthy periods of working side by side have become somewhat attentuated. However, if he is lucky the modern farm worker will find his tractor cab fitted with a radio, to which he can tune in via an earpiece. Perhaps this has a certain symbolic significance: the farm worker has become more isolated from his fellow workers, but more attuned to the world beyond the farm gate.

Changes in technology and the associated decline in the size of the farm labour force have also had a profound effect on the relationship between the farm worker and his employer. Although the trend is towards larger farms in terms of both production and acreage, the decline in the labour force is sufficiently outpacing the rate of farm amalgamation to produce a continuing decline in the average number of workers employed on each farm. In 1974 there were 1·4 regular whole-time workers for every full-time holding; ten years earlier it had been 2·1. Moreover, the distribution of workers is concentrated among the smaller farms – nearly a quarter of farm workers work on their own and nearly two-thirds work on farms employing four or less workers; only one worker in twelve is on a farm with more than twenty employees. This means that farms are becoming less bureaucratic – except where amalgamation has created very large units – and the relationship between farmer and farm worker has become a much more personal one. The economic differences between a farmer and his workers are as wide today as they ever were (probably wider when wealth as well as income is taken into account), but the social distance between them has been considerably reduced. Although the relationship is by no means an egalitarian one, it has become more harmonious and more easy-going. This is a considerable contrast with the prevailing tenor of the relationship between 'master and man' which existed on the land when labour was more numerous.

In the past the sheer size of the labour force on many farms, particularly the larger farms in the South and East of England, minimized the contact between employer and employee. This labour force was regimented through a succession of intermediaries – bailiffs on the largest farms, foremen and charge-hands elsewhere – in order to co-ordinate the frenetic periods of often complex and arduous activity, such as seed-time and harvest. The farmer was a remote and authoritarian figure and personal contact was often limited to no more than the weekly payment of wages. Control of the workforce was therefore formal and impersonal, often reflecting the tone of class relationships as they existed in the wider rural society. Mechanization, by reducing the number of workers employed on each farm has brought farmer and farm worker into a more personal, face-to-face and less formal relationship with each other. As we shall see in the following chapter, mechanization has not been the only process responsible for this, but by enabling the farmer to de-bureaucratize his farm and place greater emphasis on developing the personal loyalty of his workforce rather than relying upon regulations and sanctions, it has been an important contributory factor. Farm workers have found themselves working more often alongside their employer and the farmer in turn is often more willing to consult his workers on the day-to-day management of the farm. Indeed the relationship frequently extends beyond the work itself to the farmer's involvement in the domestic life of his employees. This can create its own peculiar problems, but such personal involvement can also increase the identification of the farm worker with his employer and with the farm.

To some degree the decreasing number of workers on the typical farm makes this close personal contact inevitable. However, many farmers believe that they must 'look after' their employees beyond the bare minimum specified by their contract of employment as a guarantee of sound and harmonious labour relations. 'Looking after' their workers most definitely does not mean paying higher than the prevailing rate of wages, but it does imply a genuine concern for their employees' welfare (including help with personal and domestic problems), the provision of decent housing facilities and frequent individual acts of generosity like small gifts on family birthdays and at Christmas, the allowance of various perquisites and even the provision of occasional 'treats' like harvest suppers and days out at local agricultural shows. In other words many farmers like to show their workers that they *care*. To the outside observer these activities bear a remarkable similarity to, and may indeed be the modern equivalent of, nineteenth-century paternalism. They represent the personal touch which takes the edge off what remains for most farm workers the harsh realities of their poor pay and dependent status. When the farmer is such a personally kind and considerate individual who recognizes his social responsibilities to his workforce, it seems churlish on the part of the farm worker to complain about low wages and poor working conditions. Thus while most farm workers recognize that they are poorly paid, few blame their own employer for their poverty. Paternalism therefore deflects the dissatisfaction of the farm worker and can act as an effective guarantor of a 'family' atmosphere on the farm.

Technological change in agriculture has increased the importance of obtaining the loyalty of the farm worker rather than relying upon a disciplined and authoritarian regime. Mechanization has increased the autonomy of the agricultural worker and has rendered close supervision difficult, if not impossible. On the other hand the farm worker has been placed in control of important and costly pieces of farm investment which may run into many thousands of pounds. No farmer can therefore afford to carry workers who are disgruntled or who have no identification with the aims of the enterprise. This partly accounts for the importance which farmers attach to cultivating their workers' loyalty. However, a paternalist style of management can stand rather oddly in the modern world. In a scientific, efficient, rationalized business, which agriculture is increasingly moving towards, the trappings of anything which smacks of paternalism can evoke embarrassment among both farmers and farm workers, and even some annoyance among the latter. Where very large units have been created by either purchase or amalgamation the 'personal touch', to which many farmers ascribe the absence of industrial relations problems in British agriculture, may in any case be inoperable. Such farms may allow for little or no daily contact with the workforce (other than by two-way radios fitted to tractors), with day-to-day supervision remaining in the hands of managers and foremen. A more formal and impersonal system of management, of the kind which other farmers disparagingly attribute to manufacturing industry, therefore prevails. These farms rely almost solely on paying high wages and offering good working conditions in order to attract and retain their labour force. Indeed the agribusinessmen who typically control such enterprises, are often impatient with any time-consuming involvement in the non-working lives of their employees. It not only conflicts with their self-conscious professionalism but they regard it as an increasing anachronism in the agriculture of the 1970s.

Most farmers view this trend with gloomy foreboding, however. They believe that personal 'gaffer-to-man' contact has been responsible for removing much of the industrial conflict which they regard as plaguing the remainder of British industry. Industrial farming, they believe, will bring industrial problems. It is unlikely that more than a tiny proportion of farms will attain the bureaucratic structure associated with agribusinessmen farmers, but they are regarded suspiciously as possible Trojan horses introducing alien patterns of labour relations into the countryside. If farmers are frank with themselves they will also recognize that paternalism is cheap. A kind word here and a Christmas turkey there is a small price to pay for the loyalty of one's employees. Giving them a wage comparable with other workers is another matter.

Pay and conditions

There are a number of fallacies which are frequently promulgated in order to explain away the low standard of living of the farm worker and which require a brisk dismissal at the outset. The first is that the poverty of the farm worker is a thing of the past and that his position has improved considerably since the war. In absolute terms this is obviously true: the farm worker has, along with the rest of the population, steadily raised his standard of living as a result of successive wage increases. In relative terms, however, it is false. Compared with other workers the position of the agricultural worker has actually deteriorated since the war. His wages have increased, but not as fast as everyone else's. Average hourly earnings in agriculture were nearly three-quarters of those in industry in the late 1940s; today they are down to less than two-thirds. Secondly, it is often argued that farm workers are compensated for their low wages by a cornucopia of payments in kind. These, however, constitute only 2 per cent of average earnings. Even the provision of free or almost free housing leaves the farm worker no better off when comparisons are made with workers elsewhere, for the latter often receive benefits – cheap meals, pension funds, medical facilities, etc. – unavailable to farm workers. Thirdly, farmers are often heard to complain of a shortage of workers on the land. However, unemployment in agriculture consistently runs above the national average and while certain specialist workers may be in short supply they form only a small part of the labour force. Finally, the satisfaction of the job is regarded by sentimental observers as sufficient compensation for the lack of material rewards. On this the farm worker is most scathing: fresh air does not pay his electricity bill.

The poverty of the farm worker today is obviously very different from that which existed in the countryside in Victorian times, but the majority of farm workers *are* poor by the standards which we have come to expect in modern Britain. In 1975 average earnings in agriculture were £45·25 for a working week of 46·1 hours, compared with £59·58 for 43·6 hours in manufacturing industry. Earnings in agriculture are the lowest of any industry covered by the Department of Employment's six-monthly earnings surveys. Moreover, the range of earnings within agriculture is relatively narrow. Highly skilled and highly trained stockmen on intensive livestock farms can, it is true, earn much more than the average wage (though often for longer and more awkward hours), since such workers are in relatively short supply, but they are the industry's élite and constitute no more than 15 per cent of the labour force. The average wage in agriculture is so low, not because it contains the odd pocket of particularly low-paid workers among an affluent majority, but because it represents virtually *in toto* a low-paying sector of the economy. Farm workers also continue to comprise the majority of the rural poor.

In common with many other low-pay industries the minimum

standards of pay and conditions are laid down by an industrial council, the Agricultural Wages Board. The AWB consists of equal numbers of employer and employee representatives, together with 'neutral' members appointed by the Ministry of Agriculture who almost invariably determine the awards. Very few workers – less than 5 per cent – receive the statutory minimum wage, however. The vast majority are paid 'premium' payments and in 1972 these were codified by the AWB into a wages structure whereby skilled and supervisory workers receive plus rates laid down by the Board. Most workers, for example, receive the craftsman's grade, which is 10 per cent above the minimum. The AWB also controls the length of the working week and the allowances that may be made in the weekly wage for various payments in kind. The specialization of farms and the mechanization of production have, however, vastly reduced the perquisites which farm workers receive – milk and potatoes are the only significant produce and by no means all farms find it convenient to make these and other small quantities of food available. Housing remains important though (see below), and the AWB controls the rent of the tied cottage. In general the AWB's awards have been niggardly – at times extremely so. It has preferred to follow rather than lead the majority of the industry's employers and seems to have interpreted its own role as that of a safety net to protect the worst-exploited workers. Centralizing wage negotiations in this way has, however, removed from most farms the resolution of the most sensitive conflict of interest between farmers and farm workers.

There are many farmers, possibly a majority, who recognize that farm workers deserve higher pay, but they resolutely maintain that they cannot afford to grant it. They acknowledge the low pay of the farm worker but, the argument runs, they cannot be paid more so long as their returns to capital invested continue to fall behind the returns available to industrial employers. Low pay among farm workers is simply an associated aspect of the low-income problem in agriculture generally, perpetuated by the government's cheap food policy. Such an explanation has often seemed plausible (though less so since the abandonment of this cheap food policy upon entry into the EEC). Its major point of weakness, however, is that what determines the incomes of farmers – the prices they receive for their produce – does not determine the income of farm workers, which is derived from the sale of their *labour*. The wages of farm workers are thus determined by the conditions prevailing in the local labour market, rather than that for agricultural products. Farmers *may* be able to pass on low prices in the form of low wages but this depends upon the conditions prevailing in the labour market in their area. Farmers near towns, for example, usually find it necessary to pay higher wages in order to obtain sufficient workers, yet farmers near towns do not receive higher prices for their produce. Similarly there is little correlation between farming profits and farm workers' wages on a regional basis. In East Anglia, for example, farmers are among the most prosperous in the country, but their workers are among the most poorly paid. The reason for this is the lack of competition for labour, not the inability of farmers to pay more. Farmers are businessmen and since wages constitute a cost of production they will normally pay no more than prevailing conditions dictate. It may salve the conscience or meet some other purpose of the farmer to pretend otherwise, but if we wish to understand the causes of low pay in the countryside and speculate on the prospects for improvement, we cannot rely upon the charity of farmers. Experience suggests that they will only pay wages comparable with those in industry when circumstances force them to do so.

One reason why farm workers' wages remain so comparatively low is that the demand for labour within agriculture has been declining as a result of mechanization. Indeed, the prospect of more expensive labour has often been sufficient to stimulate farmers to engage in a further round of mechanization so that both the supply and the demand for labour have chased each other down in an ever-decreasing spiral. Since the middle of the nineteenth century this has produced a persistent surplus of population in the countryside with a consequent depression of wage levels. Rural depopulation has rarely proceeded on a scale to compensate for the reduced demand for labour in rural areas and neither has the demand for labour in the countryside been adequately stimulated by the provision of sufficient alternative employment opportunities to agriculture. Even since the war industrial relocation schemes for rural areas have been halfhearted and inadequate. The whole tenor of planning policy has been to restrict the presence of industry in the countryside and to preserve it as a largely pastoral backwater. More recently this has received added support from the environmental lobby, which has also looked askance at all but the most picturesque forms of employment being introduced into rural areas. The quickest way to improve rural wages would be to locate a small engineering factory in every village – a utopian thought, no doubt. But as we shall see in Chapter 6 more flexible planning policies are required if the low-wage rural economy is to be alleviated and rural depopulation to be assuaged in those areas where it remains a problem. A 'traditional' English countryside can only be supported by a traditionally poverty-stricken rural labour force. Maintaining the countryside in a pristine 'rural' state merely means consigning a substantial section of its population to a level of material existence which those who propound such policies would not themselves tolerate.

Given the lack of development in many rural areas it is not surprising that the dependency of rural workers on agriculture for employment has remained, nor that so many school-leavers take a job on the land even though they have no intention of remaining there if the choice to leave should present itself. Urban labour markets have spread more deeply into rural areas thanks to improved communications, but in recent years the increasing cost and decreasing availability and frequency of public transport have cancelled out many of the gains which rural workers might otherwise have enjoyed. Moreover many farm workers still find it difficult to meet the cost of private transport which might open up the range of alternatives. The geographical area within which workers look for jobs therefore remains a restricted one. Youngsters come and go, but the older workers, with their family responsibilities, stay on. An ageing labour force cannot be expected to be a mobile one. The declining demand for labour in agriculture even militates against a move to a higher paid job within the industry itself. Furthermore rural unemployment rates are higher on average than those in towns, so that although it is less visible than urban unemployment, because the absolute numbers involved are so much smaller, rural unemployment has a significant effect in dampening down rural wage increases. In addition there is one other institution which symbolizes the continuing dependency of agricultural workers upon local farmers – the tied cottage.

Agricultural tied cottages are houses provided by farmers as part of their workers' terms of employment. A worker may be required to live in tied accommodation as a condition of employment or he may make his own decision to do so. The farmer may deduct a (nominal) rent from his tenant's wages – an amount regulated by the AWB –

but most farmers waive this. Until 1 January 1977, if for any reason – including accident, redundancy or retirement – the farm worker's employment ceased, so did his security of tenure. A farmer could apply to a county court for a possession order and evict his former employee, though the court was empowered to suspend the order for up to six months. It almost goes without saying that over the years no single topic in agriculture has succeeded in raising passions more. Agricultural trade unions have described the system as 'feudal' and 'legalized serfdom', while farmers have defended tied housing as being essential to farming (especially livestock farming) where labour needs to be on immediate call, an aid to labour mobility within the industry and a considerable tax-free perquisite.

Strictly speaking, the tied cottage is not, historically or legally, a feudal institution. It is a quite recent development of mid-Victorian agriculture, following on from the decline of farm service and the disappearance of itinerant agricultural gangs. Farmers, concerned about the disappearance of casual labour, built dwellings on their land which would ensure a pool of workers and these houses were known as 'tied' houses because they were rented from the employer rather than 'open' houses rented directly from the landowner. Thus the tied cottage system emerged directly from the desire of farmers to control labour supplies – and it is this concern which remains at the heart of the system today. During the twentieth century more houses became tied with the decline of the landlord–tenant system in farming and its replacement by owner-occupation, and since the Second World War the chronic shortage of housing in rural areas has increased the importance of tied cottages still further. By 1976 53 per cent of farm workers lived in tied housing, compared with 34 per cent in 1948. Since this period was also accompanied by a decline of the labour force in agriculture, it can be concluded that those who left the industry were predominantly not those living in tied accommodation. Tied housing therefore acted as a brake on occupational mobility.

There is ample evidence that tied cottages have been used oppressively by farmers in the past in order, for example, to strangle incipient trade unionism in the countryside, but except in a small minority of cases it is no longer used as an oppressive weapon of petty political domination: rather it is the carrot which will tempt the farm worker to accept a low wage. A farm worker with a desire for marriage and a family is often grateful, even eager, for the offer of a house with the job. However, once in the system it is difficult for him to move to higher-paid employment in another industry, for he would also have to find housing elsewhere for himself and his family. The fears of insecurity which the system once provoked were far from notional – for example, the number of possession orders granted to farmers in England and Wales in 1975 was 1268. The number of actual evictions was tiny – less than twenty per year – though when they occurred they were given widespread publicity and the fears that they raised went far beyond what their numerical significance might indicate. Some threatened evictions, it should be added, were arranged by collusion between farmers and workers in order to force the hand of local authorities who otherwise would not admit tied cottage tenants to their housing waiting lists.

The abolition of the tied cottage was for many years the notorious 'hardy annual' of TUC and Labour Party conferences but reform of the system was pushed persistently aside. In 1976, however, the Rent (Agriculture) Act made a number of important changes in the system which were hailed as 'the abolition of the tied cottage'. In fact, the Act (which is an extremely complicated piece of legislation) did *not* succeed in abolishing the tied cottage. It extended the provisions of the 1965 Rent Act to tied cottage occupants in agriculture, but at the same time provided for a procedure whereby a former worker could be rehoused by the local authority where the farmer could prove that the house was essential to accommodate a replacement worker. The Act, while improving the security of the farm worker did not, therefore, remove the key element in the tied cottage system which perpetuates his dependency – the fact that his employer is also his landlord. What the farm worker undoubtedly gained was an important right – the right to a house – but the Act did not disengage the farm worker's conditions of employment from the circumstances in which he is housed. No farm worker welcomes the prospect of having to uproot his family should he, because he is ill, injured at work, made redundant, has achieved retirement or had a row with his boss, cease to be employed on the farm. Even though he knows he can no longer be rendered homeless his feelings of dependence will not have been entirely removed. Certainly the change in legislation is unlikely to provoke a sudden rush of hitherto tied farm workers from the industry.

Despite the many improvements that have been made over the years, the poor pay of the farm worker therefore continues to reflect the very many constraints which surround his choice of occupation and employer in many rural areas. These constraints continue to contribute to his dependence upon agriculture, and even in some cases upon an individual farmer, for employment. Many farm workers recognize this as an unavoidable aspect of living away from the main centres of industry, and while they may occasionally recognize the limitations which are imposed upon their freedom to choose both employment and housing, they are not necessarily embittered by it. For the farm worker may regard his dependence upon his employer as being mitigated by the increasingly close and harmonious relationship which the two sides maintain. As a result the farm worker is as likely to resent the high wages paid to workers in other industries for what often appears to him to be little skill and less hard work as to harbour a sense of grievance against either farmers in general or his own boss in particular. Where conditions of poverty and dependency *and* harmonious and pervasive personal relationships continue to predominate in agriculture then a source of ambiguity is present in the farm worker's perceptions of the world around him. Puzzlement, as much as anger, therefore sums up his reaction as he sees the wages gap between himself and other workers continuing to widen.

Agricultural trade unionism

The organizations which have set out to improve the pay and conditions of farm workers are the agricultural trade unions. The most important union for farm workers in England is the National Union of Agricultural and Allied Workers (NUAAW) which has a membership of approximately 90000, three-quarters of whom are employed on the land. The Transport and General Workers' Union also contains about 11000 farm workers in its agricultural section, but the majority of these are located in Scotland and it is the NUAAW which is generally regarded as the industrial union for farm workers in England and Wales. Trade unionism among farm workers is not, however, a very strong movement – nor has it ever been. Only a minority of farm workers have ever been unionized and the history of rural trade unionism has been a chequered one, alternating between brief heady periods of success and long periods of stagnation and weakness. Even today trade union membership remains a some-what atypical activity for the farm worker and the NUAAW itself is not a particularly militant union. Agricultural trade unions have therefore found it difficult to make such a decisive intervention in the labour market as to substantially increase the rewards of farm workers.

The first widespread trade union movement among farm workers occurred in the 1870s under the leadership of Joseph Arch, the so-called 'Revolt of the Field'. By the end of the century, however, trade unionism had been virtually eliminated from agriculture, following the determined resistance of farmers, who in 1874 had instituted a lock-out in East Anglia which effectively broke Arch's union. The NUAAW dates from 1906 when, in response to political victimiza-tion and tied cottage evictions in Norfolk, the Eastern Counties Agricultural Labourers' and Small Holders' Union was founded in North Walsham. Its leader was George Edwards, a devout Primitive Methodist lay preacher, who had been active during the earlier period of unionization in the 1870s and in brief revivals during the intervening years. Edwards, cycling over 6000 miles a year around Norfolk, painstakingly built the membership up to 3000 within two years. Until 1910 the chief sponsor of the union was the Liberal Party, which saw political capital to be made out of organizing farm workers in the Tory rural strongholds, but in that year a strike in the Norfolk village of St Faith's evoked accusations of a Liberal sell-out and pro-voked the membership to cut its ties with the Liberal Party. What amounted to a Socialist take-over ensued. The membership remained largely moribund until the First World War, although the title of the union had been somewhat pretentiously changed to the National Agricultural Labourers' and Rural Workers' Union (NALRWU) in 1912. In 1916, however, the fortunes of the union were boosted by entirely external factors.

German submarines proved (indirectly) to be a bigger stimulus to trade unionism than all the diligent recruitment of the early pioneers. The effects of the wartime blockade led the government under Lloyd George to take steps to stimulate home food production by offering price guarantees to farmers; and as a *quid pro quo* to the unions the government also promised to establish a statutory minimum wage, to be negotiated by central and district wages boards. With wartime labour shortages and guaranteed farm prices prevailing, the union representatives on the boards found little difficulty in raising wages substantially and union membership increased by leaps and bounds as a result. Between 1916 and 1920 membership of the NALRWU grew from 4000 to 93000, while at the end of the same period the Workers' Union (the precursor of the TGWU) contained an estimated 120000 farm workers. Trade unionism in the countryside seemed to be on the crest of a wave and the sense of exhilaration was increased when in 1920 the system of price guarantees and wages boards was extended into peacetime. In the same year the NALRWU changed its name to the National Union of Agricultural Workers (NUAW).

Within a year, however, this system was dismantled. With the resumption of world trade and access to plentiful supplies of overseas food once more, price guarantees began to cost money. In 1921 they were scrapped along with the wages boards. Within months farm prices had plummeted and wages were also being driven steadily down. The NUAW looked on helplessly, but decided in 1923 to make a stand in its strongest area – north and west Norfolk. Following several occasions on which wages had been cut and the working week extended, the NUAW finally called its members in the area out in what was recognized on both sides as a trial of strength of national importance. After five bitter weeks the NUAW succeeded in holding the line – but only just. A return to work was negotiated under the conditions prevailing before the strike had begun so the union had prevented a further round of wage reductions; but this was achieved at such a cost as to convince the leadership of the impossibility of organizing effective strike action in agriculture. Even in the NUAW's strongest area less than one-quarter of the strike notices had been obeyed and the union had been reduced to penury. Farmers had demonstrated, as they had to Arch in the 1870s, that once the seed is in the ground they can happily watch it grow and starve their workers, if necessary, into submission in the meantime. Moreover they could always use family labour or import casual labour to carry out any essential work. The union found it impossible to enforce the strike – even flying pickets could not police hundreds of separate farms. The union was also left virtually bankrupt, having paid out in five weeks' strike pay nearly two years' worth of subscriptions. When victimization followed the settlement – with union members left homeless by tied cottage evictions as well as without a job – the union had no option other than to take this treatment lying down. And all this in a conflict fought halfheartedly by many Norfolk farmers who had only an eye for renewed state intervention. The lesson which the NUAW leadership drew was a simple one: strikes lead only to the demoralization of the membership and the speedy self-destruction of the union. There has been no strike in agriculture in England since 1923.

Throughout the Depression the NUAW clung on to its existence by retaining the rump of its membership – no more than 25000 – in its East Anglian stronghold. When in 1939 a repetition of the conditions encountered during the First World War once more led the government to intervene in agriculture then the conditions were also created for a renewed round of trade union growth. By creating labour shortages on the land wartime conditions again led to an increase in wages and a strengthening of the wages board (a decentralized system had operated since 1924). The immediate post-war period again provided the optimism that had existed in 1920, and the farm worker appeared to be poised for the first time to achieve equality of pay and status with workers in other industries. On this occasion, sustained state intervention in agriculture ensured that there was to be no repetition of the inter-war years. The AWB was retained and the NUAW (it became the NUAAW in 1968) remained firmly wedded to improving the conditions of its membership through such statutory channels. However, the outcome was a disappointment. During the 1950s AWB awards failed to keep pace with the cost of living and farm workers found that the gap between their earnings and those of other workers was widening once more. This provides the NUAAW today with its biggest policy dilemma. Does it remain committed to the AWB even when it demonstrably fails to deliver the goods? The insidious growth of the wages gap between agriculture and industry, which the AWB has done little to narrow, leads to the consideration once more of alternative means of raising wages on the land. Dare the NUAAW break free of its commitment to working within the statutory framework and risk a repetition of the events of 1923? So far, at least, the official policy of the union has been to support the AWB, though in recent years criticism has been growing.

The problems of creating a strong union, as the union leadership is fully aware, remain enormous – indeed in some respects they have increased. Uppermost among these is the sheer scale of the problem involved in recruiting, organizing, servicing and, above all, retaining the membership in the face of a declining labour force whose structure is hardly conducive to unionization. Agriculture still has more employers than any other industry, but the workers are scattered, mostly in ones and twos, across the countryside and in some of the most isolated and inaccessible areas. The union is forced to pour resources into simply maintaining the thousands of small branches which trade unionism in agriculture automatically involves. A less obvious but equally debilitating problem is the propensity of farm workers not to join a trade union even when availed of the opportunity to do so. Here outright oppression and denial of rights is less troublesome than the benevolence of a personally known and trusted employer; a quiet word with the boss will often be preferable to calling in a more remote and impersonal organization to settle any differences. In the past the union could be supported by the communal solidarities of the village community; now, with villages no longer consisting of a majority of farm workers and with more workers living in tied cottages isolated on farms, the village no longer fosters the collectivism which supports the union. As a result much of the energies of the NUAAW are devoted to organizational problems. There is often little remaining to contemplate any militant activity.

In recent years the NUAAW has striven to overcome some of its organizational difficulties by recruiting more workers in the agricultural ancillary industries, especially in food-processing factories. It has achieved a good deal of success in this, enabling some compensation to be made for the diminishing pool of potential recruits on the farms. However, the identity of the union remains closely tied to its agricultural as opposed to its 'allied' membership, and all the efforts of its organizers have not been able to arrest the gradual decline in membership that has accompanied the drift from the land. Compared with many of its urban industrial counterparts the NUAAW therefore remains a weak union – and a poor one. It has neither the power nor the resources to counter the pressure of the exceedingly well-organized farmers' lobby, nor is the level of unionization in agriculture sufficiently high – it is no more than 40 per cent – to permit the contemplation of widespread militant activity. An isolated farm worker in a tied house still remains vulnerable to the ubiquitous pressures of dependence and he would be unlikely to heed a strike call. Many others would not allow their animals to suffer from lack of feed or, in the case of cows, the cessation of milking. And how can a farm worker strike against an employer whom he knows to be, more often than not these days, a solicitous and considerate person, even if he pays low wages? Many farm workers join the union, therefore, not for ideological reasons, but for the friendly society benefits which it offers and as an insurance against 'problems' with the tied cottage, 'just in case'.

None of this suggests that the NUAAW is going to sanction any widespread militant activity other than a little judicious sabre-rattling by its left-wing faction during negotiations on the AWB. In the last decade there have been strike calls from county conferences in the more militant areas like Norfolk, Essex and Yorkshire, but the union's Executive Committee, which has the sole right to order strike action, has sought to maintain centralized control over any militant activity. Localized strikes have not, therefore, been permitted. With the lesson of 1923 in mind, the leadership has continued to support the AWB – for better or for worse. At the same time it has moved slowly and hesitantly towards instituting 'plant bargaining' on the very largest farms where conditions allow. For the foreseeable future, however, the inherent weaknesses of unionization in agriculture seem likely to continue to haunt the NUAAW. The falling number of agricultural workers, the urban influences that are spreading across tracts of once 'truly rural' countryside and the changing nature of the farm worker's skills may conspire in any case to lead to a reappraisal of the need for a separate farm workers' union. The TGWU has shown interest in a merger on several occasions, and there has also been a recognition among militants within the NUAAW that successful and speedy strike action could only be brought about with the cooperation of the bulk milk tanker drivers whom the TGWU organizes. The NUAAW leadership has remained understandably wary of submerging their members' interests in those of a larger union, for there are fears that in supporting urban demands for cheap food the TGWU might not always serve the best interests of farm workers. On the other hand, with the industrial might of the TGWU behind the farm worker, there might be a more realistic chance of narrowing the gap between industrial and agricultural wages.

To a remarkable degree the problems that face agricultural trade unionism today are the same as those which faced Joseph Arch more than a hundred years ago. It is apparent that trade unions in agriculture have never been sufficiently strong to raise wages beyond that level which the labour market has already determined. Many areas, such as Norfolk, which remain highly unionized continue also to contain some of the lowest-paid agricultural workers in the country. Those improvements which have been gained by the farm worker have often been by-products of trade union agitation in other industries or have been brought about by such external agencies as government action and technological innovation. The farm worker has himself contributed, though as often as not by leaving the industry rather than by joining a trade union. This is not because the farm worker is any more of an individualist *per se* than his industrial counterparts – whatever the stereotypes – but because the circumstances surrounding the farm worker render individual action, rather than collective mobilization, the only realistic alternative for the majority of those working on the land. If we are to hold out any hope of a substantial improvement in the pay and conditions of the farm worker, therefore, trade unionism seems to offer a means of achieving these ends on only the largest farming enterprises, where plant bargaining above the AWB rates becomes a possibility. Trade unions are only as strong as their membership allows them to be and their leadership cannot be expected to perform miracles. A sudden and decisive upturn in the fortunes of farm workers seems unlikely. Any improvements, if they occur, are likely to be slow and gradual and as much the result of long-term and somewhat extraneous factors.

'A place in the sun'?

In order to give a rounded picture of the changes confronting the farm worker today, we must not only consider the transformations in work and technology and the equally manifest, if less discontinuous, factors underlying his level of pay and conditions. There are other factors, less tangible and less easy to generalize, which are affecting, to use a trite phrase, the outlook of the farm worker. This relates to both the farm worker's own expectations from life and his subjective interpretations of what he sees around him. Once his horizons were limited largely to his own parish boundary and the village community which was contained within it. Most of his social cues and expected behaviour were derived from this relatively enclosed social world.

Nowadays these horizons have expanded to take in much of the world outside by virtue of changes in education, in transport and communications, and, as we shall see in the following chapter, by virtue also of changes in the social composition of village community itself. The farm worker still remains socially and geographically isolated but he is also becoming less bound by custom and habit. He is also becoming more impatient with his traditionally inferior status. Edwin Gooch, the former President of the NUAAW, once demanded that the farm worker be given his 'place in the sun', by which he meant not only better pay and conditions but a more deserving recognition by the rest of society and equality of opportunity within it. The farm worker, in many respects, has yet to achieve his place in the sun, but he is also less willing to accept the low status which the rest of society seems to offer him.

It is at this point that the paradox of change and continuity in the life of the farm worker becomes most clear. His social and economic situation continues to be regulated by the kind of disciplines that have been familiar to successive generations of workers on the land – poverty, the lack of alternative employment opportunities, the intense localism, the dependency for jobs and housing on local farmers. Yet wider cultural influences, many of them associated with the decline of the traditional rural way of life, are working to undermine the customary expectations of the farm worker – particularly when we consider this on an intergenerational basis. For example, a large majority of agricultural workers currently engaged by the industry are themselves the sons of farm workers – probably more than two-thirds. In many rural areas it has therefore been usual for local farm workers to work on the land 'man and boy'. This continuity existed among both employers and employees in many cases so that there are many farmers' sons who also had to 'serve their time' alongside the hired labour force before taking over the farm and many elderly farm workers who can remember instructing their current employer in the ways of the farm when he was a small boy. Such factors often helped to cement the relationship between a farmer and his workers, but this continuity is now being ruptured by the increasing disinclination of farm workers' sons and other young rural workers to consider a job on the land. Although farm workers may love the job itself, when it comes to advising their sons about employment, they pay more heed to the poor pay and lack of prospects. Moreover rural school-leavers themselves are increasingly aware of the stigma attached to working on the land after generations of poverty, exploitation and dependent status. In this sense farmers today are in danger of reaping the whirlwind sown by their forefathers.

The increasing reluctance of young people to consider a future in farming was illustrated in 1972 by an agricultural 'Little Neddy' national survey, *The Younger Worker in Agriculture – Projections to 1980*. This demonstrated the importance of family factors in determining the occupational choice of rural school-leavers – nearly 42 per cent of the respondents stated that they had been influenced by their family in their decision to work on the land. However, what is also handed down from father to son these days is the importance of seeking a higher-paid and higher-status job elsewhere as soon as possible. More than a quarter of the young workers interviewed had no intention of remaining in agriculture – they hoped to seek more lucrative employment, mainly in the building industry, as lorry drivers, as garage mechanics or perhaps as engineering workers in local factories. Consequently there has been a marked fall in recruitment since 1964 – although it is still not enough on its own to create a shortage of labour – and this is contributing to the ageing labour force. The report concluded that, with a further increase in mechanization, there should still be enough labour to meet the needs of the industry by 1980, but that there was little room to manoeuvre and the longer-term situation was unclear. At the time that it was published, the report received a great deal of attention since it coincided with the brief economic boom of 1971–2 and workers were leaving agriculture at an alarming rate. There were calls to strengthen the role of the Agricultural Training Board, which had been founded amid great acrimony and much suspicion among farmers in the late 1960s, and there were also suggestions of a campaign in schools to extol the benefits of working in agriculture and to counteract the industry's image of unskilled drudgery. But farmers have short memories: within a couple of years economic stagnation had stemmed the labour outflow and even led ex-farm workers in some areas to ask for their former jobs back. The clamour for action subsided and complacency over the labour situation again set in.

This complacency is self-deceiving. There is no reason to believe that, should the demand for labour in industry pick up again, the exodus of young workers from agriculture will not be renewed.

Further mechanization will enable farmers to cope with a reduced quantity of labour, but further mechanization will require a finer *quality* of labour – and it is precisely the highly educated and the highly trained who currently shun working on the land. This has led many farmers to believe that the skilled, responsible and versatile labour which they require cannot be purchased at any price, and that the future expansion of the industry will be jeopardized by a chronic shortage of the requisite workers. Tristram Beresford, for example, writes in *We Plough the Fields* that:

At a time when the prevailing attitude is to do as little as possible in return for the highest possible pay . . . farm work is losing whatever glamour it may once have had. To submit to its exactions and disciplines, and to be relatively poorly paid into the bargain, is more than can be asked of human nature. . . . It is not just a question of paying competitive wages and getting through the work in fewer hours. There is already a problem of recruitment. The skills are simply not to be bought. On many holdings this shortage of skills is now dictating the system of farming.

The awkward and uncertain hours (especially for livestock workers), the isolation and the lack of amenities are, it is true, drawbacks to recruitment which agriculture must overcome. However, the job itself, as we have already noted, is rarely the cause of disenchantment with agriculture – indeed, in a decade that has seen a renewed interest in the countryside among young people and a growing desire to escape from the urban rat-race, agriculture *could* have much to offer. The skills *are* there to be bought: the problem is that many farmers have an exaggerated notion of the kind of worker that they can obtain for the money they are willing to offer, as well as an outdated conception of what the farm worker's skills would fetch in industry. The solution lies firmly in the farmers' own hands.

Beresford is undoubtedly correct in one respect, however. It is not *just* a question of paying competitive wages. Farmers still have the problem of overcoming the stigma which all too often young people attach to working on the land. Teenage farm workers are particularly sensitive to their image at an age when they are dating girls who may or may not hope for a better future than that of a farm worker's wife. No young farm worker enjoys having his leg pulled by taunts of 'yokel' and 'country bumpkin' in pubs and discothèques and eventually he may even become ashamed of admitting to his occupation. When the young worker's social world was bounded by his village such considerations did not matter. Among friends and neighbours a farm worker's skill was appreciated and he neither knew nor cared about the reputation of farm workers outside. But young farm workers today are part of the post-war generation of rural inhabitants who have been subjected far more than preceding generations to the cultural influences and judgements of wider society. The Education Act of 1944, for example, led to the majority of rural school children being educated for the first time outside their own village after the age of eleven. It also furnished them with a curriculum in both secondary modern and grammar schools that was geared to national cultural demands and criteria of scholastic excellence. At the same time rural children became more familiar with the accoutrements of a national (indeed, international) youth culture in terms of clothes, music and other aspects of their life-style. Many, as a result, became more impatient with the social and cultural backwater which, they now realized, their village constituted. They also became aware of the low regard in which the farm worker is held outside their own rural area. It is little wonder, then, that they preferred to look elsewhere for employment.

There is little that farmers could, or can, do about these cultural changes which have come to broaden the horizons of so many rural people. However, at times farmers have been their own worst enemies. Rather than welcome social and cultural change, they have resisted it. As a result, the agriculture industry is in the ironic situation of being in the vanguard of scientific and technological progress and subject to rapid and innovatory change, yet with a reputation for being backward and conservative and the very antithesis of modernity when it comes to its labour relations. It must be added, moreover, that this reputation has often been justified. Any progress in the situation of the farm worker during the last hundred years has generally been introduced from outside the industry and against the stern resistance of farmers themselves. Even the spread of increased educational opportunities to rural areas was opposed as late as 1944 on the grounds that farm workers would no longer 'know their place'. The farming lobby has also pursued a policy of agricultural exceptionalism when it has come to the institution of a wide range of welfare and safety measures. Farm workers are usually the last to receive the protection of safety legislation, for example, or to receive benefits like sickness pay, pension schemes, paid holidays, a five-day week or even a written contract of employment and itemized pay packets. The industry has also taken a neanderthal attitude towards the training and further education of its workers. Furthermore, the farm worker has generally been among the last to receive citizenship rights granted to the rest of the population – the shadow of the workhouse was not finally removed until 1936, the Rent Act was not extended to agricultural dwellings until 1976 and even today agricultural legislation manages to override certain of the conditions of the Truck Acts. The farm worker has been allowed to participate in the modern world only sparingly, hesitantly and distrustfully. Younger workers, observing this, have turned elsewhere in order to be part of a more enlightened and progressive industry.

Because fewer farm workers' sons are willing to work in agriculture the contrasts between the traditional and the modern, between the old dependency and the new independence, are imported into the families of those older workers who have remained on the land. Many teenage farm workers' sons are soon earning as much as, if not more than, their fathers, and not surprisingly they soon demand the independence from parental authority which their economic independence confers. The opportunities for domestic conflict are obvious, but at the same time the older generation of farm workers are made more aware of the opportunities that they themselves missed and of their lowly economic position compared with workers in other industries. Farm workers can also observe the life-styles afforded by ex-workmates and neighbours who have left farming to seek higher-paid employment elsewhere. This personal acquaintance with higher living standards is a much more potent factor in increasing the restlessness of today's farm workers than the influence of television and the other mass media to which it is often attributed. What the farm worker observes on his television set are the often distant and somewhat alien *mores* of the urban, industrial world. He may regard them as curious examples of another civilization or occasionally view with incredulity the ways of city people and industrial workers, but he will only regard them with envy when television reinforces the evaluations already implanted personally by friends and kin with whom he identifies. Otherwise television merely reinforces a point of view already strong among farm workers – that there is a wide and unbridgeable gulf between people who live in the countryside and those who live in towns.

There is little reason to suppose that the consequences of these changes will in themselves lead farm workers to become more militant. While at work he is still aware of the extent to which mechanization has improved his working conditions, and his relationship with his employer generally remains a good one. It is as a consumer that he is aware of the slowly widening gap between his own standard of living and that of other workers. So the paradoxes remain and in addition the farm worker continues to observe rapid changes in his work, in his village and in established patterns of authority. Aspects of life in the countryside which he once took for granted now seem to be increasingly questioned. For the older farm worker bafflement rather than militancy is therefore the more common response – 'I don't know what the world is coming to.' Another is a search for more definite realities in the certainties of the 'good old days' – a nostalgia for the days of horses when each person knew his place, was secure within it, when the old were respected and when the world was slower-moving and more predictable. Given their continuing power-lessness, however, even the younger workers are unlikely to seek an improvement in their position by resort to militant action. Their desire to leave farming will simply be increased and they will seize the first opportunity to move. In such circumstances the abilities of individual farmers to retain the loyalty and affection of their workers will be considerably tested. They are fortunate that, for the most part, the increasing personal contact at work, the continuing isolation of farm workers from other occupational groups and the increasing proportion of workers living in tied housing out on the farms are providing opportunities for this identification to be retained, should farmers choose to cultivate it. Certainly if farmers wish to have a suitably skilled and motivated labour force by the late 1980s they will have to do more to recognize the farm worker's quite legitimate aspirations and to help rather than hinder his search for 'a place in the sun'.

'What on earth do you mean – no stuffed olives?'

5 Change in the village

So far in this book we have considered social change in rural England almost entirely in terms of agriculture. This reflects the fact that the very far-reaching social changes that have overtaken the English countryside in recent decades have been rooted first and foremost in changes within the agricultural industry – the decline of the landed estates, the technological revolution in farming, the drift from the land of agricultural workers, and so on. But rural England today consists of much more than agriculture and English rural society is no longer entirely, nor even predominantly, an agrarian society. Indeed, the single most important social change to have occurred in the countryside in recent years has concerned the changing social and occupational composition of its population. The outflow of labour from agriculture has denuded many villages of their working populations and replaced them by inhabitants who work in towns and cities and who are not dependent upon farming for their living. Increasingly, then, when we examine social change in rural England we must not only take account of changes within agriculture but of changes on the interface between the 'truly rural' (i.e. agricultural) inhabitants and the 'adventitious' population of ex-urbanite new-comers who have moved into the countryside in such large numbers since the war. As we shall see, many of the controversies and conflicts which permeate contemporary rural life either stem from this fundamental change in the social composition of most villages or are exacerbated by it; but it is also important to remember that this transformation has been provoked by preceding changes in the economic and social organization of agriculture. Social change in the village has therefore accompanied the upheavals in the nature of agricultural work itself.

Any consideration of the changing nature of the English village seems inevitably to raise the question of how far the influx of newcomers has destroyed the village 'community'. The rhetoric of 'community', however, often serves to obscure as much as to clarify the changes that have occurred. The word community itself means so many different things to different people that its use frequently adds to the confusion. For example, the 'village community' can signify nothing more than a type of settlement – a small number of people living together in a rural location usually in a nucleated pattern. This is simply a geographical expression which tells us nothing about the people who live there. The 'village community' can also mean, however, the pattern of social relationships which exist within this locality. In this case a 'community' might be said to exist when, say, everyone knows everyone else. This tells us nothing about the degree of harmony in the village – everyone might be at each other's throats – but it does indicate that within the village there is a reasonably close-knit social pattern, rather than a disparate group of individuals who happen, coincidentally, to live in the same locality. Finally, the 'village community' can mean a disembodied 'spirit' of community, a sense of belonging, of sharing a social identity in a spirit of friendliness and common emotional experience. These feelings of community are better termed communion, since they represent a form of community at the level of an individual's subjective experience or consciousness. Communion therefore relates to a particular *quality* of human relationship – a kind of meaningful social intimacy – which may have no geographical basis at all, but which, it is believed, occurs more commonly in villages.

The many references by writers on rural affairs to 'the decline of the English village community' are usually concerned with the third of these meanings – the decline of communion. This is often inferred from observations of the changing social composition of the village. Yet such inferences need to be handled with care. When the village was almost entirely an agricultural community then a case can be made, as we shall see, that the close-knit and overlapping social ties produced a situation in which everyone more or less knew everyone else, but we should be wary of sanctifying the agricultural village with a misplaced nostalgia. The village inhabitants formed a community because they had to: they were imprisoned by constraints of various kinds, including poverty, so that reciprocal aid became a necessity. The village community was, therefore, to use Raymond Williams's term, a 'mutuality of the oppressed'. Whether gossip, bickering and family feuds were or were not a more prevalent feature than a wholesome communion of the population could vary from village to village and is ultimately a matter of subjective judgement. Nevertheless the severe and rapid dislocation of the agricultural village has led to an ideology of communion being conferred upon it, a genuine sense of loss which can be contrasted with an apparently less palatable present. Since this is, in effect, as much an oblique comment on the present as a literal interpretation of the past, what such accounts tell us about the quality of village life in the past must be handled with considerable scepticism. Unfortunately there is a flourishing literary genre of what might be called 'rural retrospective regret' which is often quite unreliable on the actual history of the English village.

Because assessments of the spirit of community depend so much on highly variable subjective preferences and values, which may fluctuate according to the individual and the village concerned and even to the mood of the individual at a particular time, it is virtually impossible to generalize about whether there has or has not been a perceptible 'decline of community' in the English village. Changes in the social structure of the village community – that is, the second of the meanings outlined above – are, however, more amenable to generalization, although even here there are considerable difficulties. Part of the ideology of a healthy village community has been the pride which the inhabitants have traditionally shown in their village's unique qualities. Each village believes itself to be totally different from any other and often marks itself off in a variety of symbolic ways from those which surround it. Any attempt to generalize about the English village is therefore regarded as an affront: bland uniformity is an attribute of the urban population, but the English village is believed to be resistant to any summary. Of course, each village does contain its own unique qualities, but to dwell on these only serves to obscure the nature of the changes which have overtaken them, since a concern for the minutiae of each individual village leads us to lose sight of the widespread changes that have affected almost all villages in recent years. The uniqueness of each village has affected the timing, the pace and the extent of these changes, but virtually no village in England has been immune to them. Variations obviously occur from village to village and from area to area, so that no claim is made that what follows in this chapter applies to each and every village in England. Nevertheless a general pattern is discernible.

If uniqueness is one quality that is attributed to the English village, then timelessness is the other, but again it is easy to confer an entirely spurious antiquity on village life, and even upon the physical structure of villages, which can be misleading. As both W. G. Hoskins and W. E. Tate have shown, the English village as we know it is in its essentials a product of developments not much less recent than the growth of industrial towns and cities. In lowland England in particular the characteristic nucleated village settlement is a product of the enclosure movement and the agricultural revolution of the eighteenth century. Previously scattered farmsteads and agricultural dwellings – a pattern still common in upland farming areas – gravitated towards a definable parish centre around the church or manor house. Later, particularly during the period of mid-Victorian agricultural prosperity, farmers left the village to live in often newly built farmhouses, which were located on their own holdings of land. In lowland England, then, only the church, the manor house, and a few cottages pre-date the Industrial Revolution. The villages which can claim a degree of undisturbed continuity beyond this are not usually agricultural villages at all, but medieval textile 'towns' which have reverted to an agricultural status following the transfer of textile production to the industrial North during the nineteenth century. The continuity of settlement pattern is more apparent in the upland North and West, where villages are less common, but here the colonization of the remoter areas, such as Cumbria, was still proceeding as late as the eighteenth century. So the English village is neither as immemorial nor as unchanging as it is conventionally believed to be. Contemporary changes therefore need to be placed in the context of a continuous process of change in English rural society that has affected both the character and the structure of English villages throughout their history.

The occupational community

A convenient, though entirely arbitrary, point to begin an account of recent changes in the English village is the middle of the nineteenth century. Between 1846 and 1873 the social and ecological pattern of what we now regard as the traditional English village became firmly established, particularly in the lowland South and East. The industrial and commercial development of England had by this time succeeded in 'ruralizing' the countryside by reducing the economic viability of much small-scale manufacture and domestic handicraft and transferring it to the new system of factory production in the towns. Although the countryside did not become completely agricultural because of the continuing importance of extractive industries and the tenacious existence of some manufacture in the agricultural ancillary trades, farming was unquestionably the mainstay of the rural economy. The population of the majority of rural villages was therefore dependent upon agriculture for a living. Even if members of the village were not working directly on the land as farm workers they were involved in occupations closely associated with farming such as blacksmiths, wheelwrights, millers and other craftsmen and service workers. Because of its dependence upon a single industry the rural village formed what might be called an 'occupational community'.

As with any isolated and largely self-contained community the agricultural village was often the object of a fierce loyalty among its inhabitants. From its own customs and traditions the villagers could draw upon a strong sense of identity and morality which, looking back, one may easily mourn in a more impersonal, amoral and uncertain modern world. This sense of certainty was probably the occupational community's greatest source of strength. Inevitably the boundaries of what was and was not considered permissible in village life were much clearer in the nineteenth century, as they were in Victorian society generally. This conferred a sense of order on village life, a sense of 'place', in both a geographical and a social sense, which could be recognized and accepted as an immutable fact of life. For those villagers who accepted their 'place' this created a sense of psychological certainty and with it a not altogether unwelcome sense of security. For those who found this social order irksome – the rebellious, the ambitious or simply the single-minded – the village could become a narrow and restrictive prison, dispiriting and mean-spirited, shackling the individualist by the vicious purveyance of gossip and innuendo. This double-edged quality of village life is accurately reflected in Flora Thompson's *Lark Rise to Candleford*. Here the narrowness of social affairs in Lark Rise provides a

means of accommodation to the otherwise harsh circumstances of
rural life:

> The discussion of their own and their neighbours' affairs took the place
> occupied by books and films in the modern outlook. Nothing of outside
> importance ever happened there and their lives were as unlike as possible
> the modern conception of country life, for Lark Rise was neither a little
> hotbed of vice nor a garden of Arcadian virtues. But the lives of all human
> beings, however narrow, have room for complications for themselves and
> entertainment for the onlooker, and many a satisfying little drama was
> played out on that ten-foot stage.
>
> In their daily life they had none of the conveniences now looked upon as
> necessities: no water nearer than the communal well, no sanitation beyond
> the garden closet, and no light but candles and paraffin lamps. It was a
> hard life, but the hamlet folks did not pity themselves.

The hardness of this life stemmed from the chronic poverty and
occasionally cruel exploitation to which the nineteenth-century farm
worker – or 'farm labourer' as he was more customarily referred to –
was subjected. The conditions of the farm worker, and with them
the everyday life of the village community, could vary considerably
across the country according to the distribution of landholding, the
nature of agricultural production and the pattern of settlement.
As we noted in Chapter 2, James Caird, writing in 1878, drew
attention to the differences between the agriculture practised in the
predominantly pastoral North and West of England and that in
the mainly arable South and East, a division which affected the
organization and conditions of village life in the two regions. The
greater use of hired labour on the arable farm created a much greater
cleavage between farmers and the farm workers than in the pastoral
areas, where little hired labour was employed and where the most
significant class division was between landowners and their tenants.
Although this is a somewhat oversimplified distinction, it is nevertheless significant that rural agitation during the late nineteenth
century took the form of trade union organization (under Joseph
Arch) in the South and East, whereas unionism could make little
headway in the North and West. This was partly because the hiring
fairs in the upland areas provided a means of regulating the labour
market which appeared to render trade unionism irrelevant, but it
was also due to the reduced social distance between farmers and farm
workers there. Class conflict, when it broke out during the final

quarter of the nineteenth century in the North and West, took the form of 'tenant right', the demand by tenant farmers for greater security and the guarantee of their other interests against those of their landlords. Even today trade unionism in agriculture is more prevalent in the South and East, whereas tenants' associations, almost unknown in the arable areas, are more common in the North and West. Although the recent changes that have occurred in the social structure of rural villages have been national in their character, and therefore have impinged upon both areas, the continuing differences between the two require separate analyses of their impact. For this reason we shall consider first the changes that have occurred in the lowland village community, while the upland areas will be analysed in the section on the 'farm-centred community' later in this chapter.

In eastern and southern England, where the bulk of hired agricultural workers have traditionally been concentrated and where the class division between farmer and worker was correspondingly wide, the structure of the occupational community was a divided one. The nature of arable farming, which required a large labour force to tend the crop, conferred upon rural society a rigid social hierarchy. This was often reflected in the pattern of settlement, with most villages consisting of the dwellings of agricultural workers and with the farmers scattered around the parish on their own farms but away from the centre of the village itself. In a very real sense, therefore, the employers, whether farmers or landlords – in practice it made little difference – were not part of the rural village community as far as the agricultural worker was concerned. Although there was an 'official' village community within which landowners, farmers and clergy were included and which was occasionally celebrated in traditional (and public) rituals and ceremonies, there was another community, a locally based working-class sub-culture, which excluded 'them' in authority. This subculture represented the core of the occupational community. It was basically a neighbourly association of kin and workmates, not dissimilar to that which existed in many urban working-class neighbourhoods, but which the outsider could find virtually impenetrable. It was sustained by the isolation of the rural village, by the strong kinship links between the village inhabitants and by the need for cooperation in times of family crisis. Most importantly, it was forged out of the overlap between workplace and village, the fact that, as an occupational community, relationships established at work spilled over into leisure hours, while the accepted code of behaviour which was followed in the village also applied to the situation at work.

All of this made the rural village an extremely close-knit society. The circle of friends and acquaintances with which the farm worker surrounded himself consisted predominantly of other farm workers, both at work – where, as we have seen, workers were far more gregarious than they are today – and in the village, where most of their neighbours would also work on the land. It is little wonder, then, that ostracism and gossip were such powerful ways of enforcing the values and standards of village life, nor that the criteria of status and prestige in the community also tended to be derived from the world of work. In what Margaret Ashby calls 'this street-and-smithy parliament' every contemporary problem was discussed and lessons in human nature could be absorbed. Above all the farm worker could establish his reputation as a skilled and knowledge-able craftsman among his fellow workers. They would incessantly 'talk shop', for example, especially in that important semi-public arena – the village pub. As George Ewart Evans documents in his book *Where Beards Wag All*, it was also common to see groups of workers strolling around the parish on Sunday mornings examining each other's work, with much chafing and leg-pulling about their respective capabilities en route. He cites the recollections of James Seeley, an ex-horseman from Norfolk:

The old teamsmen would walk miles round the countryside to look at other people's work – well outside their own parish sometimes. At the time I'm speaking of, before 1914 when I was called up, the pubs were open all day during the week but on Sunday they were closed except during midday for a couple of hours, and then they'd open again in the evening. But if you'd travelled three miles you could have a drink in a pub at anytime on a Sunday. So the teamsmen [or horsemen] used to walk their three miles out of the village to get a drink, looking at the ploughing as they went. . . . Some of them made a real outing of it, looking at the land and saying perhaps: 'They've got a real good 'un here. Look at his work.'

This kind of prestige was formalized in ploughing matches for the horsemen, while for stockmen the equivalent public arenas for competition were markets and agricultural shows. In each case the basis for allocating prestige among the community was very public. A botched job, especially for ploughmen, would be visible to all the parish for the next six months – to friends, neighbours, workmates and even the casual passer-by. The mistake would be recorded in every farm and public house in the area and the resulting loss of face could be especially humiliating. The pride in the job which has often been regarded as the hallmark of the rural worker was therefore not always derived from sheer altruism. Each time a worker ploughed a field his status and even his self-respect could be at stake. The integration of the farm worker into this occupational community meant that it was his prestige among his fellow workers and neighbours that mattered most to him. Because of this, he was less concerned that he might be considered by society at large as an unskilled 'yokel' – even if he was aware of the opinion of the world outside. Within his own locality, however, a farm worker's status could be extremely high and his skill particularly valued. The identification of the farm worker with his fellow villagers was reinforced by this, and even local farmers, who also had an interest in securing skilled labour and ensuring that the farm ran as smoothly as possible, contributed to the process by seeking out the best workers according to their reputation in the locality. Nevertheless, relationships with farmers and landowners were clearly different from those between fellow workers. For relationships with farmers and landowners across most of lowland England were, almost by definition, relationships with authority.

Although the precise configuration of landowners and farmers could vary considerably from village to village, there is little doubt that they formed, from the point of view of the farm worker, a coherent and easily identifiable ruling class against which the farm worker, either individually or collectively, was relatively powerless. Within the working-class subculture of the occupational community, therefore, the village was defined in terms of two distinct and separate groups: 'us', the workers, and 'them', the bosses. The locally powerful were acknowledged rather than accepted; in Flora Thompson's words, they 'flitted across the scene like kingfishers crossing a flock of hedgerow sparrows'. They attended the church, patronized the local tradesmen and supervised the affairs of the village. They felt entitled to, and duly received, the customary genuflections that were accorded to their rank, but they belonged to the local 'house' rather than to the village. Of course, farm workers were never left in any doubt as to where the power in their village lay, but on the whole class conflict was rarely overt. Any farm worker could easily anticipate the consequences of 'going against' the local farmers, so for the most part they resigned themselves to this situation, bit their tongues rather than spoke out and developed what is by now their notorious taciturnity and ability to 'keep themselves to themselves'. In this way the traditionally placid exterior of social relations in the English countryside was allowed to remain undisturbed. However, beneath what was sometimes only a thin veneer of civility more covert expressions of resistance to the depredations imposed upon the farm worker took place. The clue to rural class conflict was therefore the existence of a thriving rural underworld which included a whole range of activities such as arson, poaching and the propagation of usually inconsequential subversive talk in the taproom of the local alehouse. Only occasionally (as in the 1830s and the 1870s) did conflict burst out in an overt and organized expression of discontent. Otherwise it took more subtle and even secret forms – such as the semi-secret societies among stockmen like 'the horseman's word'. But whatever its degree of visibility, class conflict was never far from the surface of day-to-day social relationships when the village was an occupational community.

Landowners and farmers implicitly recognized this division, but they also realized that life both on the farm and in the village would ultimately run more smoothly if the socially divisive effects of potential class conflict could be dissipated or overcome. Large landowners, in particular, often set about cultivating the loyalty and affection of the local villagers, since this also conformed to the notion of *noblesse oblige* which was part of the ethic of the country gentleman. Farm workers, too, could be persuaded to defer to the locally powerful if the latter were prepared to act in what the farm worker believed to be a legitimate manner. Hence, as has already been outlined in Chapters 2 and 3, the paternalism of the local squire could be exchanged for the deference of local workers. The institution of charity was particularly important here. Christian conscience and enlightened self-interest would often combine to enable relief to be given to the poor and the needy and for more ostentatious acts of generosity to be accorded to the village as a whole. Only the 'deserving' would receive charity, of course, for the purpose was to encourage respect and gratitude, not independence.

Gifts were the knots which secured the ties of dependency, and, it was hoped, served as timely reminders of communal identity. Thus community, as an ideology, was a gloss that was placed upon the very rigid and authoritarian divisions within the village. It was recognized that there were distinct social orders within the community, but these were widely regarded as 'natural' and their relationship was defined as an organic one: each had his or her part to play, be it ever so humble. The solidarity of 'community' at this level was very different to the unavoidable communality of the village poor. Its existence was almost entirely a symbolic one, in such rituals as 'beating the bounds', in village fairs and festivals and in sporting activities as diverse as foxhunting and cricket. Occasionally this contrivance could overshadow the less congenial reality which lay behind it and could override the more mundane, everyday exploitation of work on the land, but this, given the conditions under which farm workers lived and worked, was only sporadically successful.

As so often when we contemplate English village society much depended upon particular local conditions. As Margaret Ashby notes in the biography of her father *Joseph Ashby of Tysoe, 1859–1919:* 'They [Joseph's contemporaries] tested every man's views by his actions, by his carriage of himself on all sorts of occasions. They knew the effect of interest and class, and how in some cases these were the whole mould of mind and in others far otherwise.' It was, however, rarely possible completely to guarantee the affection of the farm worker. This was particularly the case where the occupational community provided him with a rural counter-culture that enabled class antagonisms to be sustained, albeit in a hidden form. Here the 'us and them' view of the village society could be maintained in the face of an 'official' credo in which no conflicts of interest were perceived or admitted. In such cases the most that an employer could hope for was that by his treatment of his workers he could obtain some minimal loyalty. Some farmers, however, did not even attempt this, but preferred to rely upon the application of economic and social discipline alone.

The precise way in which rural class relationships were acted out could therefore vary considerably from one village to the next according to the predilections of local farmers and landowners. Of course, a farm worker could acknowledge that the obverse side of squirearchal autocracy could be a benevolent concern for his own welfare and this could confer a sense of security and harmony on class relationships which could be extremely durable. Nevertheless, the underlying structure of the vast majority of lowland villages (and, it should be added, some in the upland, pastoral areas, too) consisted of two major social classes. Whether the farm worker preferred to defer to the authority of his 'betters', or fight against it, or merely accept it as a fact of life and accommodate to it as best he could, he recognized that there was a clear, qualitative difference between this relationship and that with his fellow workers. All members of the village knew their place and, whether they wished to change it or not, this division had to be recognized and tolerated. Those who could not contain their resentment had little option other than to emigrate.

Locals and newcomers

Today the lowland English village as an occupational community has virtually disappeared, except in a few very remote areas, destroyed by the twin assaults of the drift from the land of agricultural labour and creeping urbanization. Both have been accelerated since the war by the widespread application of the internal combustion engine. On the farm the introduction of tractors and combine harvesters has brought about a vast decrease in the number of employment opportunities and an added stimulus to the rural working population to move to the towns in search of jobs. They have been replaced in many areas by an urban, overwhelmingly middle-class population which has been attracted by a combination of cheap housing (until the late 1960s) and by an idealized view of rural life which their ownership of a car has at last allowed them to indulge. The arrival of this 'adventitious' rural population goes back further than is often assumed, and is by no means a purely post-war phenomenon. For example, George Bourne was writing about its effects in the villages of Surrey in his *Change in the Village* as early as 1912, by which time the railways had enabled a commuting population to inhabit the rural parts of the inner Home Counties. Since then the transformation of rural villages into non-agricultural settlements has taken place in a series of waves out along the lines of transportation from the major urban centres, particularly, in the first instance, London. During the inter-war years commuting was encouraged by the railway companies and by speculative builders and it was only after the Second World War that the more widespread use of the car and the continuing electrification of the railways allowed the commuting zone to be extended further. By the end of the 1960s the motorway network had linked up most of the commuting areas between the major conurbations and the in-filling of commuter villages between such radial transport routes had virtually been completed. Only a few rural areas, isolated by bad roads and non-existent railways, remained relatively untouched, but even these, by virtue of their isolation, were often gobbled up by the equally voracious demand for holiday homes and weekend cottages.

There are now few villages without their complement of newcomers who work in towns. These new 'immigrants' have brought with them an urban, middle-class life-style which is largely alien to the remaining local agricultural population. Unlike the agricultural workers in an occupational community, the newcomers do not make the village the focus of all their social activities. The possession of a car enables them to maintain social contacts with their friends elsewhere, and if necessary, to make use of urban amenities while living in the countryside. Their entertainment, their socializing, even their shopping, tend to take place outside the village. This influx of strangers can, therefore, quite rapidly affect the nature of village society: suddenly, so it appears to the locals, everybody does *not* know everybody else. The newcomer, moreover, does not enter the village as a lone individual who has to win social recognition among the locals in order to make life tolerable. Instead, particularly during the 1950s and 1960s, the newcomers arrived in such large numbers – perhaps due to the building of a new housing estate by a local speculative builder – that the individual 'immigrant' found himself one of many others whose values, behaviour and life-styles were similarly based upon urban, middle-class patterns of sociability. Although these are noticeably different from those of the local agricultural population, the newcomer does not always feel it is necessary to adapt to the hitherto accepted *mores* of the village. This, however, depends on what brought the newcomers to the village in the first place. If the incentive was a utilitarian one like cheap housing, then the newcomers will have little interest in observing the niceties of village life. They can, if necessary, establish social contacts among themselves or continue to seek them outside. On the other hand, those newcomers who wish to 'belong' may try to ingratiate themselves with the local population, sometimes – because of their misconceived expectations of village life – with disappointing results.

In either case, a new social division arises in the village which cuts across the class antagonisms of the former occupational community. On the one hand there are the close-knit locals, who are the rump of the old occupational community, and on the other the ex-urbanite newcomers whose arrival in such relatively large numbers over a short space of time cannot help but be disruptive. Some newcomers have been indifferent to the sensibilities of the local population; others, as we shall see, have been oversensitive to what *they* believe the needs of the village to be. In each case the effect has been the same: members of the former occupational community, faced with an invasion of 'their' village by outsiders, have tended to retreat in upon themselves and form a community within a community, cutting themselves off from the separate world of the newcomers. The occupational community becomes what can be called an 'encapsulated community', a village within the village, suspicious of and resistant to any intimate social contact with the commuters and second-home owners who now comprise a substantial proportion of the population. When farmers and farm workers refer to the 'loss of community' in their village it is usually to this kind of change that they are implicitly referring, for there are bound to be changing patterns of sociability developing in the village to which they are unaccustomed or from which they feel excluded. This new element in the village population also tends to create new dimensions of social conflict to replace the rural class antagonisms of the occupational community. Farmers and farm workers find that they have common interests as 'locals' which can be at loggerheads with those of the newcomers. From the farm workers' point of view, farmers therefore become 'one of us' to be counterposed to 'them', the rural immigrant population. As the recent experience of many English villages shows only too well, there are ample opportunities for conflict to arise between *both* farmers and farm workers on the one hand and the newcomers on the other.

Since the urban middle-class exodus to the countryside began in earnest in the 1950s there have typically been two issues over which such conflict has been generated: housing and the environment. Each problem will be considered in more detail later in this book, but here we may note how each issue has contributed to the initial polarization of the village population. Housing is obviously a crucial resource and one for which, moreover, the whole rural population – farmers and farm workers, locals and newcomers, agricultural and non-agricultural families – are competing. In general, this does not apply to local employment, because the newcomers either retain their employment in nearby towns and commute to work or they have come to the countryside to retire. Both they and their children are also more mobile and, typically, more highly-educated, so they compete in an entirely separate – usually professional and managerial – labour market from the local population. Housing, however, is another matter. Here, newcomers do compete with the locals, contributing to a higher demand for rural housing which, together with the restricted supply, has led to extensive changes in the nature of the rural housing market. Although rural housing, as we shall see later in this chapter, has never been in plentiful supply, the newcomers provide an easy scapegoat for the otherwise 'hidden hand' of the housing market. Resentment among the locals grows at their inability to find housing for their children in their village. Farm workers find themselves more dependent upon tied cottages and both farm workers and the non-agricultural locals join the queue for council housing. Yet here they have found that the newcomers are also opposed to the construction of further council housing in the village on the grounds that it is 'detrimental to the character of the village' and detracts from the rural environment.

The provision of council housing therefore links up the second basis of local–newcomer conflict, which relates to broadly environmental issues. The newcomers often possess a set of stereotyped expectations of village life which place a heavy emphasis on the quality of the rural environment. As was indicated at the beginning of this book, many newcomers hold strong views on the desired social and aesthetic qualities of the English village. It must conform as closely as possible to the prevailing urban view – picturesque, ancient and unchanging. The expectation that the countryside should conform to a certain idea of the picturesque and that it should present an unchanging spectacle to the appreciative onlooker has, for example, led many newcomers to be bitterly critical of the changes wrought by modern farming methods. It is they who are in the forefront of conservation societies, who complain about uprooted hedgerows in the lowland farming areas and who resent the destruction or diversion of footpaths. This is because the newcomers regard the countryside in primarily aesthetic and recreational terms. For the same reason they have been known to treat surrounding farmland as though it were a vast municipal park across which their dogs can roam or their children can ride their ponies without much thought for the consequences. The problems that this can cause, which are often unintentional and the result of a lack of knowledge about modern agriculture, are sufficient to annoy any farmer already unhappy about what he considers to be unwarranted interference in his legitimate farming operations by busybody environmentalists. An already wary relationship between the farming population and the newcomers can easily become strained by such encounters, reinforcing the divisions between the two sides.

Individual petty conflicts therefore easily accumulate to add to the differences already apparent between locals and newcomers in terms of background and life-styles. Because each side is personally unfamiliar with the other there is a tendency for stereotypes to emerge and for behaviour to take place on the basis of these stereotypes, making relationships even more difficult. Quite quickly the contact between the two sections of the rural population can become limited to the activity of a few 'go-betweens', whose employment requires them to relate to both sides. Shopkeepers and local tradesmen often carry out this role – indeed, surviving rural craftsmen, such as thatchers and blacksmiths, discover a rejuvenated demand for their skills among the newcomers. Other significant 'go-betweens' are the domestic workers hired by the more affluent newcomers – the 'little woman' who comes in to 'do' twice or three times a week, and who is often the wife of a local farm worker grateful for the money. As scouts sent out by the locals to reconnoitre the otherwise mysterious life-styles of the newcomers such people are terribly influential in defining the image of the newcomers among the locals – and of the locals among the newcomers. Gossip which is reported back easily becomes magnified in order to contribute further to the stereotypes.

For farm workers in particular the sense of loss which the influx of newcomers has prompted can be quite severe. Many newcomers share the prevailing urban view of the farm 'labourer'. They tend to be unappreciative of the farm worker's skills, not out of malice, but because they simply lack the detailed knowledge of agriculture on which to base a judgement. As they drive around the countryside the newcomers cannot distinguish between those fields which have been ploughed with a supreme exhibition of the farm worker's skills and those which have not; nor are they able to appreciate the beauty of a faultlessly drilled seed-bed, healthy stock or clean weed-free fields. The criterion by which a farm worker could once obtain high status – skill at work – is therefore threatened with being overthrown. Instead the newcomers tend to evaluate the farm worker and the other villagers on the basis of urban criteria for allocating prestige. This usually means conspicuous consumption in one or all of its varied forms – the size of the house, the size, age and make of the car, the possession of other consumer durables, the quality of furnishings, and so on. Even the garden, which can be used for the conspicuous display of flowers and shrubs rather than the more utilitarian purpose of growing food, may become part of this. Whatever form it takes, however, such conspicuous consumption – and hence the allocation of status – depends upon income and farm workers, on low wages, simply cannot compete in this league. The agricultural worker, however, reacts to the possibility of being deprived of his former status in his own village by changing the rules of the competition. Since non-acceptance on the basis of length of residence is one of the few ways in which local workers can retain any of their old status in the village, they restrict their social contacts to those who share these judgements with them.

For those newcomers who seek the social intimacy of a happy and integrated community life in the village, the reserve (and worse) of the locals can be mystifying and even upsetting. Many arrive full of goodwill and good intentions, but fail to perceive the often unanticipated consequences of their arrival on the lives of the local inhabitants, and even an oversensitivity of the need to spread good-will around the village can appear to the locals to be both patronizing and unnecessary. For example, while the newcomers may fail to understand the skill and local status of the farm worker, they do not wish to treat him as a social outcast – this would run counter to the notion of community with which many newcomers strongly identify. Moreover the newcomers do like to see farm workers around the village since this serves as a reminder that they do indeed live in a 'truly rural' village, as opposed to a kind of rustic suburbia. However, the farm worker is allotted his 'place' in the grand, and somewhat idealized, design to which the village is expected to conform. He can be a 'character', a source of quaint rustic humour or home-spun rural philosophy on such matters as the seasons and the weather, but he is rarely expected to be either forward-thinking or 'forward' in his demeanour. What are demanded are pet farm workers who cause no trouble but who form part of the landscape along with the fields and the trees.

This tendency to treat the local population as an adjunct to the scenery is a problem to which even the rural *aficionados* among the newcomers can fall prey and by which they can unwittingly cause offence. For example, the following expression of sympathy, taken from a letter to *The Times* in January 1977, at first sight appears unexceptional. The writer, who was troubled that the Lake District was losing its local population, put her case as follows:

The Lake District is one of the most compactly beautiful regions in England and so much of its intrinsic attraction lies in the way of life led by native Cumbrians. Do people who buy second houses . . . in the Lake District realise that eventually they will destroy the very appeal of the area which they have always enjoyed? Do they for a moment consider that most visitors to the Lake District want to feel surrounded by natives of the fells and not middle-class accents and protocol?

Such comments show not so much an insensitivity to the problems of the locals, but reduces them to cyphers, tourist attractions almost, along with the surrounding scenery. In this case the native Lake District population becomes what one writer on this theme, R. E. Pahl, calls 'props on the rustic stage', which help to round off the picturesque vision of the countryside. To the farm worker sentiments such as these, however well-intentioned they may be, seem patroniz-ing and, although in this particular instance the underlying attitudes were made unusually explicit, they are usually present in the assump-tions of many newcomers.

In the light of these considerations it is perhaps not surprising that new social divisions and conflicts have arisen in the English village in recent years, nor that the local population has preferred to turn in upon itself in the face of these changes. This encapsulation of the locals in their own village has also been reinforced in many cases by a physical separation of the two sections of the community. Because of the workings of the housing market the local working population tends to congregate on the village council housing estate (where one is available), where the closely knit patterns of neighbourly association which were part of the occupational community are retained. Where villages contain more than one pub these, too, usually reflect the split between locals and newcomers, or, in the case of villages with only one pub, the bars may be socially divided – the locals to the public bar, the newcomers to the lounge, often 'modernized' in rustic mode for this purpose. The whole village therefore meets socially on only rare occasions, such as the parish meeting or the village fête, but even here socializing is often highly ritualized and rudimentary, as much symbolic as real. Village fêtes in particular often show up the divisions in the village rather well. To many newcomers they can seem a celebration of village conviviality, but closer inspection often reveals that who actually speaks to whom depends very much on background and life-style. Newcomers concentrate on the winemaking and the flower arrangements, while locals head single-mindedly for the beer tent and the equally serious business of the vegetable show, a forum in which husbandry skill is still subject to public competition. It is doubtful whether such social occasions bring about any lasting reconciliation between the two groups.

It is by no means clear that many newcomers are even aware of the feelings that they arouse from time to time in the local population. Having come to the village with certain expectations they may only see what they expect to find and, since the local working population has long been used to avoiding overt conflict in the face of those who have the capacity to create trouble for them, the superficial calm of village life may remain. The civilities of politeness and social etiquette may ensure that the locals' resentment is voiced only in their own social circle. It therefore becomes easy for the ideal of village life to remain among the newcomers, even though the reality for the locals may be very different. Nevertheless, in the contemporary English village it is this feeling of having been 'taken over' by outsiders that usually prevails among the agricultural population and with it not only a sense of 'loss of community', but an inevitable animus against the invasion of 'furriners'. This is not to suggest that English villages are currently hotbeds of social unrest – far from it. But when a suitable issue presents itself these underlying feelings easily become manifested, often to the surprise and consternation of the new village-dwellers.

The farm-centred community

The ratio of locals to newcomers in the village today depends not only on the accessibility to nearby urban centres, but, now that most of lowland England has been subject to these changes, by the mixture of housing which each village contains. Since privately rented accommodation is decreasing in rural areas, in common with the national trend, the three most important housing categories are owner-occupied houses, council houses and tied cottages. Most tied cottages are located on farms rather than in the village itself, so within the village the most important housing mix is usually that between privately owned and local authority housing. Where there is no council housing then it is possible for the village to be completely overrun by ex-urban newcomers. This particularly applies to the more beautiful showpiece villages, which by their very reputation attract more newcomers and by their more picturesque appearance prompt a premium to be placed on the price of local homes. Because of their beauty such villages are also more subject to draconian planning policies which may prevent any new development at all or restrict it to only the limited in-filling of low-density private housing. Unable to buy and with no council houses available many agricultural workers are forced to seek accommodation in the only local alternative that is available to them – tied cottages. The increasing proportion of farm workers living in tied housing since the war is therefore partly accounted for by these changes in the rural housing market.

Because most tied cottages are located on farms and because the village in this case has been virtually emptied of its former working population, farm workers become both physically and socially isolated from the village. The farm becomes their 'community' while contact with the village becomes much more perfunctory. Increasingly it is merely used for its amenities – schools, shops, etc. – rather than as the social centre which it once was. There is, of course, nothing new in the development of what might be called a farm-centred community, distinct and largely separated from the village, particularly in the pastoral and upland areas of England, where this kind of settlement pattern has traditionally been more common. In this situation, where the 'community' has become the farm itself, the farm worker lives in a somewhat privatized world, for the most part socially invisible to the rest of society. The sense of isolation which might otherwise ensue is, however, mitigated by the close contact with neighbours and workmates in the other tied houses and by increasing contact with the farmer who is now a neighbour as well as an employer. There is, indeed, a much less rigid distinction between working and non-working hours, for with easier accessibility between home and workplace the farm worker tends to be involved in the job for as long as it demands, rather than working to any set hours. Similarly farmers are more prepared to be indulgent about their employees' working hours as long as the necessary tasks are carried out efficiently. In general relationships between the farmer and his workers become more informal, more personal and – because of their living cheek-by-jowl around the farm – more pervasive. Although there is a risk that life can become too self-contained and claustrophobic, farmers nevertheless find it easier to inspire some degree of personal loyalty among their workers and allow the class animosities of the occupational community to be vastly reduced.

As we have already seen, this reduction in the social distance between farmers and farm workers is also aided by the impact of the newcomers to the village. Farmers can find common cause with their workers in complaining about the 'interference' of outsiders in their own farms' and the village's affairs. Moreover farmers, at least, continue to appreciate the skills of farm workers, so that the latter obtain much higher esteem from their employers than they can expect from many newcomers. These trends have reinforced the already closer contact between farmers and their workers brought about by mechanization and the declining size of the labour force which were discussed in the previous chapter. This does not mean that the objective differences in wealth and income have been in any way reduced, but relationships have become easier and more informal. An indication of this has been the reduction in the activities of the rural underworld, which was such a thriving feature of village life when it was an occupational community, but which has now virtually disappeared. Those indulging in poaching activities today are well-organized wide-boys from nearby towns, with the use of large vans and with good contacts in the meat trade. The farm worker is as likely as not to be found standing shoulder to shoulder with his employer defending the farm and its game – a literal case of poacher turned gamekeeper.

Because of the ways in which the changes wrought by urbanization have worked their way through the village community the contrast between the more affluent life-styles of the newcomers and the poorer living standards of local farm workers have not therefore resulted in greater conflict between farmers and their employees. If anything, farm workers now identify more with farmers than they have in the past. A more likely cause of restlessness and dissatisfaction among farm workers occurs when friends, neighbours and kin among the 'locals' cease to work on the land but commute from the village to nearby towns. In those villages with easy access to local urban centres and industrial estates this has become quite common. In other words, the continuing fall in the demand for labour on farms has prompted a growing proportion of even the locals to live in the village and work in towns. This is often much more damaging to the self-esteem of the farm worker than the arrival in the village of alien newcomers with whom he does not identify. When the farm worker sees ex-workmates supporting a more grandiose life-style he becomes more aware of his own relatively lowly situation. In a multitude of subtle ways the farm worker may be reminded of his inferiority. This is the most telling way in which the loss of community may be brought poignantly home to the farm worker.

As far as the newcomers are concerned, they have wished no harm to anyone, so that any animosity which they have evoked has been entirely unintended and unanticipated. Indeed at times it has seemed difficult to see what the newcomers could do to alleviate the resentments they have occasionally caused. If they respectfully withdraw from involvement in village affairs they find themselves branded as 'stand-offish' or 'jumped-up'; if they participate fully in the life of the village they are accused of 'taking over' and of telling the local inhabitants how to run their own community. The newcomers often act as easily identifiable scapegoats who can be blamed for many of the deprivations which the contemporary rural population suffers – poor amenities, remoteness from the centres of private and public decision-making, and so on. This is not to suggest that the basis of local–newcomer conflict in English villages has been entirely illusory

– far from it, as the previous discussion has shown. However, the social separation of the two groups and the consequent tendency of each to stereotype the other has magnified the conflict involved. The newcomers feel cold-shouldered by the local population on occasions and become resentful of their almost tribal clannishness. They complain about having to live in a village for three generations before winning social acceptance or ruefully conclude that 'the first fifty years are the worst'. Moreover, the impact of the newcomers has not been an entirely detrimental one, even for the locals. There is no doubt that the middle-class exodus from the towns to the countryside has vastly improved the physical fabric of the housing in rural areas. Cottages have been restored and renovated and, whatever the occasional lapses in taste, the appearance of most English villages has been greatly improved. A comparison between a 'commuter village' and one which has suffered the ravages of rural depopulation unhindered by the arrival of newcomers soon shows this. For example, a trip to the Barringtons, a group of villages in the Cotswolds left to ruin by the local landowner rather than allow the houses to be purchased by or let to ex-urbanites, will show that the 'loss of community' in both a physical and a social sense, has not been *caused* by newcomers moving in. The Barringtons vividly demonstrate that the village as an occupational community declined because the underlying economic base could no longer support it. The disruptions caused by newcomers have been merely a tangible symptom of this change.

The newcomers to the countryside have also been able to apply more pressure upon local and central government for the improvement of local amenities. Rural education is a prime example of this. Active and articulate middle-class newcomers have been able to apply considerable pressure to local education authorities in order to improve the standards of rural schools. They have formed parent–teacher associations and other pressure groups to make their voice heard at County Hall and they have also, by becoming elected as local councillors, been able directly to influence the allocation of resources. All rural children have benefited from the improvements that have resulted, whether they are the sons and daughters of locals or newcomers. Indeed the ability of the newcomers to find their way around the local political system has often prompted the improvement of other rural amenities, albeit on a highly selective basis. For

example, newcomers have been in the forefront of the many cam-
paigns to obtain by-passes for those villages which have a main
road running through them. However, the provision of one particular
facility never seems to fail to divide the village along local and
newcomer lines: street-lighting. While the newcomers consider the
absence of street-lighting to be dangerous, particularly in the winter,
the locals, who claim they have always been able to manage without
it, regard it as an ugly and unnecessary intrusion.

The changes in the village social structure described in this chapter
have, of course, varied in their timing and extent from village to
village, yet these developments have been widespread across virtually
the entire countryside. Although they first became noticeable around
the major conurbations – for example, in the Home Counties, in
Cheshire and in parts of Warwickshire – in lowland England at least
the commuting networks have virtually joined up. The fact that the
South East contains a disproportionately high number of professional
and managerial inhabitants, that transportation is generally quicker
and easier because of the flatter terrain, and that industry and population from London have been relocated to surrounding satellite
towns have all conspired to spread the ex-urban population far out
into the metropolitan hinterland. In the North and West of England,
however, the presence of fewer middle-class people, poorer communications and more difficult terrain has imposed a more limited distance
on commuting. This is not to say that commuters have not moved
into the rural areas of the North and West, for they clearly have,
particularly where open countryside is within easy access of large
cities, such as the Peak District for Sheffield and Manchester or
the Mendips for Bristol and Bath. However, the radius of commuting
tends to be more circumscribed, so that conflict between local
residents and incoming urban dwellers has taken other forms. For
example, in areas close to the sea the newcomers have been predominantly retired couples whose impact in the local housing market
has again caused resentment in those regions where they have
become concentrated, such as Devon and Cornwall. Elsewhere,
particularly in the remoter upland areas, the issue which has aroused
most controversy has been the purchase of second homes as weekend
or holiday retreats.

Second home owners have roused the ire of local inhabitants more
than either commuters or retired newcomers, partly by the very fact

that their houses are second homes and therefore considered to be needed less than the houses of other ex-urbanites. In areas where the inflation of housing prices has made it impossible for many local people to obtain their own homes, the sight of outsiders purchasing houses when they already have one elsewhere can be an affront to local dignity. In North Wales, for example, where the factors already described in this chapter are overlaid by considerations of cultural nationalism, militant action against second home owners has ensued. In England the reaction of the local inhabitants has been generally less vocal and less publicity-seeking, but nonetheless hostile. The Lake District, for example, has been particularly affected by the purchase of holiday retreats. In 1976 a survey carried out from Lancaster University, *Rural Housing in the Lake District*, revealed that 10 per cent of the houses in the national park area were holiday homes. The report showed that some villages in the south of the area were in danger of becoming 'ghost villages' for months on end – for example, in the village of High Nibthwaite only two of the four-teen houses were occupied by people earning a local livelihood. The village contained only two resident children.

In extreme situations like this it is not surprising that the local population becomes angered. Their children have little prospect of finding any housing in their village when they wish to set up their own homes. The locals find they must leave, while houses in their village remain locked and empty for months at a time. But how typical the well-publicized case of the Lake District is cannot easily be judged, for the information on second home ownership is rather skimpy. In 1972 the number of houses used as second homes in Britain as a whole was estimated at 372 000, but it is believed that this number has declined in recent years due to the inflation in house prices since that date. The few localized investigations of the problem that have been carried out have shown that second home owners do not make an entirely negative contribution to the areas in which they purchase their property. For example, many of the houses which they buy are in the most remote or inconvenient situations and would otherwise have been abandoned by the local residents. They are frequently semi-derelict, insanitary and damp and their restoration not only contributes to the renewal of the local housing stock but provides employment for local builders and traders. Much, however, depends upon the nature of the local housing market, the location and soundness of the properties and the buoyancy of local demand. Variations in each of these factors can considerably alter the balance of benefits and costs to the local community in different areas and regions.

Second home owners often provide the easiest of targets for those who deplore the creeping urbanization of the countryside. Yet, like the impact of newcomers on village society generally, they are more a symptom than a cause of the sense of loss which the local population often feels. Without the newcomers many more villages would be ghost villages and the social demoralization would be even more acute. Even where newcomers are demonstrably forcing the local population to seek housing elsewhere through their inflationary effect on the housing market, arguably the answer is to relieve the chronic shortage of rural housing, and to build more houses suitable for local residents. In the end, however, the antagonism towards newcomers is not a rationally calculated response. It is a gut re-action to the sense of having been taken over by affluent and alien strangers. The underlying cause may be the changes in agriculture described in the earlier chapters of this book, but the newcomers represent the most visible and tangible manifestation of a disruption of community life which would have occurred in any case. The initial instinct to exclude commuters and second home owners from the countryside is not, therefore, altogether helpful. People living in towns and cities can hardly be denied their quite reasonable and legitimate desire either to reside in or to visit the countryside and without them many villages would now lie abandoned and semi-derelict. The greatest friction occurs where locals and newcomers are competing – often on unequal terms – for scarce resources. For reasons outlined earlier in this chapter these do not usually consist of jobs, but rather of space (which will be considered in the following chapter under the heading of land use and access) and housing. As far as housing is concerned, focusing attention on the disruptive social effects of the newcomers *alone* diverts attention from the fact that rural housing is not only a matter of (increasing) demand, but of supply and need. The continuing scarcity of certain types of rural housing is now having as much effect upon shaping the English village community as the influx of newcomers.

Housing and social control

The frequency with which references to rural housing have already been made in this chapter reflects the extent to which the housing market acts as an intermediary between the economic changes in agriculture, described earlier in this book, and the kind of social life which is now to be found in the English countryside. This, of course, is using the term housing market in the broadest possible sense to mean the allocation and distribution of housing, including those houses which lie outside the market sector itself, such as local authority housing and tied cottages. How this system of allocation has been operated and controlled has long had a significant effect in moulding the social composition of the rural village, for it has largely influenced *who* lives *where*. Housing has therefore been used, either consciously or unconsciously, as an agency of social control. Public debate about rural housing policy has, however, preferred not to acknowledge such social control implications and preferred instead to deal in terms of houses rather than their inhabitants. Discussions about the number of houses in rural areas, their size and density, how many should be publicly or privately owned, owner-occupied or rented, where they should be sited and how they should be designed are often presented as purely technical exercises. However, these matters are not only the province of economics, architecture or planning. The decisions that are made also help to determine the kind of people who will eventually live in the houses that are built and therefore the nature of the village community.

During the nineteenth century this link between the type of housing and the social structure of the village was made explicit in the lowland farming areas by the division between 'open' and 'closed' villages. Closed villages were those in which a resident squire owned most or all of the land in the parish, or those in which a very few large farmers maintained an oligarchy over local landownership. In cases like these local landowners allowed the construction of only the minimum number of houses needed to accommodate their permanently employed labour force, often in 'estate villages'. The building of any further houses was resisted on the grounds that the additional families which they would attract might eventually become a charge on the poor rates during periods of economic depression. As the major ratepayer in the parish a large landowner therefore had a strong incentive to limit and even – as early mechanization progressed – diminish his housing stock so that any surplus labour force did not reside locally; hence the closed character of such villages. At the other extreme were open villages where the land was divided among a large number of freeholders and smallholders. Many of them were local tradesmen who supplemented their living by acting as petty rural landlords. They therefore attracted labour without any hindrance, providing jerry-built, damp and insanitary hovels for letting to local farm workers. Such exploitation was compounded by the fact that their tenants obtained only low wages and insecure employment and could not afford a rent which would provide a sufficiently large return to keep the houses in good repair. Thus, while the far greater number of ratepayers in the open villages meant that there was no disincentive to build houses, those that were built quickly became decrepit rural slums.

The division between open and closed villages was not always as clear-cut as this may imply – many villages lay somewhere between the two – and it was less extensive in the upland areas where less labour was employed and more workers 'lived in' on the farms. Nevertheless, until the widespread construction of council houses between the two world wars, the ownership of cottages remained, as the historian Geoffrey Best has pointed out, 'a cardinal point in the grand scheme of subordination'. Those living in the shadow of the local squire found themselves, on the whole, better housed but less independent. Open villages, on the other hand, were centres of the rural underworld – some of them notoriously so – and displayed their independence of squirearchal authority not only by engaging in petty criminal activity but by becoming centres of pre-political and political activity which opposed 'official' values and attitudes. During the 1820s and 1830s, for example, the open villages were centres of the 'labourer's revolt', associated with the mythical figure of Captain Swing, in which arson and machine-breaking were the most common expression of rural protest. Later in the century the open villages were also centres of nonconformism and trade unionism. Yet nearby landowners had little option other than to tolerate the threat to law and order which the existence of open villages implied because the closed parishes to some extent relied upon the open ones to provide a pool of reserve labour which could be used during periods of peak demand like harvest, but which would not at other times become a charge on the poor rate. Rural tenants – principally farm workers – meanwhile found themselves in a vicious circle of deprivation. The biggest landowners, who could best afford to erect new dwellings with a reasonable standard of construction and sanitation, had the least incentive to do so – indeed, as the principal local ratepayers they might easily penalize themselves by attracting workers who could later apply for poor relief. On the other hand the open villages, because they attracted the surplus labour force, contained workers on depressed wages who could ill afford rents which would make housing improvements profitable.

The squalor of rural housing conditions became a mid-century scandal, highlighted by the government Blue Books on living conditions and public health which were published during the 1850s and 1860s. These investigations uncovered the topsy-turvy pattern of rural housing trends which the link between the structure of landholding, the financing of poor rates and the construction of rural houses had created. Between 1851 and 1861, for example, in 821 rural parishes covered by the investigation the population had increased from 305 567 to 322 064, while the number of houses had fallen from 69 225 to 66 109. In a sample of 5375 'typical cottages' 8805 bedrooms accommodated 13 432 adults plus a further 11 338 children. Behind the honeysuckle and the hollyhocks there was revealed a life of hitherto unimagined degradation. Calls for housing reform were led by liberal-minded onlookers. Clergymen, for example, warned about the moral consequences of overcrowding and the incidence of rural incest. Health inspectors were also concerned about the constant risk of epidemic diseases resulting from poor sanitation. A few large landowners were stirred by their consciences to build, for reasons of philanthropy rather than economy, new 'model' cottages and villages, but these were usually on their own estates where conditions were in any case generally better than elsewhere. The Union Chargeability Act of 1865 also removed many of the disincentives to build by altering the basis of poor law finance, but the onset of agricultural depression after 1873 followed so hard upon its heels that attempts to reform rural housing were rendered largely ineffective. For the same reason the Housing Act of 1890, a permissive Act allowing the newly formed local councils to build housing for rent, provided little relief. However much rural housing became a public issue, which it did periodically until 1914, the depression in agriculture generally ensured that little new building took place and it became more and more apparent that housing conditions in rural areas would receive no dramatic improvement without external intervention.

As in many other areas of rural life, events during and immediately after the First World War were to have a considerable effect upon the structure of rural housing. The introduction of the wages boards completed the decasualization of agricultural labour begun by the licensing of itinerant agricultural gangs in 1867. The open village therefore lost much of its rationale as a reservoir of surplus labour. In the upland areas the introduction of the wages boards also led to the decline of hiring fairs and the gradual discontinuance of the practice of 'living in'. In both cases the greater stability and permanency of the labour force encouraged farmers to build more tied cottages in order to ensure a supply of labour – and the significance of tied cottages was further increased by estates being broken up and sold to sitting tenants, a change which also brought about a decline in the number of closed villages. Tied cottages, indeed, performed much the same function as the closed village in Victorian times, by enabling farmers to ensure that their expenditure on housing was limited as far as possible to guaranteeing their own labour requirements. These considerations were to bear heavily upon the drive after the war to improve the housing of rural workers by, for the first time, explicitly introducing the criterion of housing need rather than an ability to pay the rent.

Lloyd George's promise of 'homes fit for heroes' was implemented in the 'Addison' Act of 1919, which first stimulated widespread local authority housing construction. This was followed by further legislation in 1924 (the 'Wheatley' Act) and a variety of measures during the 1930s. The aim of much of this legislation was to increase the sheer quantity of housing available to the rural population, thereby relieving overcrowding and improving the state of repair of the housing stock. The chosen means of achieving this end was to provide local authorities with central government funds which could be used for housing construction and enable the level of rents to be subsidized out of general Exchequer funds – in other words, the framework of the system of public housing finance with which we are familiar today. The new housing drive met with a disappointing response in rural areas, however, where local authorities were reluctant to participate in the government's house-building schemes – so reluctant, in fact, that specific legislation aimed at alleviating the plight of rural workers had to be introduced after 1935. In part this was due to the continuance of agricultural depression, which not only left many rural areas bereft of a buoyant rate base but also lowered agricultural wages below the level at which even local authority rents could be afforded. But the reluctance to take account of the new obligations imposed by government to consider the housing needs of the working classes also derived from more political motives. Since their inception in 1888 and 1894 rural councils had remained largely in the hands of landowners and farmers. A rough rule-of-thumb was that landowners controlled the rural county councils and farmers the rural district councils (which were given responsibility for housing). As the principal ratepayers in the locality – even after the de-rating of agricultural land in 1927 – they pursued a low rate/low expenditure policy and therefore were extremely reluctant to commit local authority expenditure to the building of houses which could become a burden on the rates. They were particularly reluctant to subsidize council house rents out of the general rate in order to allow farm workers access to local authority housing. Not until 1935, when the government offered rural councils no less than 80 per cent of the cost of construction of houses for agricultural workers, was legislation successful in moving recalcitrant rural authorities.

Although the provision of public housing had been established as a principle in rural areas by 1939 – by itself no mean achievement when one looks back over the history of rural housing – the results of twenty years of legislation were a disappointment. Less than 10 per cent of the housing stock in rural England and Wales consisted of council houses, despite all the attempts at pump-priming which had been carried out from Whitehall. As many wartime evacuees found to their alarm, rural housing remained at a lower standard than that to be found in most urban areas, with only slow progress having been made in the provision of piped water, sewerage and electricity. In 1942 the Scott Report concluded that: 'Thousands of cottages have no piped water supply, no gas or electric light, no third bedroom and often only one living room with no separate cooking and scullery accommodation. For the great majority of rural workers a bathroom is a rare luxury.' Such deficiencies in the number and quality of rural houses were particularly serious when viewed in the context of the inter-war legislation. This had been directed primarily at improving rural housing as an adjunct to public health policy, yet not only were the standards of rural amenities still markedly inferior (for example, 5000 rural parishes possessed no sewerage system), but the sheer volume of housing available for rural workers remained inadequate – rural district councils built only 164 083 dwellings between 1919 and 1943, compared with which the number of private houses was 706 527.

Why did this chronic shortage of rural council housing persist? The cost of housing construction, and particularly the cost of the associated public utilities, was usually higher in rural areas, although this did not deter private developers whose houses usually needed the same facilities. Low rateable values in some of the remoter rural areas also played a part. However, it seems unlikely that the political will existed among many rural authorities to embark upon a rapid and expensive programme of housing construction. Many of the principles which underlay the provision of rural housing in the nineteenth century reasserted themselves in a new institutional framework. Farmers and landowners continued to dominate rural areas, both as employers and as local councillors, and therefore as effective landlords of the housing stock within the range of farm workers: council housing, privately rented houses and tied cottages. Their desire to keep rates down made them reluctant to build council houses. Farm workers could instead be housed in tied cottages which had other advantages in addition to providing suitable accommodation, not least of which were the convenience of having workers on call, the greater stability tied housing conferred on the labour force, and the reinforcement of ties of dependency. Tied cottages also depressed farm wages, making farm workers unable to afford council house rents. Thus, the rents could not be lowered without raising the rates, while farmers were not going voluntarily to raise wages just so that their workers could afford to live in council houses. Whether as ratepayers or as employers the farmers who ran the majority of rural councils found it more advantageous to provide tied housing for farm workers and build the minimum number of local authority homes.

These trends have continued since 1945. Rural housing within reach of farm workers has come to be in even shorter supply. By

1974, on the eve of local government reorganization, rural district councils provided 20 per cent of the rural housing stock, compared with the 31 per cent supplied by local authorities elsewhere. Farm workers were thus becoming increasingly dependent upon tied cottages, while other rural workers were faced by a declining pool of privately rented housing which was apparent in rural areas, as elsewhere, after successive Rent Acts had improved the security of tenants. In addition competition for privately-rented accommodation had, as we have already noted, increased from commuters and second home owners. In view of the history of rural housing it was therefore somewhat ironic to find in 1976 that changes to the tied cottage legislation were opposed by the farmers' lobby on the grounds that there were insufficient safeguards against local authorities refusing to meet their housing responsibilities! The crux of the tied cottage problem, it was argued, was the shortage of rural housing. The cynicism of this argument is breathtaking, for the NFU and CLA could surely not have been oblivious of the fact that this shortage was one which farmers and landowners, in their role as councillors, had been responsible for creating. For many years farm workers, and other rural inhabitants who did not have access to home ownership, had been quietly and routinely disadvantaged by the housing policies of many rural local authorities.

Since the Second World War, however, the political control of rural councils has not been the only factor influencing the rate of rural house-building. A salient feature of the rural housing situation over this period has also been the incorporation of a specifically *rural* housing problem into the general problem of the nation's housing, coupled with increasing central government intervention in, and control of, rural housing provision. Rural councils have found themselves hamstrung by the centralized control of local authority expenditure (particularly during the periods of economic stagnation and crisis) and, in the case of housing, by the imposition of cost yardsticks which rarely take account of the peculiar difficulties which many rural councils face from the heavier costs incurred in housing provision in remote areas. The subsuming of rural housing under a general 'housing problem' has also been accompanied by a change in emphasis in housing policy. Between the wars the aim of housing legislation was simply to stimulate the construction of as many houses as possible in rural areas; since 1945 the aim has been to control the number of houses in rural areas as part of overall planning policies designed to contain the growth of urban sprawl, prevent the loss of good agricultural land and protect the visual quality of the countryside. Far from encouraging local authorities and private developers to build more rural houses as in the 1930s, there has been an active discouragement, involving the imposition of strict planning controls, particularly over housing in the open countryside and in other sensitive areas such as Green Belts and Areas of Outstanding Natural Beauty. The increasing affluence of the rural population wrought by the urban middle-class exodus has tended to mask the continuing and severe pockets of poverty which exist in the countryside and has led the 'problem' of rural housing to be regarded less as a problem of social welfare and more as an issue concerning land use planning and countryside preservation.

This takes us into an area of discussion – what has broadly come to be known as 'the environment' – which will be dealt with in the following chapter. However, a few indications can be given here of how environmental issues have impinged upon housing policy. Since the Town and Country Planning Act of 1947 the granting of planning permission for rural housing has arguably been concerned with the visual quality of the countryside rather than with alleviating problems of housing need. By placing strict controls upon rural development these policies have also brought about a planned scarcity of housing which, in the face of increasing demand, has made a rural house a desirable good with a premium price. Until the early 1960s the effects of rural depopulation, the dilapidation of much rural property and the cost of travel to urban centres all contributed to the lower price of rural housing compared with urban areas. But as the surplus rural housing was gradually soaked up by commuters and second home owners, and as housing which had once been a damning indictment of years of neglect and deprivation was restored and renovated, so relative scarcity began to increase prices above those prevailing for comparable suburban and even urban housing. The pressure on rural development has thus become more intense. Between 1961 and 1971 the population census recorded an increase of 1 700 000 in the rural population, and although some of this was accounted for by contiguous urban development spilling over the boundaries of surrounding Rural Districts, there is little doubt that the population pressures on most of rural England are now those of increasing demand rather than those resulting from rural de-population. The solution to this has been not to build even more houses to relieve the upward pressure on rents and prices but to impose even more stringent controls – conservation areas, village 'envelopes' and so on. As prices inexorably rise, so the population which actually achieves its goal of a house in the country becomes more socially selective.

Planning controls on rural housing have therefore become – in effect, if not in intent – instruments of social exclusivity, although this often depends as much upon implementation as on the principles enshrined in the legislation. For example, the insistence of planning authorities upon the use of certain building materials, the standards of design and external finish and the density of housing development reflect their traditional concern with how a house or a village looks rather than who will actually live in it. As a general rule, the lower the densities and the higher the standards of design, the higher the social class of those who will eventually occupy the houses that are built. As the environmental lobby has gained increasing influence over rural planning policies, so the dilemma between the requirement of maintaining an attractive village landscape and the provision of housing for those in need has become more acute. Nationally imposed cost yardsticks ensure that many rural councils can only afford to build houses to a standard design in relatively large estates, yet on both grounds they are often out of sympathy with the visual quality of many English villages. Local amenity societies and con-servation groups therefore frequently oppose their construction – and all too often the houses remain unbuilt.

Although the prime responsibility for rural housing provision has rested with the rural district councils (district councils since 1974), they must work within a strategic planning framework laid down by county council planning authorities. Thus while the district councils are responsible for development control, they must act within guidelines for zoning and land use established by the county. Traditionally, county councils have been more preservationist-minded than many of their local district councils, often because their membership showed a higher proportion of large landowners who had a keen interest in preserving the countryside, even before concern for the environment became a fashionable issue. On occasions this could lead to conflict between district and county councils over housing provision – for example, over the desire of farmers to build tied cottages in open countryside. However, the most direct influence of county councils over housing and the social composition of villages occurs in their policies for restricting the growth of some settlements in favour of 'key villages'. For reasons principally of economy, most county councils have preferred to concentrate development on a few villages which can then conveniently be provided with the full range of public amenities – schools, shops, libraries, sewerage facilities and so on. This saves on the enormous cost of duplicating amenities in every village and helps to direct and contain population growth to a few well-chosen sites. In areas of declining population the designation of key villages has become an emotionally charged issue with allegations of villages being 'left to die' by cold-hearted and remote planners. Yet the full cost of providing just piped water, electricity and sewerage, let alone the range of other amenities expected by the modern rural population can be staggering. In areas of population pressure a further rationale has been to 'write off' certain selected villages from a preservationist point of view and sacrifice them to expansion so that surrounding villages may remain 'unspoilt'. This policy of concentration has resulted in housing being provided in the form of large estates, built to uniform design by large building firms, tacked on somewhat incongruously to the older village core. Derived from policies which seek to preserve the landscape qualities of the English countryside, such estates have more often contributed to its deterioration.

In recent years there has been some awareness on the part of planners of the role of rural planning policies in exaggerating the scarcity of rural housing and achieving comparatively little for those in greatest housing need. However, the growth of environmentalism as an issue of live public concern during the 1970s has pushed planning policy more in the direction of increased control than of increased flexibility. Housing policies thus continue to be concerned more with bricks and mortar than the needs of the people who inhabit rural areas, let alone with considering how these policies *redistribute* the life-chances of the rural population. As Marilyn Rawson and Alan Rogers conclude in their review of recent policies *Rural Housing and Structure Plans:*

The general restriction of planning methods for rural housing to development control and a concern with the fabric of the built countryside pervades the whole attitude of structure planning to rural housing, not just
policies. Only rarely do plans consider more than the simple spatial attributes of the housing stock. Housing quality is examined usually by area
rather than by social group and there is little information on different income groups in the countryside and their needs and demands for housing.
This is surprising when one remembers the importance frequently given to
local housing need which can only be satisfactorily defined in relation to
an understanding of social groups and information on incomes.

It follows that policies for rural housing do not consider the social
implications which might result from their implementation. There is, for
example, little or no discussion on the possible distributional effects on
different social groups of conservation policies regarding rural housing nor
of the economic and social implications for rural housing of key settlement
strategies.

The danger is that current rural housing policies will produce a
polarization of the rural population. While the *demands* of the rich
and the affluent can be met within the framework of current housing
policies, the *needs* of the poor increasingly cannot. During the 1970s
the provision of rural housing for those who cannot partake in the
market sector has been pitiful. Between 1967 and 1973 (the last year
in which rural districts were a distinct administrative category), the
number of council houses built annually in rural areas was almost
cut in half, from 35000 to 18000, while private-sector housing held
steady at just over 70000. This enormous decline in public housing
was largely due to a government-induced squeeze on local authority
expenditure. However, since 1973 matters have hardly improved.
The Labour government elected in 1974 decided to concentrate its
housing resources on the needs of the inner city areas and coupled
this with changes in the basis of the rate support grant which disadvantaged rural local authorities. While not for one moment can
the appalling state of housing in many of the major English cities
be denied, there is no reason to believe that the problems of poor
housing and underprivilege are any less acute among the rural as
opposed to the urban poor: they are merely less obvious and less
concentrated in numbers. The result is that once those who are
unable to purchase have negotiated their way through the labyrin-
thine and highly variable eligibility rules to achieve a place on a
council housing waiting list, they join a queue which is growing at a

faster rate than addition to the council housing stock and which in some cases even exceeds the total number of families housed by the district council.

One largely unforeseen consequence of rural housing policies has therefore been to increase the relative deprivation of low-paid rural workers (and their newly married offspring). They are frequently denied the choice of living in the village in which they were born and brought up or in the village close to their employment. This has been a cause of intense resentment in some rural areas which has rebounded on those newcomers who have been able to afford to purchase their homes at prices beyond the reach of the locals. The distortions introduced into the housing market by planning controls have therefore exaggerated the divisions already existing between locals and newcomers that are derived from differences in back-grounds, cultural assumptions and life-styles. In their effects these policies have been socially regressive. They have ensured that com-petition for rural housing has been carried out on increasingly un-equal terms and that the population of many villages has become more socially exclusive. Although this has been the opposite of what was generally intended, there seems to be little sign of any reappraisal of rural planning controls which might result in a reversal of current trends.

A 'loss of community'?

The developments that have taken place in the rural housing market illustrate vividly the paradoxical nature of contemporary changes in village life. The rural population today is better housed, better educated and generally in receipt of a higher standard of living than at any time in the past. Yet alongside these improvements there have existed continuing problems of relative deprivation for particular groups within rural society who are often powerless – sometimes increasingly so – to help themselves. This paradox underlies much of the contentious discussion over whether the English village has or has not suffered a 'loss of community' through recent changes in its social composition. Clearly the relatively sudden and far-reaching nature of these changes has disrupted the established pattern of social relationships to be found within most villages. However, had a substantial number of urban dwellers not chosen to live in the countryside the consequences may have been even more severe: the complete destruction of both the social and the physical fabric of the English village. Consequently there is a good deal of uncertainty about whether the newcomers to the countryside have wrought a deterioration or a revitalization of the village community. Should we take account of only the material standards of village life or should we include such an apparently ephemeral notion as what is colloquially referred to as 'community spirit', the sense of identity and belonging, which the inhabitants feel? And from whose perspective should any assessment of gains and losses be taken? As we noted at the beginning of this chapter, because there is no consensus either among or between the different sectors of the village population over the answers to these questions, any overall conclusion about 'loss of community' is impossible.

Nevertheless it is possible to make a number of guarded conclusions on how the social changes that have been described in this chapter have altered the structure of relationships within the rural population. As we have already indicated, what has been 'lost' from the countryside has been the village as an occupational community, which has disappeared not so much because of the impact of the newcomers but because of the underlying changes in the economics of agriculture. In some villages the occupational community has been reconstituted in an attenuated form on the council housing estate or among the tied cottages of the 'farm-centred' community, but in either case a new dichotomy has emerged between those who have chosen to live in the countryside and those who remain there because of their employment or some other force of circumstances. There seems little doubt that farm workers, along with other low-paid members of the rural population, have experienced these changes with a sense of loss. When the village was an occupational community they identified closely with the other inhabitants, deriving both standards of behaviour and a sense of self-esteem from their neighbours. As rapid economic and social change has worked its way through the countryside, however, the farm worker has found himself increasingly separated from the local village community both socially and – for those living out on the farms – geographically. Farm workers are apt to complain that they now feel like strangers in their own village.

The burden of this increasing sense of isolation has fallen particularly heavily upon those members of the rural population who lack the means of personal mobility to maintain a more dispersed network of social contacts. As in the case of housing, the contradictory nature of rural development is here serving to increase the deprivation of the already disadvantaged. Both the rising expectations of the rural working population and the changing character of the village have made access to some form of transport an essential element of contemporary rural life. However, because the village newcomers possess their own cars, the reversal in the decline in rural population has not been accompanied by a revival of public transport. On the contrary, as the pool of demand has declined, so rural public transport provision has been decimated. Many rural branch railway lines disappeared in the early 1960s, while the bus services that have replaced them have in many cases been abandoned or severely curtailed. Yet the need for public transport among the poor, the elderly and the disabled remains. Indeed it may have increased as a result of the general tendency to centralize health, educational and welfare services and even shops in key villages or other local centres. At the same time rural transport has been caught in a vicious circle of declining demand and rising fares which not even the provision of subsidies has been able to break. It is therefore difficult to convince a farm worker's wife, who may have to walk two miles down a muddy lane in the pouring rain to catch the Mondays and Thursdays only (except Bank Holidays) under-threat-of-closure bus to do her weekly shopping, that she has benefited from any improvement in the provision of rural amenities, when her access to them is increasingly denied. Despite experiments with postal bus services and privately operated minibuses, the future for public transport in rural areas remains bleak. As in the case of housing, local councils find it more difficult to operate a service according to need rather than demand. Once rural bus services are subsidized they become vulnerable to withdrawal by councils dominated by car-owners wishing to limit increases in the rates, while those who need the service are often without a voice at County Hall. As a result those sections of the rural population who are unable to run a car now tend to find themselves more isolated from the outside world than at any time in their lives.

Of course, isolation is something to which the rural working population, particularly in the upland areas, has long been accustomed. However, in the past this isolation was experienced more often as a community, rather than individually. The isolation of the village from the outside world was mitigated by the existence of a close-knit village community with which the farm worker could identify and which provided him with the range of institutions and amenities which he then required in order to live the year round. Today the farm worker is more isolated as an individual. Even the closer links with local farmers cannot compensate for this, since few farmers and farm workers share their leisure activities or meet socially off the farm. The changing character of the village also diminishes its relevance as a social centre for the farm worker. For example, once the village pub changes its tone in order to cater for its new clientele, the farm worker is easily alienated – and may even be made to feel unwelcome among the gin-and-tonics and prawn cocktails. The village may even decline as a service centre as the pattern of local shops and other services becomes transformed. Mobile newcomers have less need to buy their food and other necessities in the village because they can travel into nearby towns to take advantage of cheaper prices in supermarkets. The village shopkeeper, faced with a dwindling trade, must either raise his prices or switch to providing a more specialized service for the commuters and second home owners. In the South East, for example, it has been common to find former village shops and post offices converted into bookshops, antique shops and delicatessens. Faced with changes like these, the farm worker experiences not only a sense of alienation from the village, but often a real material deprivation.

Many farmers and landowners share the sense of detachment from the village community which farm workers now increasingly tend to feel. However, as we noted earlier, farmers and landowners were detached from much of the daily life of the village even when it was an occupational community. Their social circle was more geographically widespread and they looked beyond the local village for their friends and kin. This pattern has not been altered by recent changes in village life. Being more affluent and therefore more mobile than their employees, farmers are still able to overcome many of the constraints imposed upon their socializing by remoteness and distance. The disruption which farmers and landowners have faced has been of a somewhat different kind: they have suffered a loss of their traditional authority over the village population which they once took virtually for granted. Since the newcomers are dependent upon them for neither

employment nor housing, they are not inhibited by a web of economic and social ties from expressing their opposition to the opinions
and activities of farmers or landowners hitherto considered locally
omnipotent. Middle-class and well-educated, they even compete with
farmers and landowners for positions of authority and local responsibility, disrupting or threatening to disrupt the customary hierarchy
of dominance and status in the village. This does not affect all
farmers equally, however. In terms of the typology presented in
Chapter 3, it is the gentlemen farmers – the traditional village squires
– who have probably been most affected and who have watched the
newcomers add to the general decline of squirearchal power and
influence. Similarly, the family farmers, who have typically been
very involved in and identified with the running of local village
activities, have found themselves elbowed aside. However, those
farmers who are more exclusively business-oriented – the agribusinessmen and active managerials – and are less concerned about
village affairs, may have been somewhat relieved to find that the
village population no longer expects them to engage in time-consuming and tedious parochial administration.

For some farmers and landowners the major impact of the newcomers has therefore been political rather than social, for their
arrival in the village has ensured that landownership is no longer the
automatic passport to the political domination of the countryside
that it was once considered to be. In so doing the newcomers have
contributed to the sense of urban encroachment on rural political
affairs among farmers and landowners which goes back over a much
longer period, and which has been associated with changes in the
institutions of political control in the countryside: the gradual
decline in the personalized and autocratic power of the locally
resident squirearchy and the transfer of public administration to a
more formal and impersonal framework of local government since
local politics were first placed on a democratic footing in 1888. In
some areas, of course, the changes may have been more apparent
than real and the necessity of being eligible for election may not have
changed the actual personnel who continued to dominate rural
politics. Indeed research carried out for the Maud Committee on
local government reform in 1967 showed that 35 per cent of rural
district council members were farmers, far and away the most
numerous section and more than twice as many as the next largest

group. Nevertheless there has been a slow but perceptible change in the basis of such control, which is no longer in the hands of particular landowning families and individuals as such, but part of the duties of the office to which they have been elected. Moreover, much of the day-to-day administration has been placed in the hands of salaried officials with the specialized knowledge required to understand the complexities of modern local government administration.

This separation of the responsibilities of public office from the personal qualities of the incumbent has in the long term had a number of important consequences on decision-making in rural areas. Local government has become more professionalized but it has also become more bureaucratic. Successive reforms of local government administration, which have sought to make it more efficient, have produced a more rationalized but also a more centralized system, which has brought about a necessary decline in local autonomy. Many of the important decisions affecting village life are now no longer taken locally, but by inaccessible and apparently impenetrable bureaucracies which, however well-intentioned, cannot be sensitive to local problems and idiosyncrasies. The locus of power over village decision-making has therefore receded from the Big House to County Hall and on, in many cases, to Whitehall. For these reasons many farmers and landowners sense a decline of the village community because 'the village' – that is, locally powerful farmers and landowners – no longer has control over its own affairs. The climax of this trend was seen to be the local government reorganization which was implemented in 1974. By merging rural district councils with nearby urban districts and county councils with county boroughs, it was widely believed that not only was administration bound to become even more remote, but that the control of rural affairs would be handed over to urban interests with no understanding of agriculture and the ways of the countryside. Certainly these reforms have been very unpopular in rural areas, particularly among the farmers and landowners who have seen their personal dominance finally slipping away in the merger with urban areas. The newcomers, of course, have not been responsible for this loss of rural autonomy – indeed, they have been equally affected by the growing remoteness of decision-making. However, as in many other aspects of rural social change, they have symbolized and personified the final encroachment of urbanism into English village life with which these reforms are associated. As we shall see in the following chapter, this does not necessarily mean that the interests of farmers and landowners are no longer dominant in rural society, but it does mean that this dominance has increasingly to be carried out by reaching an accommodation with these new conditions.

When the agricultural population complains of a loss of community in the English village it is usually to this loss of an enclosed, socially self-sufficient occupational community that they refer. This, however, does not represent a loss to the incoming population, to whom is left open the chance of reconstructing a sense of 'community' once the village has been transformed into a more homogeneously residential, as opposed to agricultural, settlement. It is arguable that the friction between locals and newcomers which has been a common feature of village life in recent years is only a temporary problem brought about by the dislocation of established social patterns which have been hard for the social life of the village to digest, and that once the newly arrived population has either taken over entirely or 'settled down' to a rural existence many of the initial problems will be reconciled. For example, a study of the Sussex village of Ringmer by Peter Ambrose, *The Quiet Revolution*, has suggested this pattern, but as yet his findings remain unconfirmed elsewhere. Much depends here on how stable and similar are the life-styles of the village newcomers. As we have seen in this chapter, however, the newcomers, no matter how monolithic and undifferentiated they may seem to the locals, are composed of a number of identifiably separate urban middle-class groups – commuters, weekend cottagers, holiday-home dwellers, retired couples – among whom the village may vary considerably as a centre of their social activities.

This diversity accounts for the mutually contradictory complaints that are frequently voiced by village locals: that the newcomers come in and try to run everything or that they take no part in village life and are not 'involved'. Some of the newcomers – weekend cottagers, holiday-home dwellers – are highly transitory and may take little interest in village social activities. The commuting population also contains its proportion of 'spiralists' – upwardly and outwardly mobile young professional and managerial people – who alight on the village's new private housing estate as a relatively brief transit camp in the progress of their careers. Because they arrive

with an expectation of moving on within a few years they refrain –
if only for reasons of emotional self-defence – from putting down
'roots' and involving themselves too closely in village affairs. It is
important to remember, however, that the village has declined in
significance as a social centre for even the 'locals' among the population, thanks to the growth of largely privatized forms of leisure,
such as television. Moreover, former farm workers and other locals
who have ceased to work in the village but who remain resident there
and commute to nearby towns, may also involve themselves in
leisure activities over a much wider geographical area than hitherto.
In particular, the younger inhabitants of the village increasingly
look to urban centres for their entertainment. This, however, need
not so much reflect a decline of the village as a social centre (its past
vitality has often been greatly exaggerated) as the extension of a
wider range of choice to those sections of the rural population whose
ownership of a car or a motorcycle has granted them easier access
to urban amenities. They, along with the newcomers, may hope to
take advantage of the best of both rural and urban worlds.

There are, however, many newcomers who intend to stay permanently in the village and who are attracted, at least in part, by
the very prospect of living in a 'real community'. Rather than remain
uninvolved in village activities and risking the accusation of being
'stand-offish', many of them enthusiastically throw themselves into
the life of the community, provoking the opposite complaint from
the local population of 'wanting to take the place over'. Where
the indicators of a thriving community life are ostensibly absent,
they may even try to create the 'community' which their preconceptions of rural life have led them to expect. The major problem here
is that their image of what this community consists of tends to be
markedly different from that of the local population. In particular
it tends to be associational rather than communal – that is, they
regard as a key indicator of a flourishing village the number of
clubs, societies and other associations which it supports. A common
characteristic of social life in the modern village is thus the attempt
by newcomers to create an *ersatz* sense of community by founding
and running local organizations – branches of the WEA, amateur
dramatics societies, art clubs, etc. – and even building a new 'community centre' in which to house them. Given the diversity of
employment among the newcomers this *formal* method of association

is usually necessary to bring the population together. To the locals, however, it appears to lack the spontaneity of what *they* consider to be a 'real community', which they regard as arising 'naturally' out of living and working together over succeeding generations. It is worth speculating on whether, from the locals' point of view, the proliferation of village organizations reflects not so much a flourishing of community life as a symbol of its downfall. Certainly the tendency of a number of planning studies to equate the vitality of a village with the number of organizations it contains reveals a decidedly middle-class bias and fails to give sufficient weight to the overwhelmingly informal basis of rural working-class association. To a farm worker, for example, a community centre represents the antithesis of what he understands by 'community'.

We therefore come back to different meanings which the term 'community' expresses to different people. The word itself is so value-loaded that no judgement on whether contemporary trends in rural society have or have not brought about a 'loss of community' in the English village is realistically possible. What is clearer is that the arrival of a non-agricultural population in the village has created new cleavages and social divisions which have proved difficult to reconcile. Moreover, as we have seen, not all the effects of these changes relate to something so intangible as a sense of community, for material resources have also been redistributed in a way which has disadvantaged certain sections, principally the poorer sections, of the local population. As the example of housing palpably shows, conflict arises in the most acute form where these resources are in short supply and where all social groups are competing in pursuit of the same objective. Unfortunately, one of these resources is the very countryside itself, which is subject to increasing pressure from the competing demands of the rural population. Friction between locals and newcomers has been as much a function of this as of any other factor, a conflict between the aesthetic appreciation of the qualities of the English countryside and a utilitarian assessment of its productive capacity. This is a conflict of interest which cannot easily be overcome and hardly augurs well for the future reconciliation of the differences between the agricultural and non-agricultural rural population. Indeed the concerns of land use and access have become the most pressing public issue relating to rural areas in the 1970s.

'*Did you ever meet a farmer who* didn't *claim to be ruined?*'

6 Environmentalism and the countryside

During the last decade or so a wide range of what were once considered to be mundane or esoteric problems concerning the English countryside have been thrust to the forefront of public attention by the apparently sudden and widespread increase in anxiety about 'the environment'. Thus what began as a specific and separate set of issues involving such matters as landscape change, pesticide use, urban and industrial development, resource depletion, recreational demand and the preservation of rare flora and fauna have been linked together in a much more comprehensive debate about environmental matters. As a result, what is often loosely referred to as the 'environmental movement' or 'the environmental lobby' now encompasses an enormous range of groups from anarchic 'eco-freaks' to establishment institutions like the Countryside Commission and from small, parochial amenity societies to multi-national pressure groups like Friends of the Earth. During the last years of the 1960s environmentalism also became fashionable, transforming the esteem granted to those individuals and organizations seen to be upholding 'environmental' values. Ecology, for example, had hitherto been granted a rather lowly status by professional scientists on account of its association with the kind of amateur botanical pursuits beloved of Victorian country vicars. Now ecologists found themselves the veritable gurus of our age. Similarly bodies such as the Council for the Protection of Rural England, often depicted as the last refuge of ex-Etonian Guards officers and assorted upper-class cranks, was able to speak with a new confidence and a new authority, attract a new breed of membership and turn itself into a highly professional custodian of the English countryside. It was little wonder, then, that one leading ecologist, Max Nicholson, was able to speak, with pardonable hyperbole, of an 'environmental revolution'.

As our awareness of 'the environment' has grown, so has the

meaning given to the term expanded until it has come to signify the whole of the non-cultural world. We are now faced with a situation, therefore, in which the debate about 'the environment' has become so wide-ranging that it has impinged upon almost every aspect of contemporary industrial society. Consequently it is neither possible nor appropriate in a book of this kind to analyse all of the issues which currently preoccupy environmentalists. It will be necessary instead to limit our discussion to only those aspects of environmentalism which are immediately relevant to current social changes in rural England. This excludes such important matters as the threatened global environmental crisis, personified by the 'doom-watch' school of thought, and a whole range of peculiarly urban problems relating to redevelopment, transport and industrial pollution. Within these limitations, however, an amorphous and diverse spread of topics remains to be explored, particularly since a persistent theme of this chapter will be to emphasize that environmentalism in rural England is not simply a technological or ecological affair, but a social, political and even philosophical question, too.

For example, it is arguable that the qualitative change which engendered an environmental movement in the early 1960s involved not so much the presence of environmental destruction as the fact that the new forms of pollution and disruption became much more difficult, if not impossible, to avoid. A simple piece of historical reflection will show that industrialization rendered many localities virtually uninhabitable as long as two hundred years ago. However, it was always possible for the rich and the powerful to isolate themselves from the consequences of industrial growth by moving away from the factory areas to the more tranquil and less squalid atmosphere of the countryside. This demonstrates that the combination of 'amenities' which constitutes the rural environment is what Fred Hirsch, in his book *The Social Limits to Growth*, calls a 'positional good' – that is, something which is fixed in supply and whose consumption is dependent upon one's position in society. Positional goods, therefore, come into the hands of the *early* rich. As in the case of all positional goods, however, those features of the rural environment that are so widely admired can only be retained if access to them by other social groups can somehow be restricted. In other words, a positional good cannot be shared without losing some of its value; consequently as the countryside became more

accessible during the 1960s, thanks mainly to increasing car ownership, so the value of the rural environment began to fall to those
already in possession – and they quickly mobilized to defend their
interests. Stanley Johnson puts this point most forcefully in his book
The Politics of the Environment:

The title of the movement launched in this country is not without significance. It was called 'The Countryside in 1970' because the mood of the
time was predominantly one of unease and anxiety about what was
happening to the countryside. The fact that the patron of the movement
was the Duke of Edinburgh is also not without significance. Whatever
evolutions took place in later years, a good deal of impetus in those early
days came from the middle and upper-middle classes. These people, owners
of homes and second homes in rural England, sensed the threat of alien
hordes, closed ranks, and, as is customary, looked to royalty to sanctify
their cause. As far as decent environments were concerned, they were the
'haves' and they wanted to keep it that way. They themselves might 'motor'
down to their country retreat at the weekends but they looked with signal
disfavour on the idea that the vast mass of the populace might enjoy a
similar mobility and have access to pleasures which for the moment were
peculiarly their own.

Of course, we should not be surprised that pressure groups pursue
self-interested aims – that is usually why they are created. Neither
does the fact that private and publicly espoused interests occasionally coincide render those interests illegitimate on that account alone.
However, it is perhaps significant that environmentalism received
little attention as long as it was only the poor and the powerless who
suffered from the detritus of industrial society. By the 1960s, on the
other hand, it was becoming increasingly difficult for those further
up the social scale to avoid the consequences of industrialization any
longer – even by indulging in rural retreatism. So perhaps more
instrumental in influencing the spread of environmentalism in
England than the writings of apocalyptic 'doom-watchers' were
such factors as the widespread construction of motorways – which,
because they were routed around rather than through cities, shattered
the peace of so many middle-class localities – and the changes in
agricultural technology which altered the ecology and the landscape
of extensive areas of rural England.

In the intervening years the environmental lobby has probably
gathered a broader basis of support, although, as we shall see later

in this chapter, the values which are upheld are often more sectional than many environmentalists might suppose. Those who wish to preserve the traditional features of the English countryside have, however, been extremely successful in alerting public and political opinion and have gained an increasing adherence – at least in principle – to conservationist values. Nevertheless, the peculiar quality of the rural environment as a 'positional good' ensures that environmental conflict remains part of the 'politics of affluence'. The long-standing resistance to urban and industrial encroachment continues, but increasingly in recent years the defenders of the rural environment have found themselves fighting on two fronts. Not only have they continued vigilantly to oppose the many external threats to the countryside, but they have developed an awareness that the rural environment is also being subverted from within – by farmers and landowners, and the demands of modern agricultural practice. By 1973 one of the leading figures of the environmental lobby, Sir Colin Buchanan, felt it necessary to accuse farmers, in a speech to the CPRE, of being 'the most ruthless section of the business community'. As he put it: 'The planners and the road engineers have had a good bashing, but they have learnt their lesson. The real danger to the countryside now lies in the agricultural community.'

Agriculture and ecology

We can date the beginning of the disillusionment with agriculture as a force for rural conservation fairly precisely: the publication of Rachel Carson's *Silent Spring* in 1962. With relentless detail she documented the effects that the petrochemical 'elixirs of death' – the pesticides which farmers still regard as an integral part of modern agriculture – were wreaking on the wildlife of the countryside. Although not unaware of the benefits in increased production which the new agrochemicals had allowed, she drew attention, in a passionate book, to the long-term dangers:

It is not my contention that chemical insecticides must never be used. I do contend that we have put poisonous and biologically potent chemicals indiscriminately into the hands of persons largely or wholly ignorant of their potentials for harm. We have subjected enormous numbers of people to contact with these poisons, without their consent and often without their knowledge. . . . I contend, furthermore, that we have allowed these chemicals to be used with little or no advance investigation of their effect on soil, water, wildlife and man himself. Future generations are unlikely to condone our lack of prudent concern for the integrity of the natural world that supports all life.

With words like these Rachel Carson placed farming practice at the centre of what was to be an often rancorous controversy about the compatibility of efficient, profitable and cheap food production with the ecological balance of the countryside. As we have already seen in the previous chapter, this conflict has also been reinforced by the social changes which have occurred in rural areas, so that disputes concerning environmental preservation often coincide with local–newcomer, rural–urban, and agricultural–industrial divisions in the rural population. There is a good deal of evidence to show that the reinforcing nature of these divisions has helped to perpetuate the conflict between farmers and environmentalists.

Agriculture, by definition, involves a disturbance of the natural ecology. Indeed, most forms of agriculture do not so much disturb the natural environment as destroy it and replace it by a manmade artefact. Rachel Carson realized this: her argument was based not upon idyllic sentiment, but upon the fear that the artefact which modern agriculture was creating was neither safe nor to our own long-term advantage. Her attack was not therefore directed towards the use of pesticides in general, but towards their indiscriminate use – particularly of organo-chloride insecticides. These were entirely novel synthetic substances and no species (including man) had acquired any previous experience of them. When they were first introduced they were an enormous boon to the farmer and the initial response was almost euphoric. The most common, the insecticide DDT, was very stable, had a very low toxicity to humans and was cheap to manufacture. It was used extensively during the Second World War, and is still used in parts of the Third World to help eradicate malaria and typhus. DDT was followed by other organo-chlorides, including aldrin, isodrin, entrin, and dieldrin, which was widely used in Britain as a sheep-dip and as a seed dressing. When they were introduced the mechanisms by which these insecticides worked was not known, but their low acute toxicity and, above all, their stability appeared to make them safe to use. Yet it was this very stability which made them so potentially harmful, for their effects upon a whole ecosystem, as opposed to an individual species, were not considered before they were adopted and so, as farmers enthusiastically seized the opportunities which these new insecticides offered, little thought was given to any possible chain reaction which might follow. It was left to Rachel Carson to bring to the attention of a wider public just what the unintended consequences might be.

The most widely publicized of these consequences involved the accumulation of DDT and other organo-chlorides in the food chain. So stable were these chemical compounds that they were passed on from prey to predator by their accumulation in fatty tissue, involving a metabolic process which led to higher concentrations as the insecticide was passed along the chain. The very stability which so commended itself to farmers – any transient compound is less useful in agriculture unless it can be applied directly to the pest – was the factor which so alarmed ecologists. In Britain Rachel Carson's vision of a 'silent spring' provided a potent symbol of the dangers. While many hitherto disinterested onlookers could, perhaps, stomach the loss of several insect species (even dragonflies and butterflies), there were few who were not moved by the prospect of extermination for a number of species of birds. Those under threat also included some of the most majestic of all birds – the golden eagle, the peregrine falcon – because, as birds of prey, they were at the head of the food chain. The danger was not so much from direct poisoning, but from the effect of sublethal doses of organo-chlorides on eggshell thinning. This produced a spectacular decline in the number of birds successfully reared and eventually in the total population of adult birds. For example, in those areas where golden eagles fed extensively on carrion sheep which had been dipped in dieldrin, the proportion of pairs successfully rearing young fell from 72 per cent to 29 per cent during the late 1950s. Similarly, the number of peregrine falcons was more than halved between 1939 and 1963. Much of this decline again occurred in the late 1950s, when aldrin and dieldrin were introduced as seed dressings, and was almost certainly due to peregrines eating pigeons which had fed on the seed. By no means all species of raptors suffered in this way, but sufficient alarm was engendered to lead to demands that organo-chlorides be prohibited. Restrictions were placed on the use of aldrin and dieldrin as seed dressings in 1962 and the use of dieldrin as a sheep dip was restricted in 1966. When DDT was found to have carcinogenic properties it, too, was restricted. However, the persistence of organo-chlorides in the environment has ensured that the rate of recovery of affected species has been slow.

Fortunately continuing research by agrochemical manufacturers has to a large extent enabled the persistent organo-chlorides to be suspended. Modern pesticides are often more selective and less persistent in their effects and thus less environmentally hazardous. Nevertheless the indirect ecological effects cannot always be foreseen. Some pesticides, for example, have encouraged the development of mutant strains of pests, like the famed 'super-rats' resistant to Warfarin or DDT-resistant mosquitoes. Others have had a boomerang effect by wiping out natural predators or by obligingly clearing the habitat for another, though equally troublesome, pest. Herbicides which killed poppies in wheatfields cleared the way for wild oats, so that until the (very expensive) sprays had been developed to cope with them, a trip through the eastern counties in midsummer could create the strong impression that oats had made a spectacular comeback as a cereals crop. Pests therefore continue to flourish despite the widespread application of pesticides, although ironically this occurs within the context of a general impoverishment of the wildlife of the countryside. Indeed recent research has suggested that the outbreak of infestations by cereals aphids is inversely correlated with species diversity, so that the trend towards monoculture and the reduction of natural predators may have increased the risk of sudden epidemics. Ecologists with a morbid sense of *déjà vu* have even warned of the possibility of modern equivalents of the Irish potato famine, while those with more fertile imaginations have invoked science fiction fantasies of plagues of mutant insects devastating the countryside. The more lurid and alarmist versions may perhaps be discounted, but they have fed the popular distrust of the use of artificial chemicals in agriculture and this, however much farmers may deplore the fact, has become an important factor in the politics of environmentalism.

The use of chemicals in agriculture is not limited to pesticides. Paradoxically the ecological problems deriving from the application of artificial fertilizers are often equally complex and extensive. Fertilizer encourages weeds as well as crops to grow, so the increasing use of fertilizer promotes the increasing use of selective herbicides. If this seems an abstruse form of cultivation it is not one that is limited to modern agriculture, but can be found in many suburban gardens where, acre for acre, the concentrations of both fertilizer and pesticide are higher than on the average arable farm. Nevertheless, the sheer quantity of nitrate fertilizer that is applied to much farmland – and it has increased five times since the 1930s – creates problems from the surface run-off of rainwater which finds its way into drainage channels and ditches and eventually into streams and rivers. Here the nitrate contributes to 'entrophication' – the excessive growth of vegetation and algae in the water. Over-abundant growth may selectively promote a few aquatic plants to the detriment of others, clog the water-course and reduce the number of fish and other aquatic creatures (and hence their predators). This has created particular problems in parts of the Norfolk Broads, for example. A more sinister development is the seepage of nitrate into aquifers which are used as sources of the domestic water supply. During the drought of 1976 this resulted in an unusually high concentration of nitrate in the aquifers under parts of East Anglia and warnings were issued in some areas that babies should be given only bottled water to drink. Since it may take decades for water to percolate into these aquifers the problem is a long-term one, and bearing in mind the increasing use of artificial fertilizer since the war, one which may return.

Controversy has also surrounded the long-term effects of artificial fertilizer on the soil structure. This is an issue surrounded by farming lore and even prejudice, which is often at odds with scientific investigation, and this, together with the extreme variability of soil conditions in England, makes any generalized assessment virtually impossible. In some cases cultivation maintains a good soil structure, while in others it may break it down, and what constitutes a 'good' soil structure may depend upon its mineral composition and upon the use to which it is put. Much of the recent discussion about soil structure has centred on the decline of its organic matter content, particularly in the arable areas, following the decline of outdoor grazing and mixed farming patterns, the replacement of animal manure by artificial fertilizer and the use of heavy machinery to apply it. The fear that is often expressed is that these new forms of cultivation will result in soil conditions analogous to the Oklahoma 'Dust Bowl' of the 1930s. Occasional springtime dust storms in the Fens are even invoked as an ominous example, although these are caused by the drying out of the peat soils and have occurred since the Fens were drained in the seventeenth century. (Nor, incidentally, are 'Fenland Blows' caused by the absence of hedgerows – another common belief; conventional hedges are simply not tall enough to be effective, only shelter belts of poplars or other tall trees.) However, an inquiry by the Agricultural Advisory Council in 1973 revealed that the use of artificial fertilizer and the deficiency of organic matter in light sandy soils increased the risk of wind erosion in parts of the Midlands and East Anglia. Although this has led some farmers to renounce the more extreme forms of continuous cropping, the new minimum cultivation methods (described in Chapter 3) may allow a return to monoculture on suitable light soils. By eliminating ploughing, soil disturbance is kept to a minimum and wind erosion is reduced by the fact that the soil is never without either a crop cover or a binding layer of roots. The number of occasions on which heavy machinery must be driven across the land is also reduced, although compaction and 'panning' are more of a problem on heavy clay soils which are not prone to wind erosion. Nevertheless, minimum cultivation methods are much more dependent upon agrochemicals, especially herbicides, so there are few benefits for wildlife.

Modern farmers are often accused of 'soil-mining' rather than farming – of not replacing the fertility which they extract from the soil by a balanced rotation of crop and animal husbandry. Be that as it may, there is certainly one sense in which modern agriculture literally, albeit indirectly, mines the earth: by its increasing dependence on fossil-based fuels. Although in principle agriculture ought to be a net producer of energy, converting the sun's energy into the calorific value of food, modern agriculture is actually a net consumer. We are consequently eating up our energy resources. Apart from the fuel used directly to power farm equipment and to transport food, processed or unprocessed, to the consumer, the fertilizers and pesticides which are an integral part of modern cultivation methods are overwhelmingly derivatives of oil. The increasing specialization of modern agriculture means that while arable farmers use over one million tons of artificial fertilizer each year, intensive livestock producers experience considerable difficulties in disposing of their animal waste. Our energy resources would go literally down the drain if many water authorities, worried by the pollution problem, did not force farmers to find other methods of disposal. Nevertheless modern agriculture's contribution to the energy crisis is that each of us eats the equivalent of approximately 100 gallons of petrol each year. The amount is comparatively small – in a crisis it could be met simply by placing a ban on Sunday motoring – and with the proximity of North Sea oil it does not present an immediate problem. But it hardly offers a long-term solution to the problem of resource depletion. As oil resources become more scarce by the end of the century, can agriculture continue in its present form? And at what cost to the consumer? Such thoughts do not immediately exercise the minds of farmers, but they are becoming concerned by the rises in the price of fertilizer and other oil-based inputs and by their own powerlessness in the face of 'agribusiness' corporations, which was referred to in Chapter 3. So the dependence on agrochemicals and the effect which this has on the ecology of the countryside are not *simply* the moral responsibility of the individual farmer. It involves the whole political economy of modern agriculture – and that includes consumers and politicians as well as producers.

This point can be more clearly illustrated by considering the prolonged controversy surrounding the effects of modern farming methods on the rural landscape. This has created as much, if not more, acrimony between farming and environmental interests in recent years, with the destruction of traditional landscape features replacing the extermination of birds of prey as a rallying point for public attention. This shift in emphasis has taken place partly because the restrictions on the use of organo-chloride pesticides introduced in the 1960s have enabled some of the more extreme threats to wildlife preservation to recede and partly because pesticide manufacturers countered nature conservationist claims that they were responsible for the reduction in bird population by arguing that hedgerow and woodland removal could be the prime culprits. The relevant pressure groups maintain their vigilance, but during the 1970s the changes in the rural landscape, especially in the lowlands, have become much more visible and have certainly received much more publicity. These changes have been touched upon several times in this book already and the reasons for them were considered in Chapter 3. They relate basically to the widespread changes which have occurred in agricultural technology and husbandry techniques during the 'second agricultural revolution' of the last thirty years. Where these changes have been most extensive, the landscape has reflected them. Therefore it is not surprising that the lowlands land-scape has changed most, especially in arable areas, for farming in the lowlands has been subject to the most thoroughgoing technologi-cal changes. The factors which lie behind the removal of trees and hedgerows, the erection of new and imposing farm buildings and the ploughing up of downland and heath were listed in Chapter 3: increasing mechanization, increasing labour costs, the introduction of more intensive livestock systems and the drive towards maximizing crop production on an expensively priced capital asset. The upland areas have suffered fewer changes, but this is not to say that the upland landscape has remained unaltered. Fell and moorland have been cleared of bracken and heather in order to provide extra grassland and, most notoriously, the 'serried ranks' of conifers have marched across the hillsides. In all areas the sustained prosperity of British agriculture since the war has encouraged farmers to expand their output by taking marginal areas of land into cultivation. Yet, as we remarked in Chapter 1, it is the agriculturally marginal which is often, by prevailing urban aesthetic standards, the most pictur-esque.

The nature of the rural landscape is, of course, inextricably linked to the variety of wildlife species which it supports and the removal of traditional landscape features – hedgerows, trees, ponds, marshes, even permanent pasture – necessarily involves the destruction of wildlife habitats. The urban daytripper and the village newcomer have therefore found common cause with the ecologist to greet these landscape changes with bitter resentment. Farmers have in turn responded to this hostility with a mixture of anger, contempt and disdain. The anger has arisen because most farmers believe that the allegations that they are 'ruining' the countryside are exaggerated and too indiscriminate. This indignation is also accompanied by a contempt for the 'ignorant' protectionist who, many farmers allege, has no knowledge or understanding of modern agriculture, and especially of the economics of food production. Farmers are quick to point out that the desire to retain hedgerows and other familiar landscape features emanates from exactly that social group – the 'urban mass' – whose demands for cheap food have indirectly brought about those changes which they so deplore. The farmer therefore accuses the preservationist of hypocrisy. However, the charge is often returned by environmentalists who note how much

farmers pride themselves on being 'stewards' of the English countryside for the benefit of future generations and for the nation at large,
but then deny the right of anyone else to have a say in how it should
be maintained for them. Drawing upon the historical legacy of an
independent yeomanry the farmer will then reply that no one is going
to tell *him* how to run his farm or meddle in his affairs and that
environmentalist 'busybodies' should go and mind their own business. Needless to say, once the battle lines have been drawn in this
way, there tends to be a deterioration in relationships all round.

Those organizations, most notably the Countryside Commission,
which have earnestly attempted to reconcile the viewpoints of
farmers and environmentalists have had a hard time. Once the
stereotypes have been established there has been a tendency towards
self-fulfilling prophecy in the behaviour of each side towards the
other. Farmers, their pride stung, can easily become aggressively
unhelpful to even the most politely worded and well-reasoned appeal
to curb some of the unnecessarily destructive aspects of their farming
practices. Equally it must be understood that there are many farmers
who perpetrate these changes with genuine personal regret, but who
feel compelled to do so by economic circumstances. Many experience
a sense of guilt at taking out a hedge or destroying a copse of trees
for purely economic reasons and farmers, no less than anyone else,
do not like to be reminded of something which, in the abstract, they
might find difficult to justify. Touched on a raw nerve, they can
react accordingly. The hostility which farmers have recently provoked
from many environmentalists also helps to confirm them in their
characteristic persecution complex, associated with being a small,
closely knit minority in an urban industrial society. Any attempts to
persuade farmers of the necessity of environmental conservation must
take all these factors into account. However, it would be quite mistaken to regard the conflict over farming and the environment as
stemming from a 'breakdown of communications', to use the fashionable cliché, because a direct conflict of interest is also involved. It is
arguable that if each side could communicate its opinions more
clearly to the other, the resulting conflict would be even more embittered. Farmers regard the landscape as a factor of production
and a source of profit; supporters of the environmental movement,
on the other hand, look upon the countryside as a source of visual
pleasure and as a habitat for wildlife – as something to be 'consumed'.

As long as this aesthetic appreciation does not coincide with profitable necessity then this conflict will remain.

If this perspective is adopted, environmentalists ought perhaps to be grateful for the fact that the vast majority of farmers are not more economically rational when they come to organize the husbandry of their farms and that the inertia introduced by the historical pattern of landownership and farm structure in this country has acted as a brake on landscape change. A landscape determined *solely* by what is most profitable under current conditions would look very different from that which exists today, despite the rapid changes which have recently taken place. There is, for example, virtually no economic justification for retaining any hedgerows at all on the majority of farms in the southern and eastern counties of England. Indeed it has been estimated that the presence of hedgerows reduces the output of cereals farms by up to 15 per cent. As we have already seen, they are no protection against wind erosion, which can in any case be overcome by other means, and even if there are stock grazing on the fields a movable fence is more efficient, convenient and requires less maintenance. Hedges also obstruct farm machinery, rob crops of food and water and shade the crop, producing uneven growth and preventing it from drying out at harvest. Moreover, the roots from trees and hedges clog drains and hinder the plough. It is little wonder, then, that until quite recently the Ministry of Agriculture, mindful of its responsibility to increase the production of as much cheap food as possible, gave grants to farmers for hedgerow removal. But what is more remarkable is that so many farmers were sentimental (and some impecunious) enough to keep their hedgerows in for so long. As Nan Fairbrother points out in *New Lives, New Landscapes:*

It is useless trying to justify [hedgerows and] trees in terms of farming, for such unreal arguments are no protection against ten-ton bulldozers, and our wartime farmer had no illusions about the trees on his farm. Every one of them, he said, lost him money every year; he kept them because he liked them, and because he had no children and could afford to indulge his old age. .

Possibly the only use for hedgerows today is that they help to keep people and litter out of fields, rather than animals in, but if hedges and trees were uneconomic during the war, how much more so are they today?

The logical arable landscape is therefore the prairie and, no matter how much this type of landscape may be deplored, the economics of modern food production are compelling more and more farmers to create it. From a relatively small base among the most profit-conscious farmers of Lincolnshire and East Anglia, a prairie land-scape has spread to other farms and to other areas. As more animals have been brought inside by the introduction of intensive feeding systems, so more land has been given up to arable production. During the 1960s the barley acreage doubled and an increase was recorded in every county in England. The arable/pastoral boundary also began to creep northwards and westwards as a result of more land being brought into arable cultivation so that counties like Nottinghamshire, Northamptonshire, Berkshire, Wiltshire and Hampshire recorded some of the highest increases. What is happening is that the English rural landscape is *slowly* becoming divided into three major types in the lowlands. These are listed by Nan Fairbrother as follows:

One is intensive arable as in the Fens, New Holland in Lincolnshire, and on much of the chalk; there are few or no hedges or trees, but open country with no sense of enclosure or division. Simply the land surface with level crops emphasising the smoothness of the worked earth. The second type of rural landscape is the traditional mixed farm . . . but mechanised and often enlarged. This is common in the Midlands . . . ; the smaller fields have been run together and evened-off, but the old pattern is still recognisable in its new mechanised version. There are hedges still, but low now and neatly clipped, many of the small woods and copses have gone, and most of the trees in the hedges are the ageing survivors of enclosure planting. It is only a matter of time before they die . . . and there are few new saplings in these machine-cut hedges to replace them, even if farmers wanted them.

The third type of landscape is the predominantly grass farm with animals on permanent pasture, and this is still common in a belt running north-south from Lancashire to Dorset and into the south-west. Here the fields are small . . . and the hedges often tall and deep, leafy with trees of all ages as hedgerow saplings grow up to replace the dying giants. . . . It is the least mechanised of our farming scenery, the least efficient and the most resist-ant to change because of the multiple ownership and the often rented holdings.

The distinctions are not, of course, quite as clearcut as this, since considerable local variations remain, particularly around urban centres and on the very poor soils of little agricultural significance. However, this represents the shape of things to come, with the first type increasingly in the ascendancy aided and abetted by the demand for cheap food and the agricultural policies of successive governments aimed at ensuring the expansion of home production.

In the lowlands it is the prosperity of agriculture which is contributing to landscape change by allowing increasing investment in new capital-intensive forms of production. In the uplands, on the other hand, the greatest threats to the traditional landscape arise out of poverty, neglect and decay. As we have seen in Chapter 3 marginal farmers engaged in sheep and beef cattle rearing dominate the upland areas, and many of them are on a 'deferred death sentence'. The resulting poverty is occasionally picturesque – as in the case of antiquated farm buildings – but broken walls, derelict farmsteads and scrub-covered hillsides often present grotesque eyesores. Within the context of current agricultural policies there are sound economic *and* social reasons for abandoning farming altogether over large areas of the uplands and using the land for other purposes which would both be profitable and create employment. It has been estimated that up to one-third of hill land could grow timber and the aim is to increase the forestry acreage by 60 per cent by the end of the century. But just as the removal of trees from the lowlands has created considerable opposition from environmentalists so has the policy of planting them across the hillsides. Much of the Forestry Commission's early planting was certainly crude and insensitive, but in recent years it has become more attentive to its landscaping responsibilities (not least because the Forestry Commission has found that there is money to be made out of tourism if it does so) and now employs landscape consultants to advise on its planting policies. As long as trees are more profitable than sheep and beef cattle and as long as softwoods are more profitable than hardwoods, the trend towards conifer-covered hills will continue. Sheep-mown hills can only be retained where sheep farming prospers; otherwise the hillsides will revert to equally disfiguring scrub as farms are eventually abandoned. The upland areas have already suffered extensive depopulation because the local agricultural economy will no longer support the standard of living which their inhabitants quite reasonably demand. It is both unfair and unrealistic to expect those who remain to make further sacrifices in order to service the sensibilities of visitors. As in the lowlands, the traditional landscape has to some extent been preserved by the economic irrationality of farmers – although in the uplands it consists of their ability to hold on against all the odds rather than disavow the pursuit of maximum profits.

To anyone committed to the preservation of the traditional landscape of rural England, much of this must make gloomy reading. Certainly the landscape will continue to change in response to new technological factors and the evolving structure of the agricultural industry. The idea of a static and unchanging countryside is a misreading of history and, as far as the future is concerned, a totally unrealistic expectation. As long as we, as consumers, demand cheap food and as long as this demand is implemented by state-directed agricultural policies, the end product will be the disappearance of the traditional rural landscape and associated farm buildings. However, the conflict between modern farming practice and environmental conservation is by no means an irreconcilable one and, although entrenched positions have been taken up on both sides, there are now a few signs of a more sophisticated awareness of the problems involved and a more constructive desire on the part of both farming organizations and the environmental lobby to overcome them. It is, for example, quite mistaken to believe that all farmers are hostile towards environmentalism. The gentleman farmer has long sought to preserve the aesthetic qualities of the English countryside and has provided the backbone of the CPRE. There are, moreover, many small farmers who prefer to follow a traditional 'way of life' and abjure the profit maximization that often provides landscape change. The most aggressively anti-environmentalist farmers are probably the agribusinessmen who allow little to stand in the way of enhanced profit margins and who are largely indifferent to aesthetic considerations. Nevertheless, the majority of farmers engage in landscape change as a result of the economic constraints imposed upon their farming practice rather than as a result of any personal whim. Only those who can afford to ignore these constraints feel capable of exercising a *choice* to retain a more traditional agricultural landscape. This suggests that the attitudes of farmers towards environmental conservation are considerably more complicated than the stereotypes adopted by the more extreme members of the environmental lobby would suggest. By no means all farmers are as antipathetic to the conservationist case as is sometimes assumed, but eventually they must all make a living.

Taking these factors into account, there have recently been put forward several imaginative proposals aimed at encouraging farmers and landowners to create a more aesthetically pleasing landscape. The Countryside Commission, for example, has funded an extensive research programme in both the lowlands and the uplands in order to assess the extent of existing landscape change and to demonstrate how profitable farming and an attractive countryside may be combined. The lowlands study *New Agricultural Landscapes* by Richard Westmacott and Tom Worthington was published in 1974. Based on a series of case studies in seven counties, it confirms that the most significant change in the arable landscape has been the loss of hedgerows and trees, but the authors argue that the present landscape is not always inferior to that of the past. A careful rearrangement of field patterns may actually enhance the natural contours of the landscape and, although the indigenous wildlife may be seriously affected, the 'new agricultural landscapes' may be both functional and aesthetically pleasing. Westmacott and Worthington argue that an essentially voluntary scheme of advice and persuasion within the present system of agricultural advisory services can enable such a landscape to be fashioned. Moreover, the Countryside Commission's own favoured policy is to promote landscape agreements and tree-planting schemes in cooperation with sympathetic farmers and landowners. The major problem with essentially voluntary schemes like these, however, is that they appeal to only those farmers who are already convinced environmentalists. They are unlikely to influence those farmers – such as agribusinessmen – who react most readily, and most exclusively, to financial incentives; and these are usually precisely those farmers who wreak the greatest landscape change. Agribusinessmen, for example, are unlikely to be moved by permissive policies: for them the creation of a desired landscape must either be profitable or unavoidable. And as the economic constraints push more and more farmers towards the rationalization of their enterprises the proportion of farmers (and of the countryside) to whom this applies is likely to increase.

This suggests that some system of control must be introduced if farmers are to be persuaded to retain the wildlife habitats or landscape features which they would otherwise destroy. The problem is that there is little agreement over how this control should operate and what form it should take. The Countryside Act of 1968 allowed local authorities to take a more positive role in environmental conservation and gave the Countryside Commission general responsibility for safeguarding the rural landscape. Despite some notable local successes, the results have, however, been disappointing: certainly little impact appears to have been made upon the *laissez-faire* attitude of the farmer towards his own property. By the mid-1970s the general policy of winning the confidence of the farming organizations and working on the basis of persuasion and advice was being increasingly questioned. But there has remained considerable disagreement over the most viable alternative – financial incentive or state compulsion. Some forms of incentive are feasible – for example, the attachment of landscape conditions to agricultural grants – but would be difficult to operate in practice without a comprehensive (and expensive) advisory service to back them up. Any such proposal would almost certainly provoke resistance from the NFU and CLA who have hitherto ensured that their members remain largely outside the scope of town and country planning legislation and who would be suspicious of 'bureaucratic interference'. The outcry would undoubtedly be even greater if some form of compulsion were involved, such as placing the rural landscape under the same kind of protective legislation as already exists for 'listed' buildings so that farmers would have to notify the local planning authority of any intention to remove a protected landscape feature, such as a hedgerow or a section of heath. It is by no means clear how farmers would react to *any* system which threatened to control their freedom to do as they please with their own land. There is also little evidence to show that farmers welcome an opportunity to become glorified park wardens or landscape gardeners – nor, indeed, have they the necessary skills to do so. Although there have been a number of successful experiments in providing advice to farmers at the 'grass roots' – most notably the Upland Management Scheme in the Lake District – farmers still remain suspicious of environmentalists however sympathetic they may be to environmentalism.

This suspicion runs very deep. It is not simply xenophobia, but a reluctance to admit any other 'proprietary interest', including that of the environmental lobby, into the control of private property. Any infringement of the owner's exclusive rights will be resisted, and for this reason, if no other, attempts to provide a planned resolution of the conflict between farming and the environment will prove difficult. Fortunately many nature reserves and other wildlife refuges are situated on land of little agricultural value; and many farmers can still be persuaded to retain important and irretrievable landscape features if only they are informed of their unique significance. But in the future a diverse ecology will only be able to coexist with an efficient agriculture within the context of a *planned* land-use strategy, and such an attempt to resolve the various and conflicting demands on the countryside cannot be successful without farmers surrendering at least some of their freedom of action to do as they wish with their own land. It is not, therefore, simply bloody-mindedness which will lead some farmers to resist planning controls over the rural landscape; it will be a defence, however tenuous, of the interest of private property – and that, needless to say, is an interest which is fundamental to the fabric of contemporary English society. The essentially *political* nature of this issue is rarely addressed publicly and explicitly, but sooner or later a decision will have to be made over whether or not those in possession of the rural landscape should be forced to cede some of their control.

In the meantime, the rationalization of agriculture continues. The resolution of the many conflicts between farmers and environmentalists remains a hit-and-miss affair. A tactful environmental lobby, a sympathetic farmer and a smattering of goodwill on both sides may continue to produce encouraging results. But for how long? In the final analysis a farmer must make a profit and all the economic pressures on farmers will eventually lead them to place agriculture before environmental conservation. So a conflict of interest remains. Already, for example, birds of prey which are saved from accidental poisoning by pesticides are being deliberately shot, trapped or poisoned as their numbers increase once more. Voluntary landscape agreements have not saved acres of hedgerows, heath or woodland and even those trees that remain in lowland England are an ageing population because insufficient planting has taken place over the past thirty years. Therefore the fundamental problem of property rights cannot be evaded indefinitely. Although most farmland is privately owned the landscape is publicly consumed. As a result we all feel we should have a say in its appearance, but as yet we have no *right* to be heard. This is a much older problem and one which precedes the rise of environmentalism, because in addition to the environmental lobby the exclusive rights of the farmer have long been under threat from another source – the massed ranks of the urban population, intent on using the countryside as a source of recreation and determined to gain access to what *they* consider to be semi-public territory.

Recreation and access

The vast majority of farmers and landowners take an inordinate pride in the countryside and will show off their land to the occasional interested and respectful visitor. But when visitors to the countryside are considered *en masse* rather than on an individual basis, then the farmer's traditional nervousness towards the urban population begins to take over. In moments of mature reflection the farmer may pity the 'townie' – a pity based upon what the farmer regards as the dehumanized and alienating quality of life in the larger cities – but that genuine twinge of concern is easily swept aside by the nightmare of being 'invaded', 'swamped' or 'overrun' by a 'mass' of 'ignorant' daytrippers and holidaymakers. Some of these fears have been forged out of bitter experience. Many of the problems associated with the uncontrolled access to farmland are long-standing and have been enshrined in the Country Code, the list of 'do's and don'ts' concerning open gates, litter, dogs which worry livestock, fire risks and so on. However, recent trends in farming practice have made agriculture even more incompatible with uncontrolled recreation. Intensive livestock methods increase the susceptibility of animals to diseases easily spread by humans, and visitors threaten good farm hygiene; and the danger can easily be reversed – some farming operations, particularly spraying, threaten visitors. So farmers increasingly object to visitors 'roaming all over' their land and will point out with some vehemence that they would not be allowed, nor even expect to be allowed, the same licence to wander around urban factories. For the exasperated livestock farmer, with fears for the future of his pig unit or broiler house, for the fruit-grower alarmed by the possibility of a poisonous spray inadvertently finding its way into the metabolism of a casual passerby, and for the cereals farmer who does not take kindly to his best malting barley being trampled down in order to create an impromptu picnic site, the simplest solution is to go in for siege tactics. Up go the 'Trespassers Will Be Prosecuted' and 'Keep Out' signs, the extra barbed wire is ordered and the shotgun is cleaned and prepared. Those who dare to venture off public rights of way find themselves harassed and evicted. As a further disincentive footpaths may suddenly disappear under the plough or new fences are erected across them, signposts mysteriously vanish and perhaps an unsociable bull is (illegally) posted in a field transversed by a path. Once again the battle lines are drawn.

The ensuing conflict has been sharpened by the phenomenal growth of outdoor recreation during the last two decades. Increasing leisure time, thanks to the near-universal introduction of a five-day working week and paid holidays, has combined with increasing affluence to produce a rapid increase in daytrips to the country and, more recently, in the number of long-weekend and off-season holidays. The Countryside Commission's *Digest of Countryside Recreation Statistics* charts many of these changes and offers a glimpse of the increasing demands being made on the countryside. For example, the number of visitors to the Department of the Environment's Ancient Monuments rose from 6·8 million in 1960 to 15·4 million in 1972; visitors to National Trust properties also increased in number from 1·02 million to 3·9 million over the same period. By the early 1970s it was estimated that there were already over five million campers and caravanners and three million anglers. Not only are more and more people willing and able to go and look at the countryside, but the trend is towards more active recreational pursuits, involving the more extensive use of space and paralleled by an extension of the time spent there. Nothing more aptly illustrates the quality of the English countryside as a 'positional good'. Millions of us now look to the countryside to 'get away from it all', only to find many favoured spots overcrowded by people and traffic as a result. The place for a quiet picnic on a Bank Holiday is now in the centre of the City of London – few people, little or no traffic and an ample supply of peace and quiet. Since the countryside is a 'positional good', it is hardly surprising to find that the demand for rural leisure activities is socially skewed. The *Digest* suggests that managerial, professional and other non-manual workers (social classes A B and C1) are overrepresented by a factor of between two and three, whereas semi- and unskilled manual workers (social class D E) are underrepresented by a factor of three or more. This is obviously accounted for in part by the affluence of the higher social classes, but it also reflects their different pattern of recreational preference. Primarily, though by no means exclusively, it is the English middle class which, somewhat self-consciously, 'appreciates' the countryside – and which is determined that others will not 'spoil' it for them.

In so far as this involves finding more and more ingenious ways of keeping as many people as possible away from unspoilt parts of rural England, there is common ground between some visitors to the countryside and many of those who live and work there. This goes to show that alliances formed in the conflict over recreation and access to the countryside are by no means the same as those which coalesce over issues of wildlife preservation and landscape change. Indeed there are even differences of opinion among environmentalists over how this increasing demand upon the countryside is to be accommodated. Some environmentalists prefer preservation-by-exclusion, so that visitors are rationed because some areas are made deliberately inaccessible (particularly 'wilderness' areas) or a toll or entrance fee is imposed, or even, as a last resort (as in the case of most nature reserves), access is made dependent upon the membership of an amenity society and/or the possession of a permit. A more subtle form of restriction is to proceed by a philosophy akin to that of *apartheid*. Environmental *bantustans* are set aside where virtually unrestricted leisure activity is allowed and even encouraged, so that the surrounding area can be strictly controlled and rationed for those interested in a more solitary appreciation of the countryside. Thus Bowness-on-Windermere is sacrificed for the greater good of the Lake District or Matlock Bath in the cause of the Peak District. A third alternative is to keep one step ahead of demand by increasing the provision of rural leisure facilities and expanding the range of choice. Although arguably the most constructive approach, this is usually the one which creates the greatest controversy. In the marginal farming areas of the uplands, where revenues from tourism are an important part of the farming economy, farmers may welcome further recreational development, but conservationists are usually more hostile. In the lowlands both farmers and environmentalists may combine to oppose development, but are often at loggerheads over the issue of access to farmland. The debate over recreation and access in the countryside therefore easily fragments into a plethora of parochial disputes, with constantly shifting allegiances and alliances, and one which oscillates between each of these three alternative solutions. As yet, no coherent policy has emerged, only a confusion of purpose over whether to impose greater restrictions or offer more choice.

Of course, each of these solutions will be valid in particular circumstances. For example, there may be good grounds for the total exclusion of the public from some nature reserves. On the other hand, the onus is on those who advocate the view that the countryside offers spiritual uplift to the modern urban dweller to make it more, rather than less, accessible to those who live in towns. Recent public policy, as exemplified by the Countryside Act of 1968, accurately reflects the dilemma between the belief that 'the countryside is Good for You', so that people should be encouraged to visit it, and the necessity of reassuring agricultural and environmental interests. The Act enabled local authorities to create and administer country parks and picnic sites, thereby expanding choice but directing it towards specially planned recreational reservations. Their provision has, in any case, varied considerably between different parts of the country, and, because of the precise way in which it has been implemented, the Act has done little to increase the opportunities for rural recreation among the more deprived sections of the urban population. Consequently most visitors to the countryside continue to come from a fairly circumscribed group of affluent suburban car-owning families while those arguably in greater need are scarcely catered for. But again there is ambivalence over whether they *should* be encouraged into the countryside: to the farmer and conservationist alike a vision is conjured up of marauding inner-city teenagers and other undesirable aliens, wreaking havoc in an environment best kept well away from 'those kinds of people'.

In the true manner of a 'positional good', the appreciation of the countryside thus continues to depend upon limitations placed upon its accessibility. Various groups act as social as well as literal gatekeepers to the rewards which rural England has to offer, and visitors are allowed through only on a selective basis. Isabel Emmett has referred to the formal and informal mechanisms of selection as the 'social filter in the leisure field', allowing different groups access to different facilities, more or less easily. As she points out:

No piece of ground used for leisure is merely a physical place: it is always a social entity too – the filters are always there.

. . . In the countryside the gross, legal filter is formed by those who own rights in and control the countryside . . . and their employees who police the countryside on their behalf.

. . . Private landlords, local authorities and others have limited the provision of facilities which would make it easy for other social groups [than well-to-do people] to use the countryside, often with the conscious intention of limiting use. . . . Only now are we beginning to try to reckon the costs of democracy; beginning, for instance, to see queues to climb some rocks in Snowdonia.

There may be technical decisions to make about how to control the larger numbers in their access to the countryside: decisions about spacing and placing of car-parks, toilets, refreshments, picnic sites and footpaths. But let us also watch for the reaction from those in possession, which group often includes ourselves in another role. The sense of affront, the defences put up will be hard to see amidst the paternal concern to do what is best for all. But those of us feeling and putting into action this paternal concern should try to observe within ourselves the elements of outrage, self-defence and exclusivity which will warp our policies.

Remarkably little research has been carried out on the question of how these filters operate, and by whom they are operated, yet any policies aimed at harmonizing the interests of agriculture, conservation and recreation in the countryside must be based upon an understanding of this problem. The more sociological aspects of leisure and rural amenity have been overlooked in favour of the purely physical aspects of recreational planning or a mere head-count of who goes where, when and for how long.

Although attempts are being made to remedy this lack of knowledge, there are still many assumptions about recreation and the countryside which are taken as facts. The biggest myth of all, of course, concerns that of a static and unchanging countryside fighting a rearguard action against urban encroachment, with the corollary that the natural must, by that very fact alone, be superior to the manmade. When this is combined with a series of élitist and mostly facile generalizations about the 'swinish multitude' of unappreciative urbanites prejudice easily hardens to become common 'knowledge'. It *may* be – although we cannot be sure because our knowledge is so uneven – that many of the frequently expressed fears of the effects of expanding leisure opportunities on the countryside are exaggerated, that well-publicized cases of overcrowding and ecological damage in the Lake District, in parts of the Derbyshire Peak District or on the Downs in Kent and Sussex are localized and atypical rather than the shape of things to come elsewhere. It is possible, for example, to recall the fears expressed by conservationists in Devon and Somerset during the construction of the M5 beyond Bristol at the prospect of hundreds of thousands of the denizens of Birmingham and the Black Country descending upon Dartmoor and Exmoor. In the event the vast majority continued to make for the seaside resorts in the area, leaving the conservationists to fend off the more predatory designs of farmers and water authorities. The unspoken assumption here, as so often elsewhere, was that crowds would impair enjoyment – a typically individualistic assumption which it is taken for granted applies to the entire population. In fact, it is a value which exists predominantly among only the middle-aged and the middle-class. Common observation suggests that other social groups enjoy the conviviality and sociability of being part of a crowd and find open spaces 'with nothing to do' dead and unappealing. Moreover, statistics collected by the Countryside Commission suggest that the overwhelming majority of visitors to the countryside venture no more than a couple of hundred yards from their car. Most of them demand little more than a 'view with a loo' – a place to park, a cup of tea and adequate toilet facilities. Nevertheless a peculiar social blindness easily affects environmental judgements: we hear much more about the 'detrimental character' of refreshment kiosks than of boathouses and about the erosion of footpaths than the more severe ecological impact of persistent horse-riding or ski-ing. This may not be unconnected with the social composition of their respective devotees.

It would be foolish, however, to argue that the problems created by the increasing urban demand for recreation in the countryside are entirely illusory or simply a matter of arbitrary taste: they clearly are not. Nowhere is this more apparent than where access to farm-land is most easily accomplished and is least organized – in those rural areas which abut directly on to the main centres of the popu-lation: the so-called 'urban fringe'. Here the problem of trespass from neighbouring urban areas can be almost a way of life for some harassed farmers with continual problems of damaged or stolen crops, dumped rubbish, damage to fences, gates and farm buildings and machinery and the worrying of livestock. Some of this is due to malicious vandalism, but much more interference is probably caused by ignorance or thoughtlessness. But whatever the cause, there are no benefits for the farmer, only an increasing sense of frustration and anger. Consequently urban-fringe farmers find themselves taking unusually thorough measures to defend their land against intrusion – extra barbed-wire fencing along boundaries and footpaths, an unsightly rash of warning notices and even electronic detection devices are all employed. Farmers may even switch their pattern of production in order to minimize the risks – from arable to intensive livestock farming, for example. Most of the conflicts concerning agriculture and amenity also occur in a particularly acute form on the urban fringe. Thus urban neighbours may attempt to curb farming operations because of problems of noise or smell. Farmers growing trees for profit can find a Tree Preservation Order placed on them because they enhance the view from a nearby housing estate. Spraying crops and burning stubble also provoke outcries from nearby residents. There are, of course, compensating advantages for urban-fringe farmers – proximity to markets and consumers, the possibility of grafting on lucrative recreational facilities for horse-riding, fishing, shooting, and so on, and not least the prospect of being able to sell out at development value. However, the experience of farming on the urban fringe illustrates the scale of the problems encountered when urban recreation and agriculture are indiscriminately mixed without any attempt to manage their inevitable incompatibilities. Without this no one seems satisfied: the farmer cannot farm efficiently; the environmentalist is despondent about the blighted landscape; and the nearby urban population is not allowed the freedom it would wish in order to relax in the countryside.

Many observers have argued that some form of planning is therefore essential if the optimum outcome for all concerned is to be achieved, but carefully administered recreational facilities in the countryside will not be sufficient on their own. Too many urban dwellers regard 'a day in the country' as an escape from the regimentation that planned leisure sometimes implies. The licence to 'roam all over' farmland is precisely what many of them require. So changes in attitudes are also needed and given that real interests are often involved – the profitability of agriculture, the rights of private property, the defence of national scenic assets – these changes will be difficult to engineer. Alongside the need to engage in a more explicit discussion of the values which underlie rural planning (which, as we shall see in the following section, is rarely a purely technocratic exercise) there is the need to ensure that the relevant knowledge about today's countryside is more widely disseminated. Little information about contemporary agriculture is conveyed in schools or by the mass media (*The Archers* and *Emmerdale Farm* notwith-standing). Yet, given the opportunity and some imaginative presen-tation, the urban population has shown that it is capable of respond-ing, judging by the numbers who take an interest at county shows or who turn up at the pitifully few farms which organize public open days. Farmers, too, need to understand more about the social impulses which prompt an increasing number of urbanites to look to the countryside for relaxation and enjoyment. The self-contained social circle of most farmers, commented upon in Chapter 3, does not particularly lend itself to such empathy, but farmers will ignore the aspirations of the other 97 per cent of the population at their peril – and so, for that matter, will conservationists. This will mean conceding the impossibility, whatever the strict legal interpretation, of farm land ever being treated by the urban population in the same way as a factory or even their own back gardens. Equally, however, the farmer is entitled to demand that the countryside be viewed neither as a more extensive version of an urban recreation ground, nor as an arcadian idyll set aside for the pursuit of an indulgent atavism. Otherwise mutual incomprehension and avoidable conflict will continue.

Rural planning: the containment of urban England

The ecological changes wrought by modern farming practice and the increasing urban demand for recreation in the countryside have emerged only quite recently as publicly acknowledged threats to the quality of the rural environment. They have highlighted the complex nature of the interrelationship between urban and rural life in an advanced industrial society like Britain and have focused attention on fundamental dilemmas concerning economic development, distributive justice and the preservation of quality in the modern world. It has become the role of professional town and country planners to arbitrate many of these controversies for, in practice, it is they who have operated the machinery of planning control through which the conflict over the rural environment has been channelled. In some cases this may have placed planners in the position of attempting to solve problems which are insoluble, if only because they stem from the mutually exclusive values which different groups of people hold with regard to the countryside, with all the attendant risks to their reputation which this has involved. However, planners have been forced to pronounce on a wide range of environmental disputes within a framework of legislation introduced to deal with an apparently, though deceptively, more straightforward problem – the development of agricultural land for industrial and residential purposes. Although, as we have already seen, contemporary rural planning problems reach far beyond the issue of development control, much of the current planning legislation continues to be concerned with the conflict between agriculture and other forms of land use. Moreover, the British system of land-use planning originated from attempts to solve urban problems – overcrowding, sanitation, hygiene, etc. – with, until recently, relatively little attention being paid to the countryside. Historically, therefore, rural planning has been virtually a by-product of a system designed to cope with urban growth, partly because the countryside was regarded as a bucolic backdrop to life in urban areas and partly because the idea of a planned countryside was, to influential public opinion, anathema. The task of planning was, rather, to ensure that the countryside retained its 'natural' unplanned character by protecting it from the incursions of urban industrialism. Only in the last decade or so, therefore, has rural planning not proceeded by default.

Simple inspection of planning legislation reveals the continuity of this approach. The first, and largely ineffective, Housing and Town Planning Act of 1909 contained permissive powers for the control of land 'in the course of development or likely to be used for building purposes' and development plans for all towns with a population of more than 20000 became compulsory in 1919. The aim was to rationalize the hitherto haphazard pattern of urban growth, but county councils were not granted similar powers until 1929. A further Act was introduced in 1932 and a Restriction of Ribbon Development Act in 1935, but much of the legislation was ineffectual. As a consequence the rate of loss of agricultural land was increasing during the 1930s and this provoked a startling mobilization of interest groups and committees of inquiry whose ideas and policies were to be enacted in the immediate post-war period. Central to this process were the deliberations of the Royal Commission on the Geographical Distribution of the Industrial Population, better known as the Barlow Commission, which was appointed in 1937 and reported in 1940. As Peter Hall and his associates conclude in their review of post-war planning, *The Containment of Urban England:*

The Barlow Report can be said to be the essential basis of the postwar British planning system. From its recommendations sprang the reports of the Uthwatt Committee on compensation and betterment and the Scott Report on rural land use, both of which can fairly be regarded as appendices to Barlow. From its minority report . . . sprang the decision to set up comprehensive controls over the location of industry, which was embodied in the Distribution of Industry Act of 1945. From its comments on new towns came the appointment of Lord Reith's Committee in 1945, and then the New Towns Act of 1946 which carried the Reith proposals into action. Finally, from its insistence on comprehensive and effective land use planning came the great Town and Country Planning Act of 1947 which was the legislative basis, as Barlow was the philosophical basis, of the whole planning system. . . .

This is obviously not the place to enter into a detailed history of this system, but it is worthwhile dwelling for a moment on the 'philosophical basis' of the Barlow Report because of the way in which it has remained so influential on policies relating to planning and the rural environment until the present day.

The Barlow Commission was concerned with two major policy objectives. The first, clearly given urgency by the Depression years, was the correction of the manifest regional imbalance which had arisen in the distribution of employment and the population. The second objective was that of urban containment, to which the problem of regional imbalance was believed to be indissolubly linked. By controlling the growth of the largest conurbations, especially London, it was believed that employment and industrial renewal could be directed towards the depressed areas in the North of England, Wales and Scotland, thereby also sparing the fertile agricultural land and threatened countryside of the Midlands and South East. In this way a humane desire to improve the distribution of industrial development and improved living standards in the urban centres was combined with a fairly rigid preservationist approach to the countryside. Given the acute agricultural depression of the 1930s this might seem strangely myopic, but it was engendered by an essentially arcadian vision of rural England, to which urbanism was assumed to be opposed. Patrick Abercrombie, in the standard planning textbook of the inter-war years, *Town and Country Planning*, stated that

The essence of the aesthetic of town and country planning consists in the frank recognition of these two elements, *town* and *country*, as representing opposite but complementary poles of influence. . . . With these two opposites constantly in view, a great deal of confused thinking and acting is washed away: the town should indeed be frankly artificial, urban; the country natural, rural.

Abercrombie was a member of the Barlow Commission and later responsible for the first Greater London Plan. He was also a founder-member of the Council for the Preservation of Rural England in 1926, after which, under his chairmanship, the CPRE had conducted a well-organized campaign against the encroachment of urban sprawl into the countryside. Abercrombie was also an outspoken advocate of Green Belts around the major conurbations, *cordons sanitaires* intended to keep urbanism at bay. Through an articulate and influential body of opinion, of which Abercrombie was the most prominent spokesman, rural preservationist sentiment therefore came to pervade the philosophy of post-war planning. Moreover the traditional English reverence for the rural way of life ensured that precisely *what* it was that was being preserved was never examined too closely.

The Scott Report on Land Utilization in Rural Areas, published in 1942, was particularly abstemious in this regard. It reinforced the Barlow conclusions on the need to impose physical controls on urban growth and it sanctified the prior claims of agriculture over both land use and labour in rural areas. Its general approach could be summarized in the phrase 'every acre counts', for the Report put forward a new planning principle for rural areas – that the onus of proof must lie with the prospective developer to show that 'a clear case of a national advantage was made out' before planning permission could be granted. It is true that since the war this principle has been frequently honoured in the breach, but the general presumption of a rural *status quo* has nevertheless been incorporated into planning practice. The rationale, easily understandable in wartime, was that agricultural land had to be protected as a priceless national asset, irrespective of its value, its productive capacity or the support cost to the consumer or taxpayer. In a Minority Report Professor S. R. Dennison had pointed to a possible fallacy in the argument – that a prosperous agriculture did not mean a ubiquitous agriculture but an *efficient* one and that this might well entail the release of marginal land allowing resources of capital and manpower to be more profitably employed elsewhere. Restricting the location of industry in rural areas in the wake of such changes would depress rural wages levels, increase rural–urban migration and hinder the viability of rural services – that is, exacerbate the problem of regional imbalance which the Barlow Commission had been so intent on redressing. Looking back, Dennison's comments have a gloomily prophetic ring about them. They foreshadow the chronic problems of low wages and poor service provision for rural workers which are such a prominent feature of rural England today; and they also address the problem of how much was to be paid for preserving the rural environment and *who* was going to pay for it. In the end Dennison's fellow-members of the Scott Committee ignored his arguments because their commitment to rural preservation was not based upon marginal utility economics, nor any rational calculation of costs and benefits. As Hall *et al.* point out:

It is hard to resist the conclusion that the objectives were not rational in a strict sense. They were mystical. In the special circumstances of a major war, that is perhaps understandable. But the effects were felt long after the war was over. The most important was to give the new planning system a pronounced preservationist bias. Those who operated the system in the counties accepted, in effect, the value judgements of the Scott Committee.

One of the major problems of restricting development in rural areas is that, as the discussion of rural housing in Chapter 5 indicated, it can create a planned scarcity of development land, and, without any parallel control over prices, provides a windfall for the fortunate few who possess land with planning permission. Without some control over 'betterment' – the increase in land values which accompanies permission for industrial or residential development – local plans become speculators' guides and the increase in value becomes, in effect, a highly regressive form of indirect taxation on home-owners and others who eventually use the land after it has been developed. The Uthwatt Committee on Compensation and Betterment was set up to consider this problem and it reported in 1942. Given the approving reception granted to the Barlow and Scott recommendations, it is instructive to see what became of the Uthwatt proposals, impinging as they did on a very different set of interests. The Committee rejected the nationalization of all land as politically unacceptable, but suggested that development rights on urban-fringe land should in effect be nationalized and that they should be purchased by a state agency when required. The Town and Country Planning Act of 1947 accepted this solution in principle, creating a Central Land Board to assemble development land, but it extended the nationalization of development rights to all land. In the event these provisions proved to be a dead letter. The Central Land Board was abolished in 1953 and a similar fate befell the Land Commission which briefly performed a similar task between 1967 and 1970. In 1976 the Community Land Act introduced a municipally run system, but local authorities were starved of the cash to intervene in the market. The system of compensation awarded for compulsory purchase and similar statutory changes in land use has not, however, met with quite the same vicissitudes. In normal circumstances compensation consists of the market value of the land, decided, where appropriate, by reference to alternative possibilities of development. Only in the case of development under the New Towns Act of 1946 or the Town Development Act of 1952 (i.e. overspill agreements) where a public agency is involved, is land purchased at existing use (agricultural) value. Whatever the intentions of the 1947 Act betterment has remained largely in the hands of the private property owner, while compensation has also favoured the private interest (notional development value) rather than the public interest (existing use value).

With this highly significant exception the 1947 Town and Country Planning Act remains the centrepiece of the legislation which fashions the kind of rural England which is familiar to us today. Although amended and extended, particularly in 1968, and consolidated in 1971, the basic planning system formulated by the 1947 Act remains intact. Under this legislation development control has been linked to the construction of local plans, which in rural areas have sought to limit the spread of urban growth into the countryside by designating 'white land' where agriculture should remain undisturbed. Whatever the fears of farmers or conservationists this policy has been successful, for, as was noted at the beginning of Chapter 2, the rate of loss of agricultural land has been only half the pre-war level. The 1947 Act also sought to control the encroachment of urbanism in other ways – for example, by controlling the proliferation of outdoor advertising in rural areas or by granting only short-term planning permission for caravan sites. Since, however, it was assumed that the conservation of the countryside could safely be left in the hands of those *in situ*, and there was no wish to pick a fight with either the NFU or the CLA, from the outset 'the use of any land for the purposes of agriculture or forestry' was excluded from the provisions of the Act. With the exception of very large or very tall buildings, beyond the requirements of any normal farm at that time, farmers were granted a freedom from planning restrictions enjoyed by no other industrial activity. This doctrine of agricultural exceptionalism remains in force today, although the widespread criticism of recent landscape changes and the insensitive design of many modern farm buildings have recently brought this principle under increasing challenge.

The steps taken to protect the countryside under the 1947 Act were reinforced by accompanying legislation in the immediate post-war period. The most important was the National Parks and Access to the Countryside Act of 1949, which was concerned with the establishment of a system of National Parks, modelled closely on the American experience following the designation of Yellowstone Park in 1872. Their introduction to England and Wales followed the production of the Dower Report in 1945 and the Hobhouse Report in 1947. Dower initially defined a National Park as:

. . . an extensive area of beautiful and relatively wild country in which, for the nation's benefit and by appropriate national decisions and action,
(a) the characteristic landscape beauty is strictly preserved,
(b) access and facilities for public open-air enjoyment are amply provided,
(c) wildlife and buildings and places of architectural and historic interest are suitably protected, while
(d) established farming use is effectively maintained.

These objectives remain, but the task of achieving all of them simultaneously has proved to be extremely difficult. Since 1949 ten National Parks in England and Wales have been designated: Northumberland, Lake District, Yorkshire Dales, North York Moors, Peak District, Snowdonia, Pembrokeshire Coast, Brecon Beacons, Exmoor and Dartmoor. They constitute only 9 per cent of the land surface, but include the major areas of upland landscape beauty, which their designation has helped to preserve. Dower also recommended the designation of the Norfolk Broads, a proposal which has recently been revived, while a recent suggestion for a Cambrian National Park in mid-Wales was abandoned after opposition from local farming interests. In accordance with the intention that the landscape should be 'strictly preserved', development control in the National Parks has been particularly draconian, although the implementation of planning policies has been somewhat haphazard. Until local government reorganization in 1973, for example, only the Peak District and the Lake District possessed their own planning boards, while the remainder were under the control of somewhat loose and ineffective planning committees or joint advisory committees of their constituent county councils. An advisory National Parks Commission overlorded the system. Since 1974, however, each park has been run by a single authority with a specialist officer. The National Parks Commission was renamed the Countryside Commission in 1968 and given general responsibilities for conservation and recreation in the countryside. It operates, perhaps appropriately, from a converted police station in Cheltenham.

Until recently the major threat to the 'strictly preserved' landscape of the National Parks came from proposed development, especially mineral workings and road construction. There have been a number of 'test cases' – limestone quarrying in the Peak District, copper mining in Snowdonia, potash mining in the North York Moors, the A66 improvement in the Lake District, the Sheffield–Manchester motorway in the Peak District – which have gained national notoriety but have as yet failed to establish any case law which would serve as a precedent for future proposals. These, however, have been external threats of the kind which prompted the designation of the National Parks in the first place. As far as indigenous conflicts are concerned, the original Act foresaw only two and these were dealt with in the remainder of its provisions. The first concerned public rights of way.

In rural areas county councils were required to publish footpath maps which might eventually provide a definitive guide to public rights of access. In addition the Act enabled long-distance routes to be painstakingly assembled by linking together existing footpaths and, where necessary, negotiating new sections. Not surprisingly, progress was slow, but a number are now open including the Pennine Way, the Ridgeway Path, Offa's Dyke, the South-West Peninsula Coast Path and long-distance paths on the North and South Downs. These have proved to be extremely popular, even to the point of creating their own management problems at certain easily accessible spots, but have probably contributed to a diminution in disturbance to the surrounding farming areas.

The second problem which the 1949 Act attempted to resolve concerned the preservation of wildlife which the encouragement of 'public open-air enjoyment' might otherwise jeopardize. Part III of the Act made provision for National Nature Reserves under the control of the Nature Conservancy, a research and advisory body created by royal charter in 1949. By 1973 there were sixty-five National Nature Reserves in England (134 in Britain as a whole), owned or leased by the Nature Conservancy or run under a Nature Reserve Agreement with the local landowner. The aim has been to preserve a cross-section of the most interesting ecological communities or geological sections and to protect areas with particularly rich habitats or rare species of plants and animals. Except in a few cases public access is not encouraged and may even be prohibited altogether on particularly vulnerable sites. The 1949 Act also gave the Nature Conservancy a duty to notify planning authorities of land which was ecologically of 'special interest'. There are now over 3000 of these Sites of Special Scientific Interest in Britain, where before development can take place the planning authority must inform the Conservancy so that its views can be taken into account when deciding on whether to grant planning permission. In 1973 the Nature Conservancy was abolished and replaced by the Nature Conservancy Council, an independent statutory body responsible for reserve management and conservation advice. It also took on the role of general ecological 'watchdog' and disseminator of information on nature conservation. Its former research stations were, however, retained in the Natural Environment Research Council and are now known collectively as the Institute for Terrestrial Ecology.

Apart from some provisions for tree planting and eyesore removal these were the major positive proposals of the 1949 Act. But the main aim of the Act was a negative one: to preserve those rural landscapes considered to be of irrefutable national importance from the prospect of development. The approach was defensive and protective. This philosophy was also applied to other beautiful stretches of countryside which could not be absorbed in National Parks. The Act designated these as Areas of Outstanding Natural Beauty (AONBs) where public recreation was not encouraged and where the emphasis was on landscape conservation; development was therefore strictly controlled. Designation has been frankly based upon aesthetic criteria and the AONBs include some of England's best-loved countryside – the Cotswolds, Dedham Vale, the Downs, the Quantock and Mendip Hills, the Lincolnshire Wolds and so on. They form the 'second division' of protected rural landscapes and are followed by Areas of Great Landscape Value which are of local importance and are controlled under the Town and Country Planning Act.

The 1947 Act also places an embargo on development in Green Belts which, as we have seen, are concerned with urban containment rather than landscape value. Green Belts now cover 5800 square miles of England and Wales, some of it scenically undistinguished. The purpose of designating Green Belts has therefore not been the same as that of National Parks and AONBs, although somewhat similar planning controls apply. Many Green Belt areas have no particular landscape value at all: their purpose is also to preserve the character of *urban* areas by limiting the growth of suburbs. For this reason the designation of Green Belts has often been associated with the provision of New Towns in the countryside beyond them where a proportion of erstwhile suburbanites are directed by a policy of planned urban dispersal. This, however, has enabled development to leapfrog the (often sterile) rural area on the immediate urban fringe and pushed urban growth even further out into the countryside than might otherwise have occurred. This is particularly apparent, for example, in the 'metropolitan fringe' beyond the London Green Belt in Hertfordshire. Nevertheless traditional groups in the counties concerned have grudgingly accepted the New Towns as a preferable alternative to *ad hoc* and unplanned urbanization elsewhere, enabling rural areas 'worth saving' to be equipped with even more braconian development restrictions. Admittedly this blanket refusal to contemplate any development in selected rural areas has been increasingly questioned in recent years, but it is an approach which continues to be employed in 'unspoilt' country-side considered to be particularly at risk. Thus in 1970 the Country-side Commission suggested that thirty-four of the most beautiful stretches of coastline in England and Wales should be designated Heritage Coasts in order to save them from development.

In theory the system of town and country planning created by the legislation of the immediate post-war period involved a radical reform of the *laissez-faire* approach to land use which had brought unwanted and sometimes unintended changes in the countryside. The underlying political aims were liberal and progressive, a Fabian desire to eradicate the worst irrationalities and social injustices of industrial and residential development that had been mostly derived from the unrestricted application of market forces. The practical results have, however, been very different. By the late 1960s 'the planners' were a byword for remote bureaucracy and heartless inhumanity, and although these feelings were more often prompted by the consequence of urban redevelopment programmes, they were echoed in rural areas over sensitive issues like reservoirs, motorways and 'key village' policies. Planners have, of course, often represented convenient scapegoats who could be blamed for problems beyond their control and if the ideals of the original architects of the British planning system have not always been fulfilled, then the fault has sometimes lain elsewhere, in the deliberate distortion of the early aims by subsequent politicians and in economic and social changes that no one could have anticipated. Each of these factors must be taken into account in attempting to explain one of the central para-doxes of rural planning since the late 1940s: the fact that the idealized blueprint contained a strong element of planning for the least for-tunate whereas in practice it seems almost systematically to have had the reverse effect. So far it has been the most privileged members of English rural society who have benefited most from the operation of the planning system in rural areas, while the poor and the deprived have gained comparatively little. Rural planners themselves are by no means wholly responsible for this state of affairs, but equally they have been slow to recognize the social consequences of their policies or to cast them within a philosophy of distributive justice.

The reasons for this state of affairs are by now deeply institution-alized within the planning profession. For example, physical planning has been institutionally separated from regional economic planning on the one hand and various forms of social planning on the other. In rural areas, a particular point of weakness has been the lack of liaison with the policy-making of the Ministry of Agriculture, so that quite frequently agricultural policies and rural planning policies have been tugging in entirely opposite directions (for example, over the preservation of the rural landscape). Even at its best this piece-meal planning has hindered the development of a corporate approach to rural issues in which the interrelationship between various and often conflicting problems could be assessed. This fragmentation occurs not only at the national level – where, for example, proposals on capital taxation emanating from the Treasury seem to take little account of their effects on either agricultural or environmental policies – but also locally and *between* central and local government agencies. In the last few years this problem has been recognized, leading to demands for a new Royal Commission on the countryside, but all that has so far emerged is a Civil Service committee, the Countryside Review Committee, with all the attendant problems of interdepartmental intrigues and a partiality for compromise.

Not only has the organization of planning served to hinder the achievements of the system, but the values of the planning profession have tended to define the stated objectives in narrowly technocratic terms. In their drive to obtain professional status planners have preferred to avoid the inevitably contentious debate about the ultimate ends of planning (considered 'political' and therefore 'unprofessional') and have concentrated instead upon refining their expertise in particular planning techniques. Because planning was originally defined in terms of land use these techniques initially involved little more than the production of ever more sophisticated maps. The means then became the ends. There were few explicit attempts to relate such physically defined policy objectives – zoning, design and so forth – to the *social* needs or demands of the population except by default. It was in this way that planning policies often worked in a manner which was counter to many of the social policy objectives which were supposed to be their ultimate ends, a point which was not lost on a succession of academic observers during the 1960s. Planners were depicted as 'evangelistic bureaucrats' with no creed other than a vague architectural or environmental determinism (a view to which some sociologists, flattered to be asked, occasionally pandered). As far as rural planning was concerned this environmental determinism translated into the preservation of the countryside and the provision of basic public services. By such means, it was believed, the 'traditional rural way of life' could be retained, but there was no attempt to monitor how these policies might affect the distribution of resources and opportunities *within* the rural population because planners were neither trained nor particularly inclined to investigate such matters. In rural areas at least the accusation that planning was no longer 'for people', a frequent refrain of the 1960s, was wide of the mark; instead the fateful fallacy involved the belief that the 'traditional rural way of life' was beneficial to all rural inhabitants. This influential but unexamined assumption was a product of an unholy alliance between the farmers and landowners who politically controlled rural England and the radical middle-class reformers who formulated the post-war legislation. The former group had a vested interest in preserving the *status quo*, while the latter, epitomized by the nature-loving Hampstead Fabian who enjoyed country rambling at the weekends, possessed a hopelessly sentimental vision of rural life. The rural poor had little to gain from the preservation of their poverty, but they were without a voice on the crucial committees which evolved the planning system from the late 1930s onwards. Consequently the 1947 Act framed the objectives of rural planning in terms of the protection of an inherently changeless countryside and a consensual 'rural way of life' which overlooked important social differences within the rural population.

Since 1947 the limited value of this approach has become increasingly apparent. The philosophy of urban containment may have been a success, and we may in consequence have an arguably more beautiful and more extensive countryside, but the problems of rural planning can scarcely be claimed to have subsided as a result. This is because current problems which afflict the countryside cannot be reduced to the formula of 'urban *versus* rural' very readily or very meaningfully. The mere fact that such a large proportion of the rural population now works in towns is illustrative of this, but many of the social changes which have affected the everyday life of the countryside cannot easily be fitted into a rural–urban dichotomy. Important developments like the spread of education, the rise of the welfare state, the influence of the mass media and even the increasing rationalization of agriculture itself reflect not so much the influence of urban or rural ways of life, but of the *national* upon the *local*. They represent the diminution of local differences in the face of nationally inspired changes. Those recommendations of the Barlow Commission which led directly to the Distribution of Industry Act seemed to have recognized this within the context of regional economic planning, but the framework of physical planning policy remained couched in terms of rural–urban antagonism. This ideology accounts for many of the details of the rural planning system – the almost total exemption of agriculture, the formal prescription against the development of agricultural land, the residual nature of much countryside planning, and so on – but it also accounts for how this system has been overtaken by changes with which it was ill-equipped to cope, such as those involving agriculture and landscape change.

By the late 1960s many rural planners were becoming increasingly aware of these weaknesses. One leading County Planning Officer, Ray Green, in his book *Country Planning*, even went so far as to argue that 'the . . . years since the Town and Country Planning Act of 1947 represent two decades of wasted opportunity for *positive* rural planning'. Some attempt was made to remedy this situation in the Town and Country Planning Act of 1968. This Act introduced a system of structure plans – strategic plans covering not only land use but population, employment, transport and housing – which marked a distinct change in emphasis from the old approach. In rural areas, the structure plans were to aim at implementing positive resource development rather than to reflect the former predominantly negative planning policies. There was also less emphasis on the production of maps and a move towards surveys of relevant social and economic inputs (until curtailed by public expenditure cuts in 1974). This symbolized a movement away from the former concentration upon the purely physical aspects of planning policy towards a more sociological approach. The structure plan system also offered a means of transcending the divide between urban and rural areas, although this did not become a real possibility until after the reorganization of local government in 1973–4. Progress has, however, been slow and the potential for changing the approach to rural planning, which the Act envisaged, has not always been fulfilled. No doubt the inertia created by planning offices steeped in older traditions has played its part, but a more worrying aspect has concerned the gap between the evidence uncovered by the surveys and the actual policies which have eventually emerged. In 1976, for example, the Countryside Commission was moved to comment in its *Annual Report*, that 'the content of structure plans in general does not convince us that the potential of the new development plans system for tackling rural problems has been realised'. The reasons for this have lain not so much in the outlook of rural planners but in the balance of political forces which underlie the planning process in the counties.

The precise nature of this political balance has obviously varied from place to place, as well as over time, but in general political power in rural areas has remained firmly in the hands of the most prosperous residents. In a few counties this has involved the continuation of the old squirearchal rule of farmers and landowners, although, as was indicated in the previous chapter, their omnipotence has been declining. Elsewhere they have been displaced in local government by professional and managerial newcomers, but on the issue of strategic planning policy this has made little or no difference to the ensuing decisions. Both groups are profoundly preservationist in their sentiments and have maintained a strong accord over the desire to exclude as far as possible virtually any significant industrial or residential development from the countryside, whether for agricultural or environmental reasons. This policy has therefore triumphed, despite the changes which have occurred in the personnel of county council planning committees. It is not therefore coincidental that many of the set-piece rural planning conflicts have concerned the impact of nationally taken decisions, usually under the auspices of central government, upon particular rural localities, for this is often the only occasion on which the routine of rural strategic planning is placed under direct pressure. On other occasions the alliance of traditional gentleman farmers and landowners and the more affluent newcomers on many county councils continues the everyday routine of directing development proposals away from the countryside, and even applies its veto to applications for agricultural housing passed by the smaller farmers on the district councils. The regressive effect on rural housing of this preservationist policy was outlined in the previous chapter, but the consequences of preserving the rural *status quo* go beyond the question of housing provision. They also affect the employment opportunities in rural areas and therefore the entire standard of living of the rural working population.

Since 1947 the presumption that the countryside should be preserved, almost exclusively, for agriculture has ensured that the major source of employment in rural areas should be the farming industry. Yet the number of employment opportunities in agriculture has, as we have seen, declined rapidly since the war. By directing new industrial development away from rural areas, conventional strategic planning policy has had two important consequences: it has restricted the rate of economic growth in the countryside; and it has weakened the bargaining power of existing rural workers by reducing the number of competitors for local labour. Strategic planning has therefore contained a strong element of planning for the interests of the better-off. Rural employers have clearly gained from the preservation of a low-wage rural economy – indeed, in some areas it has been given indirect encouragement. Even the ex-urban newcomers have gained from being able to call upon a pool of local cheap labour to perform the standard middle-class range of domestic services. On the other hand farm workers, for example, have been trapped in a low-paying industry with declining employment opportunities and often in tied housing, too. Denied alternative employment in their own locality they have been forced to move to the towns in order to benefit from a higher standard of living, while those who remain exist on depressed wage levels. As in the case of housing, a policy of preserving the rural *status quo* has thus turned out to be *redistributive* – and in a highly regressive manner. Occasionally rural planners have become aware of these tendencies, but the political will has been lacking to bring about a change of policy. For example, in 1975 the report of the East Anglian Regional Strategy Planning Team placed considerable emphasis on the need to attract more industry into the area so that local wage levels could be raised: 'Away from the major centres, poor job prospects cause considerable local concern. Opportunities are limited to agricultural employment and incomes tend to be low. . . . There should be opportunities for individuals to increase their incomes and widen their interests through a better choice of jobs and training opportunities.' Not surprisingly the report met with considerable opposition from the region's county councils and was later quietly shelved by the Department of the Environment, which had publicly disagreed with many of its conclusions.

In the absence of any spontaneous move on the part of many rural authorities to attract industry into rural areas the remaining agency specifically devoted to this task is the Council for Small Industries in Rural Areas (CoSIRA). The work of CoSIRA dates back beyond the establishment of the current planning system in 1947, having been formed out of the Rural Industries' Bureau (founded in 1921) and a number of other organizations to stimulate employment in rural areas. It acts as an agent for the Development Commission, a body established in 1910 to promote the rural economy, sponsoring employers of not more than twenty skilled workers who want to expand or set up in a rural area where the local population does not exceed 10000. For many years CoSIRA was a half-forgotten backwater of the Civil Service, considered by many to be an agreeable and well-meaning joke. It had a reputation for supporting quaint rustic crafts which, while suitably picturesque, were hardly a dynamic force in transforming rural employment opportunities. Basket-weavers and blacksmiths might apply, but an engineering factory could be frowned upon. In 1974, however, a determined attempt was made to revitalize CoSIRA: its budget was increased and its work has expanded considerably. It has also striven to change its image, placing more emphasis on technologically advanced industries like plastics and electronics, becoming involved in technical training and constructing advance factories in depressed rural areas. Predictably, this more active role has brought CoSIRA into conflict with village preservation societies and other environmental groups suspicious of CoSIRA's plans to build new workshops and warehouses in hitherto wholly agricultural areas. Even in its new progressive guise, however, the activities of CoSIRA are insufficient on their own to overcome the inertia introduced by the anti-development assumptions of most rural planning policies.

The powerful alliance between agricultural and environmental interests therefore remains largely undisturbed over strategic planning issues. It is only at the more local level that this agreement dissolves in the disputes over modern farming practice and environmental conservation. Planners are, of course, largely powerless to intervene in this conflict because agriculture has been virtually exempt from planning restrictions and because the planning system is concerned with the *use* of land rather than how it is *managed*. Since 1968 the Countryside Commission has grappled with this problem, but it has few powers at its disposal to affect the situation and those which it does possess it has been reluctant to use in order to avoid risking the goodwill of the farming organizations. In any case these powers can only be applied in National Parks or Areas of Outstanding Natural Beauty. Here the local planning authority may invoke an 'Article Four Direction' in order to preserve the rural landscape from certain agriculturally induced changes. But these powers have been used very sparingly indeed and in one AONB – Dedham Vale – a voluntary liaison system involving planners' and farmers' representatives has been adopted as an alternative to outright compulsion. In practice Article Four Directions are only possible where the form of landscape changes takes some time to achieve, as in the erection of new farm buildings. In the day-to-day operations of modern farming, however, where the crucial decisions which affect the rural landscape are being made, a formal system of regulation is too slow and too unwieldy to have much influence. Consequently the Countryside Commission has recognized that it would not be feasible, either economically or politically, to operate through formal regulation. Instead it has preferred persuasion, in the form of 'landscape agreements' reached voluntarily with farmers in order to afford some protection to particularly valuable environmental features. These measures have, however, met with only very limited success in the face of the massive economic pressures on farmers to adopt new techniques which necessitate landscape change.

It is not surprising, therefore, that environmentalists have recently become extremely restless over the apparent inability of the rural planning authorities to obtain some control over the activities of farmers, especially in the National Parks and AONBs. In 1974 the Report of the National Parks Policies Review Committee, the Sandford Report, investigated this problem and made a number of recommendations which emphasized the need for positive management rather than the use of yet more negative restrictions. These included new powers for park authorities to acquire land for the purposes of preserving or enhancing the landscape and reimbursement for farmers who suffered lost revenue by agreeing to manage their land in a manner which preserved the traditional landscape. However, the Sandford Report provided no real answer to the growing conflict between agriculture and amenity in areas of high aesthetic value. Although the dilemma was clearly recognized, signalling the end of the customary belief that the countryside could safely be left in the hands of farmers, the Committee seemed uncertain over how to proceed. There remained a reluctance to bring agriculture within the ambit of development control planning – a significant political victory for the NFU and the CLA. Instead the Committee decided to rely upon the traditional values of stewardship associated with the ownership of land by extending the policy of voluntary co-operation with farmers and landowners. As we have seen in Chapter 3, *some* farmers are undoubtedly receptive to this approach, but equally there are many, particularly those in the vanguard of modern agriculture, who are not. It could only be a question of time before this conflict would reassert itself, given the general economic tendencies of farming today, and this duly occurred during 1976 in a bitter and prolonged dispute over the conversion of moorland in Exmoor. Both sides of this dispute, farmers and environmentalists, have recognized its national significance, for on its outcome will hinge the future balance between the needs of agricultural efficiency and environmental conservation in all of our National Parks. This has undoubtedly involved a certain amount of kite-flying by the environmental lobby in order to discover the political feasibility of bringing the hitherto unrestricted activities of farming under the control of the planning process.

In this respect the problem is not one that is peculiar to Exmoor. However, Exmoor has long been regarded as one of the most exquisite examples of English landscape beauty and it has a vociferous and well-connected preservationist pressure group, the Exmoor Society, prepared to defend the areas of moorland to which Exmoor owes much of its scenic reputation. For many years the Exmoor Society had expressed concern at the disappearance of moorland under the plough – an estimated 9500 acres, out of 59000 acres, were lost in this manner between 1947 and 1976. In 1968 the National Park Authorities in Exmoor designated 41000 acres of moorland as a Critical Amenity Area and reached a 'gentleman's agreement' with the NFU and CLA whereby farmers in the Area would voluntarily give six months' notice to the Park Authorities of intention to plough. In return the Park Authorities agreed to desist from invoking a 'Section 14 order' under the 1968 Countryside Act which would make such notification compulsory. The Park Authorities hoped in this way to persuade farmers to enter into management agreements which would conserve the moorland. Between 1968 and the summer of 1977, however, a further 1000–1500 acres of moorland were ploughed up, including 650 acres within the Critical Amenity Area between 1972 and 1977. Ironically, much of this conversion would have been impossible without grant aid from the Ministry of Agriculture (local hill farmers receive around 56 per cent of their income from grants and subsidies) which can pay up to 70 per cent of the cost. During 1976 the Exmoor Society became increasingly angry at the continuing loss of moorland and allegations began to fly around in the local and national press that the Exmoor National Park Committee (constituted in 1974 as a committee of Somerset County Council) was 'soft on farmers' or had even been infiltrated by agricultural interests. The Countryside Commission, in its role of National Parks overlord, also became concerned. It regarded the case of Exmoor as an opportunity to push for further powers over the compulsory purchase of land in the National Parks, and against the opposition of the NFU and CLA proposed that a material change of use of defined areas of open country should be regarded as 'development' under the Town and Country Planning Act, thus requiring planning permission. This would involve a new principle in planning legislation – that a change from one kind of farming practice to another would amount to a 'material change of use', something which would have very wide implications indeed for the future relationship between farmers and planners in the countryside.

It is only possible to imagine the infighting which then ensued between the Department of the Environment and the Ministry of Agriculture, who were, in effect, the governmental sponsors of the two sides of the dispute. In April 1977 they invited Lord Porchester, a landowner and chairman of Hampshire County Council, to conduct a study of Exmoor, to 'consider what courses of action . . . are open to relevant public authorities in order to ensure that a proper balance is struck between the various national and local interests involved' and to 'advise the Ministers, the Countryside Commission and the National Park Committee in the exercise of their functions'. The Porchester Report was published in the following November. Lord Porchester confessed to 'having grave doubts' about the efficacy of the management agreements advocated by the National Park Committee. 'Their track record', he wrote, 'is against them.' Although such agreements had been a recommended tool of moorland conservation, Lord Porchester found that there were none in operation on Exmoor and that attempts to obtain agreements had 'all foundered, sometimes amid a flurry of publicity'. However, he also found the Countryside Commission's proposals too cumbersome in practice to form an acceptable means of exercising control. He recommended instead that a new survey should be carried out, aimed at tightening up the existing Critical Amenity Area Map, so that within this area a 'final commitment' could be made to conservation 'and accordingly a presumption against agricultural reclamation'. This would secure for all time those areas of Exmoor of exceptional landscape value. It was also recommended that the Ministry of Agriculture should recognize and support this policy by feeling obliged to withhold improvement grants within these areas.

The Porchester Report refused to make any general observations on the use of planning controls in the National Parks (an inevitable outcome of the narrow terms of reference of the investigation), proposing only that new powers be given to make Moorland Conservation Orders which would restrict farming activities in return for a capital payment of fair compensation to the farmers affected. Whether this ostensibly minor break in the principle of agricultural *laissez-faire* is used as a precedent in order to preserve the rural landscape elsewhere from the depredations of modern agriculture remains to be seen (at the time of going to press the government was still considering the Porchester proposals), but a clear national policy on such matters cannot be postponed indefinitely. By the end of 1977, for example, a similar dispute was already brewing in another part of Somerset, outside the National Park, where the unique landscape of the Somerset Levels was being threatened by the drainage of the low-lying fields – again with the encouragement of the Ministry of Agriculture. Indeed the problems highlighted by the conflict in Exmoor will no doubt be repeated up and down the country in the years to come unless some new planning policy initiative is taken.

Exmoor is therefore simply the place where the environmental lobby, aided by the Countryside Commission, has chosen to make a stand on this issue. Apart from the intrinsic landscape qualities which make Exmoor worth preserving, the dispute has symbolized the way in which the mantle of stewardship, so long claimed by the private landowner, has passed, in the minds of many environmentalists, to the planning profession. As a landowner himself, Lord Porchester was clearly aware of the way in which the philosophy of stewardship had rebounded on the farmers of Exmoor to their considerable embarrassment. His report is full of reminders of how the beauty of Exmoor cannot be maintained without the contribution of local farmers. Nevertheless the local environmentalists have become thoroughly unconvinced that a sense of stewardship overrides the opportunity to increase profits when the two are in conflict. It is significant that the environmental lobby is increasingly looking to planners to intervene. In this context, at least they are regarded as the final court of appeal on the preservation of the national heritage (having long been castigated as arch-villains). Fortunately this is a responsibility which the planners involved in the preservation of the English countryside have been willing to accept. As Hall *et al.* have pointed out:

Stewardship of the land, in its modern form as a basic value of those involved in planning and the planning movement, is a concern for the proper care and use of all the land in the country, urban or rural. Obviously an extension of traditional aristocratic values in society, it provides the ideology behind the power and responsibility of the contemporary land-use planners. . . .

The civil servants in national and local government who together apply the value of stewardship of the land on a national scale in Britain, see themselves for the most part as bearing a heavy social responsibility. It is true that they often feel that they do not have sufficient authority to properly exercise this responsibility. But . . . their attitude is paternalistic and often conservative with regard to the care of their charge . . . .

There are, however, two important distinctions between the stewardship operated by planners and that of the private landowner. The first concerns the rights attaching to property ownership – control, benefit and alienation. The private landowner retains all of these, even though the ideology of stewardship admits a hypothetical 'national interest' in them. The planner, on the other hand, retains only the right of control (and this may be inadequate), for given the non-implementation of the Uthwatt proposals the benefits of property ownership have been allowed to remain largely in private hands. Moreover planners have intervened only indirectly, and then with inflationary effect, in the property market so that the buying and selling of land has remained undisturbed. Although both planners and private landowners appeal to an apparently impartial and similar ideology of stewardship, therefore, any increase in the activities of planners cannot help but be a threat to the remaining property rights of the private landowner and this is a fundamental issue which underlies the dispute in Exmoor and will no doubt influence the subsequent political deliberations.

The second important difference concerns the fact that planners are agents of local and central government and therefore, nominally at least, subject to democratic control. Although the notion of stewardship is inherently paternalistic, the logic of the argument that in a democratic society those who are subject to the planning process should have some say in the formulation of the plans which will affect them has been hard to refute. For this reason public partici-pation in planning was encouraged by the 1968 Act, although the Act was equivocally vague about what form this participation might take or how this broad principle was to be applied. A major problem concerns precisely what constitutes the relevant constituency which should be granted the right to participate. Most rural planning remains under the control of county and district councils, who are responsible to their existing electorates and not to any which lie beyond their geographical boundaries. Unfortunately, however, decisions taken over rural planning matters often have repercussions elsewhere. For example, the policy of strict development control in rural areas has had an effect on the space available for *urban* house-holds by restricting the spread of urban areas and raising the cost of land for housebuilding – compare the size of building plots in 1930s suburbia with suburban housing estates built in the 1970s. But the urban population which is affected in this way is not consul-ted over rural planning policies. Moreover, three decades of rural planning have, as we have seen, contributed to the *social* segregation of rural from urban areas. They have reinforced, or at least failed to prevent, the tendency for rural England to become middle- and upper-class England. These planning policies may have been socially regressive, but given the current rural constituency which they have helped to create, they are likely to receive continuing local political support. It is naive to suppose that an increasingly middle-class rural electorate will altruistically vote away its advantages, any more than any other section of the population would be likely to do so. Furthermore, the particular form which public participation has taken – the active intervention of articulate and well-organized environmental pressure groups – has only served, albeit unwittingly, to increase the opportunities presented to prosperous rural inhabitants to protect their local vested interests. By no means all environmental groups are of this kind, but there is little evidence to show that increased public participation has redressed the balance of inequity which the rural planning system has so far engendered.

The environmental lobby

The proliferation of environmental organizations has been one of the most significant aspects of what might be called (following David Donnison) 'the micro-politics of the countryside' during the last decade. A number of factors have contributed to this, many of which have already been touched upon, including the accelerating pace of agricultural change, the growing public awareness of environmental problems, the changing composition of the rural population and the increasing use of the countryside as a source of leisure and recreation. There has emerged a large and amorphous environmental lobby (although the phrase itself implies a coherence which is often entirely absent in reality) which has helped to establish a frame of reference for public debate over environmental matters that has had undoubted influence upon official attitudes and policies. In part the growth of this lobby has represented a spontaneous grass-roots movement, with amenity societies and other environmental groups being formed locally to pursue some particular interest and only later joining one of the nationally based 'umbrella' associations, which could put them in touch with other like-minded groups. One of these, the Civic Trust – which embraces both urban and rural amenity societies – saw an increase in the number of its affiliates from 300 in 1960 to 1250 in 1975. Elsewhere, however, the growth of environmentalism has been expressed in the transformation of older established, national environmental organizations whose membership has recently increased in leaps and bounds. For example, the membership of the Conservation Society increased from 1150 in 1969 to 8000 in 1974; the National Trust, which had 10000 members in 1945, had 200000 in 1972, 400000 in 1974 and 600000 by 1978; and the Royal Society for the Protection of Birds increased its membership from 6803 in 1952 to 241019 in 1977. Philip Lowe, who has carried out one of the few systematic investigations of this phenomenon, has accepted an estimated gross membership of environmental pressure groups of nearly two million, although this does not take account of extensive multiple memberships by particularly committed individuals. By any reckoning, however, this is an impressive achievement, the flavour of which can be captured from an editorial in the R S P B's journal *Birds* in the summer of 1977:

Twenty-five years ago . . . it was considered unusual to be a birdwatcher. Conservation was a word rarely uttered. There were more important tasks in a country still lurching forward after war. Birdwatching was a harmless eccentricity indulged in by doctors, clerics, retired service officers, teachers and the like. Most people had neither the time nor the mobility to show much interest. Most still worked a five-and-a-half-day week; car-owning families were in the minority; many had only a fortnight's holiday a year and most were too busy adjusting to the world after the war to concern themselves with conservation.

But now look! . . . The annual report for 1952 proudly announced a record annual recruitment of 342 new members, the number we now recruit in a couple of days!

No doubt many of the other environmental groups concerned with nature conservation, the preservation of the countryside, the promotion of rural leisure activities and the prevention of pollution and dereliction could offer similar accounts of their success.

It would be mistaken, however, to suppose that this loosely knit environmental lobby relies upon its sheer weight of numbers in order to press its case effectively, for of greater importance has been the degree of active involvement of the members, the skills and resources at their disposal and, above all, the quality of the groups' organization and leadership. The arguments put forward by organizations like the CPRE, the National Trust and the Ramblers' Association have never been based upon a purely popular appeal and their effectiveness has depended less upon the size of their respective membership than an ability to obtain access to crucial areas of decision-making in local and national government. This has not only placed a premium upon tactical political skill but also upon the technical expertise which some environmental organizations have to offer to decision-makers at both the national and local level. Such expertise can easily become valued and sought after by the government, by local authorities and by various statutory bodies which have responsibility for environmental matters, allowing relationships with the relevant environmental organizations to become consultative rather than antagonistic. For example, local amenity societies and some national organizations like the CPRE may now be consulted over planning decisions which affect their interests. Nevertheless, a sizeable membership is often required in order to provide the income necessary to maintain the required level of organizational effectiveness, and a large and active membership is also essential in order to retain political legitimacy – that is, to establish a right to consultation and avoid the accusation of being unrepresentative of anyone other than a handful of vociferous individuals with a supply of impressively headed notepaper.

In recent years the growth of the environmental lobby has been encouraged by the government, which sees in the proliferation of organized environmental groups a convenient expression of public opinion to which it can relate in the formulation and implementation of its policies. For example, the Skeffington Committee on public participation in planning, which reported in 1969, placed particular emphasis on the role of local voluntary associations in the planning process. It suggested that these groups should be represented on advisory committees which could convey their views to local planners, and that planning authorities should make greater efforts to consult local opinion before their plans were finalized. More recently, in circular 46/73 the Department of the Environment has advised local authorities that:

Voluntary bodies, national and local, can play an important role in conservation and indeed in the planning process generally. . . . It is hoped that this circular will encourage still further co-operation between local authorities and voluntary bodies. In particular, it is hoped that this will enable voluntary bodies to play a constructive role whether by helping the local authorities to work out and implement positive conservation policies or by initiating schemes for conservation and improvement. Ways in which voluntary effort can be harnessed to improve the appearance of towns and villages . . . are set out in the Civic Trust's recent publication, *Pride of Place*, and no doubt all local authorities will wish to arrange action on these lines in their own areas.

This kind of involvement on the part of environmental organizations has undoubtedly strengthened their position, as well as stimulated the formation of still more local environmental groups in order to take advantage of the new climate of participation in planning. Participation and organization have therefore gone hand in hand, each contributing to the effectiveness of the other.

The huge increase in the number of environmental groups has made the environmental lobby a political force to be reckoned with in the countryside. However, its impact remains diffuse and unevenly spread, not only because at the local level the number of active participants can be quite small and their consequent effectiveness dependent upon idiosyncrasies of energy and political skill, but because there remains a problem of coordination between the various arms and the many levels of the environmental movement. This is why the term 'environmental lobby' can convey a quite spurious uniformity, for the amount of formal coordination between environmental groups has been limited. The Council for Nature orchestrates nature conservation interests and some national organizations, like the Civic Trust, the National Trust and the CPRE, achieve a modicum of coordination among the plethora of national and local societies by being themselves federal or partly federal bodies. Nationally there are also a number of joint committees or standing committees on environmental matters which periodically bring together organizations with an interest in particular issues like the National Parks or countryside access. But the widespread mobilization of environmental interests continues to take place on a largely *ad hoc* basis and usually only in response to specific and urgent issues as and when they occur. It was the recognition of this weakness which provoked the Nature Conservancy and the Council for Nature to organize a series of conferences on the theme 'The Countryside in 1970' in 1963, 1965 and 1970. The aim was to bring together all the major organizations with an interest in the use of the countryside and it led to the first attempt formally to coordinate the whole of the environmental lobby in the Committee for Environmental Conservation (CoEnCo) in 1970. Its role has, however, been limited mainly to the exchange of information and the initiative still lies with the multitude of local and national associations.

This relative lack of formal coordination has forced much of the necessary mobilization of the environmental lobby to take place informally along a 'grapevine' of actively involved individuals. A number of key people are able, by their multiple and interlocking membership of different environmental groups, to activate the resources of a whole range of organizations. Appearances can therefore be misleading. As Philip Lowe has pointed out:

... when we hear that the National Trust, CPRE, Commons Preservation Society and Ramblers' Association have each decided to oppose, say, a proposed road development, we must be aware of what this may mean in terms of the number of individuals involved in each of these decisions. For, though environmental groups may be able to claim, quite rightly, to represent over a million people, the numbers actively and effectively involved at the national level in policy and decision making are minuscule, perhaps less than a hundred, in total, for the established groups.

As Lowe goes on to indicate, this situation is common among voluntary associations of any kind, and although there have been occasional grass-roots rebellions against some members of this alleged 'self-perpetuating oligarchy', they have been infrequent and mostly ineffective. Nevertheless, by giving their personal views an aura of institutional legitimacy, this small group of people can obtain much greater publicity and command much greater attention than might otherwise be the case. There is an obvious danger that public opinion could be cynically manipulated by such tactics, but it is worth repeating here a point made in another context in Chapter 3 – that the resort to public rhetoric is often a sign of weakness in a pressure group, symbolic of a failure to obtain the desired result by more private means. In this regard the publicity which the environmental lobby has courted in recent years may merely have reflected its arrival on the political scene as a raw newcomer. It has managed to create a closely intimate relationship with only a few of the statutory agencies within the Department of the Environment, and many of these are politically marginal, not being in areas of party political controversy and possessing little money or power. Certainly, when it comes to effective lobbying tactics, environmentalists can only cast an envious gaze on the kind of influence which, say, the NFU enjoys within the Ministry of Agriculture.

The environmental lobby's influence has, however, increased considerably in recent years, particularly at the local level through the consultations which now take place between planning offices and amenity societies. This growing access to important areas of decision-making, together with the fact that, as we have seen, conservation policies often turn out to be regressively redistributive in their effects, has alerted a number of commentators to the possibility that the environmental lobby may be obtaining an undue and not entirely welcome influence over planning policies. This was the theme of David Eversley's polemical article 'Conservation for the Minority?' in the journal *Built Environment Quarterly* in 1974. Eversley bitterly attacked the irrational and indiscriminate resistance to change which he perceived in certain sections of the environmental movement and the selfish desire of some conservationists to sacrifice the living standards of the majority of the population in order to protect their own notion of environmental quality:

The catalogue is endless. Whenever there is a conflict engendered by the desire to create an asset which can bring higher living standards to the many, the few claim the power of absolute veto. Electric pylons bring relatively cheap electricity into homes where 40 years ago a 25-watt bulb was a luxury. Since the war, a million acres of land have been lost to agriculture (less than 2 per cent of the total stock of farm land), but perhaps 15 million more people now have a house of their own with a garden.

Eversley reserves much of his vitriol for the élitism which he believes to dominate the environmental movement:

A tiny minority of self-appointed arbiters of taste dictates what the living standard of the rest of us shall be. . . . One rapid glance at the composition of the official bodies which can prevent any plans for change by their edicts, the unofficial pressure groups which back them, the leading individual writers who monopolise the subject in the press, will show us who they are: the ever-present ancient establishment, the landed aristocracy, the products of Oxford and Cambridge, the landowners, the officer class, and, behind them, their hangers-on: the trendy academics with less pretensions to gentility who prove their club-worthiness by espousing these élitist views . . . .They are continually mourning for a past where they, and they alone, had a right to tranquillity, the open countryside, distant coasts, spacious surroundings, plentiful and humble servants, and were in receipt of the safety and convenience provided by public expenditure. They loathe an extension of these privileges to the majority of the people.

In his Fabian tract *A Social Democratic Britain*, Anthony Crosland made a similar point, albeit in a more moderate tone:

To say that we must attend meticulously to the environmental case does not mean that we must go to the other extreme and wholly neglect the economic case. Here we must beware of some of our friends. For part of the conservationist lobby would do precisely this. Their approach is hostile to growth and indifferent to the needs of ordinary people. It has a manifestly class bias and reflects a set of middle and upper class value judgements. . . [for which] preservation of the *status quo* is the sole consideration.

Both these writers, Eversley in particular, are trying to jolt the reader out of the complacent assumption that what is good for 'the environment' (defined largely in landscape terms) must, by that fact alone, be good for everyone. Yet it is this plausible and beguiling assumption which the environmental lobby has used to such good purpose in spreading its influence in recent years.

Both Eversley (as former Chief Strategic Planner for the GLC) and Crosland (as Secretary of State for the Environment) may be depicted as scarcely impartial judges of the environmental lobby, since both have found themselves at the receiving end of the lobby's persistent political pressure. How far this has jaundiced their appreciation of environmentalism is difficult to say, since there are few systematic studies of environmental groups over the recent period in which they have gained so much in membership and influence. However, what little evidence is available gives some support to the charge of élitism – indeed it is doubtful whether many of the most influential organizations would wish to deny this since they are very self-consciously engaged in the preservation of quality. Certainly the membership of the environmental lobby comes overwhelmingly from the middle and upper classes, a fact on which all the investigators of the phenomenon agree. Lincoln Allison, for example, in his book *Environmental Planning*, shows that of the chairmen and secretaries of the county branches of the CPRE, 19 per cent are members of the House of Lords and 31 per cent are retired military officers. Moreover: 'An examination of the lists of branch subscribers shows a similar picture: a high proportion of JPs, double-barrelled names and members of historically important families. It would be wrong to describe CPRE activists as "middle-class", they are upper and upper-middle class in a large part.' Indeed, such is the respectability of the CPRE that most of its branches are in close and informal contact with their respective planning authorities and in some cases, as Allison demonstrates, the chief planning officer may even be a member. Significantly, Allison concludes that it is difficult 'to detach achievements of the group from achievements of certain planners or planning ideals', but nevertheless his own assessment is that the

CPRE, 'even conceived rigidly as an organisation, has had a great impact on planning'. The influence of the CPRE, as a recognizably 'establishment' organization may be unusually high, but as Philip Lowe has shown in a more wide-ranging study of local environmental groups, its social composition, ideology and political efficacy are by no means unique.

As we noted at the beginning of this chapter, there is nothing illegitimate about a pressure group pursuing its own sectional interest by every means at its disposal – that is what it exists to achieve. But the social profile of the environmental lobby does raise the question of political equity: does the political mobilization of environmentalists accentuate the already existing disparities between the favoured environments of the powerful and wealthy and the degraded environments of the deprived? On the evidence already presented in this book it would be surprising if this were not the case. We have already seen how farm workers, for example, have found it extraordinarily difficult to organize themselves, even over such bread-and-butter issues as wages and conditions. Inevitably it is the least prosperous and the least educated who find the greatest difficulty in protecting their interests, something which is almost true by definition but which also relates to deeply rooted political and cultural factors in British society as a whole. The environmental lobby is not, of course, responsible for this state of affairs, but the social composition of its membership, together with the values and aesthetic judgements which characterize its interpretation of 'the environment', can hardly be said to have enhanced the situation of those rural inhabitants already lacking political and economic power. The latter simply do not possess the resources, financial or otherwise, to challenge these assumptions or to organize their own 'participation' in the statutory planning process. The field has therefore been left clear for a particular and partial definition of environmentalism to dominate public discussion and to act as a legitimate influence over political decision-making, while other, equally valid, viewpoints remain in danger of being unheard or ignored because of the inability of those at the bottom of the social scale to organize and promote their views.

This is most clearly apparent in the way in which the environmental lobby has annexed the notion of 'national heritage'. Appeals to 'the nation' are frequently used to legitimate policies which are otherwise quite explicitly sectional and élitist in their aims. Environmental groups rarely present their arguments in terms of a sectional demand, but prefer to employ an idiom of *national* benefit which encompasses all social groups. The most beautiful areas of the countryside are therefore to be preserved 'for the benefit of the nation' – a clear echo of the aristocratic concept of stewardship. This enables the values which underlie environmentalism to be presented in a form which appears to be disinterested. Yet on closer inspection this invocation of the national good quickly disappears, for it embodies an appeal to a certain kind of cultural excellence believed to be possessed by only a few discerning individuals. As Philip Lowe remarks: 'Thus we see built into much preservationist thought an ambivalence: preservation for the nation, but not necessarily for the public.' Indeed 'the public', regarded as unappreciative and philistine, represents a *threat* to this 'national heritage'. Thus we find Octavia Hill designating the National Trust as '. . . men and women who should be free from the tendency to sacrifice such treasures to mercenary considerations, or to vulgarise them in accordance with popular cries – should be, in fact, those to whom historic memories loom large, also love the wild bird, butterfly and plant, who realise the *national* value of hill slope lighted by sun or shadowed by cloud'.

This represents a persistent theme in the ideology of the environmental lobby – the appeal to an abstract ideal of 'the nation' whose values are embodied in the cultural choices of an élite minority. The abstract ideal is then used to justify the preservation of the countryside *from* 'the nation' in its less palatable reality – 'the public', 'the tourists', 'the masses'. At best such a juxtaposition leads to an uneasy accommodation between élitist values and populist rhetoric, but where difficult decisions have to be made the latter always gives way to the former. For example, Sylvia Law, Principal Planner for the GLC, has associated conservation with 'the centuries of literature, painting and music [that] seem to have become part of our national [*sic*] consciousness'. Although she warns of the danger of 'extremist views', she also argues, in a candid if somewhat alarming statement from a planner, that 'we must continue to affirm by faith if not by research' the protectionist argument. Undoubtedly many environmentalists would agree with this kind of statement, for in the last analysis this brand of environmentalism is a gut feeling rather than a calculated political stance. The more dogmatic aspects are rarely revealed because they are subtly obscured by annexing the 'national heritage', thereby successfully hiding the less altruistic motives which lurk just beneath the surface of the argument.

All of this suggests that the well-intentioned attempts to increase public participation in planning will fail to reverse the socially regressive tendencies which rural planning has manifested since the war. The way in which participation has worked out in practice has only served to benefit further the already influential upper and middle-class representation in the planning process and it has also made any attempt to redress this imbalance appear less democratic and therefore less easy to justify politically. The popular appeal of environmentalism in the 1970s does not augur well for a reversal of these trends, nor is it likely, in view of the increasing middle-class population of rural England, that such a reversal will be politically feasible. There must be some doubt over whether the wider social implications of environmentalism will be recognized and considered. Many environmentalists still claim to be 'non-political', a view which, as this chapter has tried to show, must be regarded with some scepticism. The debate over environmentalism and the countryside is in reality a deeply political one, revealing issues which are the very stuff of politics: distributional justice; individual freedom *versus* a planned allocation of resources; the impact of science and technology on society; the defence of private property rights; the expansion of individual choice and the satisfaction of social needs. Beneath the conflict over 'the environment' there is therefore a much deeper conflict involving fundamental political principles and the kind of society we wish to create for the future. To sanitize these competing ideologies and utopias by arguing that they lie outside the realm of political discussion is both to trivialize politics and to obscure the true significance of the issues involved. Until this inherently political dimension is at least acknowledged then attempts to construct rational solutions to the very complex problems relating to the rural environment will continue to be thwarted.

7 English rural society: retrospect and prospect

At this point we must begin to draw together the separate threads of the analysis presented so far in this book. This is an important task because the fabric of rural life does not divide neatly into the sections implied by the previous six chapters and nor do the inhabitants of rural England experience their daily lives in this compartmentalized fashion. It is, however, a somewhat hazardous exercise, since in reality rural England still presents the much celebrated 'patchwork quilt' of people, places, activities and environments which almost defies summary and certainly renders any simplistic generalization impossible. Finding a way through this constantly changing, almost kaleidoscopic structure is not, therefore, a simple matter, for in considering each aspect of rural society in detail it is easy to lose sight of rural England as a totality and of how issues relating to landownership, farming, the village community and the rural environment are ultimately related to each other and to broader aspects of contemporary English society as a whole. But find a way through it we must if we are to gain some overall perspective on current social changes in rural England and with it some inkling of the likely direction of future trends. So first it is necessary to review the material contained in the previous chapters by placing particular emphasis upon the links between the many facets of rural life hitherto considered separately.

It has been a major theme of this book that in order to understand the nature of social change in rural England it is necessary to begin with an examination of the rural and particularly the agricultural economy. This is not to argue that the many changes which have occurred in rural life in recent years can only be considered in economic terms, for this is patently not true. However, it is an argument which continues to place the production of food at the centre of rural life (together with associated manufacturing, processing and service activity) and which sees many of the observed changes in rural England as being related, either directly or indirectly, to changes in the system of agricultural production. It has therefore been possible to discern a unity in the general direction of change in rural areas, even though there have been considerable variations in timing and extent. Since the Second World War, whatever the short-term fluctuations, the state has implemented the urban demand for cheap (by historical standards) and plentiful food, while simultaneously offering the farmer the guaranteee of stability and, for the efficient producer, profitability. The state has also acted as midwife to what has become known as the second agricultural revolution – the transformation of the technology of food production and the many social changes which have flowed from this. England's farmers have been granted the conditions under which they could embark upon a programme of increasing productivity and cost-efficiency which has been unmatched virtually anywhere in the world. The consequences of this are all around us in rural England today. Farms have become fewer, larger and more specialized. The rationalization of agriculture has forced more and more small farmers out of business and increased the concentration of production among the very largest farming enterprises which have remained. We have witnessed the rise of the agribusinessman.

As we have seen, these changes have not brought about the disappearance of the small farmer, although they have made his situation increasingly precarious. Instead there has been a slow but steady polarization of farm businesses, with the larger units formed by amalgamation or purchase cornering the lion's share of production, while those which do not expand are becoming gradually marginalized. Nevertheless, the state has taken care to ensure that the rate of attrition of small farms should not become too severe, particularly in areas, such as the uplands, where they are heavily concentrated. Elsewhere the small farmer has survived by virtue of his tenacity and his adaptability, but circumstances have generally been against him. The common observation that 'there will always be a place for the small farmer' is undoubtedly true as it stands for there will always be highly idiosyncratic forms of production with which the bigger producers cannot be bothered, but increasingly there will be little direct competition between them. An analogy may be made with retail shopping where supermarkets have generally superseded the family-run corner shop, but where small businesses survive by specializing in forms of trading outside the ambit of department stores and supermarket chains. A similar situation is emerging in agriculture. It is noticeable that those sectors which have undergone the most profound technological transformations – most notably poultry and cereals production – already exhibit the highest incidence of concentration and offer the least hope of successful competition for the small farmer. The spread of this tendency throughout the remainder of agriculture is inhibited only by technological obstacles, a state-inspired safety net and the ability of the small farmers themselves to hang on.

The small farmer has traditionally provided an awkward dilemma for agricultural policy-makers, who have always defined their task in narrowly economic terms. An economically 'rational' policy would hasten his demise, but enough rural constituencies have been dominated by small farmers to render this a dubious proposition for politicians of all parties. In addition the plight of the small farmer has introduced the otherwise neglected problem of the social implications of post-war agricultural policy. Here there is a quite startling contrast between the undoubted success of this policy in terms of its stated goals (the expansion of home production, the increase in cost-efficiency, the maintenance of a prosperous agriculture) and its mostly deleterious *social* effects on the countryside in either depopulating rural areas at an even faster rate than hitherto or polarizing them socially. Such polarization may occur between the expanding large producers and the marginalized smaller ones, between both of these and rural workers who suffer inadequate service provision and, indirectly, between the local poor and affluent newcomers. These social effects have rarely been monitored, let alone built into the policy calculations of the Ministry of Agriculture, where the assumption that what is good for farmers must be good for the rural population as a whole has been perpetuated by a mixture of 'bureaucratic and commercial vested interest, self-justification and reluctant necessity', as one academic observer, T. E. Josling, has put it.

In the face of a good deal of evidence to the contrary it has taken three decades for this assumption to be questioned – and even now it remains a central tenet of faith. Thus, although the Ministry has recently appointed 'socio-economic advisers', with a remit to consider the wider social implications of agricultural change, it has done so only as an obligation under EEC policy. Perhaps a charitable view of their role would be to regard them as the 'do-gooders' of ADAS, the Ministry's advisory service – tolerated, but ignored when the tough decisions have to be made. In the early days, at least, most were ex-ADAS advisers sent out to grass, already steeped in the Ministry's conventional wisdom and at something of a loss over what their function should be; even now few have received any training in subjects other than agriculture or agricultural economics. They therefore tend to accept the view that the vitality of English rural society can be measured by the prosperity of English farmers.

Since farmers comprise a varying but significant proportion of the rural population there is, of course, a grain of truth in this proposition. But by no means all sections of the rural population have benefited equally from post-war agricultural policy and, as we have already seen, some have been *relatively* disadvantaged. The small producer might therefore beg to differ from the conventional view – and so might the farm worker and his wife, the environmentalist, the unemployed rural school-leaver and even the young couple on the waiting list for a rural council house. As earlier chapters in this book have attempted to demonstrate, it is possible to trace a chain of events from the political economy of modern agriculture to aspects of rural social change which ostensibly have no connection with agricultural policy matters at all. Yet the formulation of agricultural policy has mostly ignored the possible social consequences and at best been indifferent to them. To a large extent this has been the result of a division of labour within the government and the Civil Service which has allowed the Ministry of Agriculture to respond to a clear and unambiguous demand to reduce the cost of food production, while other departments, both locally and nationally, have been left to mop up the social consequences. Moreover the urban majority of the population has shown little interest in rural change except in its most visual aspects – tractors and combine harvesters replacing horses, the disappearance of hedgerows, etc. – as long as food has remained cheap. They too have remained largely indifferent to the *social* problems of rural areas, particularly as their perception has often been clouded by misplaced sentiment. As long as agricultural policy was, literally, delivering the goods, what was happening to the fabric of life in the countryside could be complacently over-looked.

As far as the formulation of agricultural policy in the immediate post-war period was concerned, it is doubtful whether any serious consideration was ever given to its possible social implications in the countryside, for all its encouragement of rapid technological change. This was because of its essentially retrospective foundations, built upon the contrasting experiences of agricultural depression during the interwar years and the need to maximize food production at almost any cost during the Second World War. The invocation of one or the other could always be relied upon to silence any critic, whether from within the farming industry or outside. The affluence of succeeding decades also ensured that the cost of agricultural support never intruded into the consciousness of the taxpayer and was therefore not too closely examined. Even when the result was chronic overproduction or the 'feather-bedding' of barley barons, the consumer generally benefited from lower prices and the propor-tion of public expenditure devoted to agriculture was so small that the extra revenue required was hardly noticed. During the 1970s, however, the political climate surrounding agriculture has changed quite dramatically. Entry into the EEC has switched the burden of agricultural support from the taxpayer to the consumer and this, together with the general inflation in the British economy during this decade, has ensured that the cost of food production has become once more a hot political issue. Now that the cost of overproduction is borne directly by the consumer resentment has grown over the support of 'inefficient' farmers, whether at home, or, more often, on the continent. The purely defensive aspects of agricultural policy have come under increasing political pressure with the main emphasis of recent debate being on the need to protect consumers rather than producers. This has undoubtedly strengthened the political hand of the large-scale producers still further, for they can point to their greater cost-efficiency and potential for expansion by virtue of further hefty injections of capital investment. Such a political reaction to inflation, however, continues to be discussed with little or no consideration for what the future of English rural society will look like as a result.

In general terms the most likely future projection is an acceleration of already existing trends. The degree of concentration of production on larger farms is likely to increase and agriculture will continue to become more capital-intensive. Farming will continue its progression towards a rationally calculated, scientifically based system of food manufacture, becoming increasingly indistinguishable from other industries. Farmers, in turn, will become more and more constrained to maximize their profits as they attempt to maintain their incomes and accumulate the capital necessary to adopt the technological innovations which ensure continuing low-cost profitable production. The factor which agricultural economists cryptically refer to as '*x*-efficiency' – the tendency to follow the orthodox rules of profit maximization rather than seek other rewards – will therefore continue to improve. The education and training of farmers will continue to advance in order to take account of these changes, so that in these and other important respects farmers will be drawn closer to the prevailing pattern of entrepreneurial behaviour found in other industries. The gradual 'disenchantment' of agriculture – the replacement of intuition by calculation and the elimination of the mysteries of plant and animal husbandry by exposing them to scientific appraisal – will therefore continue apace. In more tangible terms it is possible to foresee the further reduction of the agricultural labour force, and with it the reduction, other things being equal, of employment opportunities in rural areas. Without the introduction of new employment into the countryside the tendency for rural villages to become commuter dormitories or weekend retreats – already well advanced – will increase.

Such a scenario can be constructed by projecting existing developments a little way into the future. Much more difficult to assess is the likely outcome of current structural changes in agriculture which have had only a tangential relationship to explicit policy objectives. The most important example of this concerns recent changes in landownership, particularly the intervention of the City institutions. It is now generally accepted by agricultural economists that some of the chief beneficiaries of post-war agricultural policy have been landowners (who, as Chapter 2 indicated, include a large proportion of farmers). As Josling has pointed out in a review of agricultural policies in developed countries:

The predominant conclusion is that land, as the input least elastic in supply, gains the most in per unit returns, and hence in the asset price of the stock from which land services are obtained. Though this may not hold for individual farm programmes, and may be modified over time by the availability of land-saving technology, the impact of these conclusions has now been incorporated into the conventional wisdom of farm politics.

In other words, sustained state intervention in agriculture has not only guaranteed the incomes of efficient producers, but has enhanced the investment value of agricultural land. As was discussed in Chapter 2, the inflation in land prices has increased the liability of owner-occupying farmers and other private landowners to Capital Gains Tax and Capital Transfer Tax – systems of taxation introduced with non-agricultural objectives in mind and with, apparently, little thought for their possible agricultural consequences. It is the marginal farmer who can best appreciate the contradictions in policy which this situation reflects, for he is regarded by the Ministry of Agriculture as inefficient and unable to make an adequate living from farming, while the value of his capital assets enables the Treasury to define him as a rich man. 'Better off dead than alive' is often his embittered summary of this predicament.

It is precisely this potential for capital growth rather than income-bearing yield which has attracted the institutional investors, however. Although, as we have seen, institutional investment in agricultural land is by no means a new phenomenon, the nature and scale of recent involvement is pregnant with a wide range of possibilities for the future conduct of rural life. There seems little reason to suppose that the City institutions will withdraw from landownership even if changes in CTT were to be undertaken. On the best-quality land their involvement is rapidly becoming an important one and unless the whole direction of post-war policy is to be reversed and decisive external intervention in the agricultural land market is to ensue (both unlikely propositions) institutional landholding is much more likely to increase than to decline. This alone will give a greater role to the agribusinessman and hasten the rationalization of the agriculture industry. On most holdings, however, day-to-day control will remain in the hands of the farmer with the institutions simply taking over the capital value of the land and using a proportion of this to provide new investment in fixed assets. At present only a small fraction of the land is actually farmed by the institutions, although how long this will remain the case is uncertain. As we noted in Chapter 2, a great deal has been made of the remoteness and impersonality of institutional control, but institutional involvement has also brought advantages in the form of new investment, a career structure for employees on City-run farms and opportunities for expansion for the ambitious, progressive farmer. The economic case for institutional ownership has been grudgingly conceded; critics now tend to fall back on the allegedly iniquitous social consequences of City control, although these are usually overstated and the merits of local patronage exaggerated almost beyond recognition by a mixture of nostalgia and wishful thinking. It seems quite likely in any case that economic pressures will lead the traditional landowner to adopt a managerial style more akin to that of the City institutions, while the latter, anxious to preserve a responsible image among their investors, may not be averse to a little local patronage as an inexpensive form of public relations.

Certainly there is little evidence to suggest that farms owned or run by the City institutions are unpopular as employers. The older farm worker would possibly regret the absence of a 'gaffer' with whom he could talk on a personal basis, and for whom neither a manager nor an agent may be an adequate substitute. The younger generation of farm workers are less likely to be concerned by the loss of a personal touch, however. Instead they appreciate the higher rates of pay, better working conditions, more modern machinery and better prospects for promotion on the larger farms, whose company structure – whether City-backed or otherwise – can sometimes offer a career ladder frequently entirely absent elsewhere. Indeed the intervention of outside capital in agriculture and the formation of extremely large farming units which has often accompanied this process offer new hope – possibly the only hope – to the young, ambitious and highly trained recruit to the industry. For as a factor of production labour has not fared as well as land in the period since the war. The increase in production may have increased the demand for land and therefore (given a fixed or even declining supply) have considerably raised its price, but almost the reverse situation has applied to farm labour, particularly hired labour. Demand has been reduced drastically because of mechanization and other technological changes and although the supply has also fallen it has not done so in sufficient quantity to provide a sustained relative increase in farm wages. As we saw in Chapter 4, the wages gap between agriculture and industry has widened steadily since the war, despite the need to attract a more highly skilled and highly trained labour force.

Given the continuing fall in the demand for labour it seems unlikely that any dramatic improvement in the relative position of the farm worker will occur in the near future, but with an ageing labour force the long-term position is more uncertain.

It is clear, however, that in the future hired labour will be even more concentrated on the largest enterprises providing the bulk of agricultural output. Because mechanization has had the effect of increasing the skill level demanded of farm workers, rather than de-skilling the job as has so often occurred in other industries, this need not necessarily involve any loss of job satisfaction and there may be benefits in terms of better pay and conditions. Thus, although the severe social stigma which is now attached to working on the land will continue to deter large numbers of school-leavers from seeking employment in agriculture, these larger enterprises may offer a more attractive proposition, always assuming that farming employers can offer a more enlightened attitude to their workers. The great imponderable, however, is the continuing rate of technological change. If the price of skilled labour becomes too high and if these large farming companies can tap suitable capital resources for investment, then automation cannot be far behind, at least on arable farms. This is a pattern already emerging in the United States (especially in California) and the technology for computer-controlled tractors and harvesting equipment is already available, albeit at what is currently a prohibitively high cost. Such considerations must obviously remain a matter for speculation. Nevertheless, there are enough innovations which are already waiting to be further utilized here and now, and enough farmers continuing to hoard elderly workers who will not be replaced when they retire to give a further push to the 'drift from the land' in the immediate years to come. The relative poverty of the farm worker is unlikely to be relieved under these circumstances.

All of these predictions flow from the assumption that the basis of post-war British agricultural policy will remain unchanged in the future. This seems a reasonable assumption in view of the fact that all the political pressure to change the Common Agricultural Policy is to push the structure of agriculture even further, and more quickly, down this road. The CAP's method of financing agricultural production has so increased the visibility of farm support programmes to the consumer that the marginal, inefficient producer is now regarded, rightly or wrongly, as a stubborn and irrational obstacle to lower food prices. During a period of high inflation the pressure has been particularly strong to force farmers to increase their cost-efficiency so that the population as a whole can benefit through a fall in food prices as a result of modern farming methods. There is little or no publicly expressed desire to make farms smaller, more labour-intensive and less productive. Instead there is now a general recognition that the accumulation of surpluses in the EEC will only be finally removed if farm prices are so low that the less efficient producers are forced out of existence and output is concentrated on those farms with the necessary capital resources to increase productivity and yields still further. This will require a significant drop in the number of both farmers and farm workers within the industry, yet the social costs arising from a politically popular reform of the CAP have barely been considered in the public debate which has arisen since Britain entered the EEC.

The only sustained and articulate opposition to this trend has come from the environmental lobby, which has not only been highly critical of the effects of modern agricultural practice on the ecology of the countryside, but has also called into question some of the basic assumptions of agricultural policy – such as its measure of 'efficiency' – and presented an apocalyptic vision of the future if current developments are allowed to continue. The most serious indictment concerns the contribution of modern agriculture to the depletion of energy resources by its increasing reliance upon petro-chemicals. Agriculture, it is then argued, will fall foul of the predicted world energy crisis of the mid-1980s. This argument has a reasonably sound, although controversial, empirical basis and the fact that modern agriculture is a net consumer of energy when it ought to be a net producer may well produce some unforeseen problems in the long run. Clearly an acute energy crisis is a factor which could over-turn all the commonly held assumptions about the future of British agriculture (and not only agriculture). However, the proportion of petrochemical production used on Britain's farms is sufficiently small, and the likelihood of agriculture being given priority in any system of allocation so great, that only moderate adjustments ought to be necessary – a small reversal of the trend towards special-ization, perhaps, though not necessarily any reduction in scale. A brief rehearsal of this situation could be observed in 1973–4 following the Arab oil embargo, the formation of OPEC and the rise in oil prices. The inflation in the price of fertilizers, pesticides and other oil-based farm inputs was certainly severe, yet the basic direction of agricultural change has remained. There is a long way to go before the oil crisis reverses current trends in agricultural production, before tractors are allowed to rust as farmers return to using horses and before food surpluses in Europe are replaced by shortages.

The most likely future is therefore 'more of the same' – the continuation and extension of the kinds of changes which we have observed in agriculture since the war. The numbers of both farmers and farm workers will continue to decline and, although many small farms will survive, the industry will be dominated, in terms of both output and hired manpower, by a comparatively small number of very large farms, many of which will emerge under the aegis of outside capital investment. It is to the wider social implications of these purely agricultural changes that we can now turn, for as we have seen in the previous two chapters, the growing presence of a non-agricultural population in the countryside provides a new set of social conditions with which the farming population has been forced to come to terms. This has often been a somewhat painful process. Yet ironically it has been largely brought about by changes within agriculture – most notably the drift from the land – as well as by the rising affluence of the population and improved forms of private transportation. The presence of this sizeable new element in the rural population means, however, that the direction of future social change in rural England cannot be reduced to that of agriculture alone. We also need to look at the demands and aspirations of the newcomers to the countryside and at the changing nature of the relationship between the rural population as a whole and the remainder of contemporary English society.

Rural England: polarization and eclipse

The outflow of labour from agriculture has brought about some radical and decisive changes in the social life of the English village. Few villages these days contain a population which is solely, or even predominantly, dependent upon agriculture in order to earn a living. As we saw in Chapter 5, the village as an occupational community, centred upon farming, has therefore declined. This transformation has occurred within a single generation in most rural areas and has been so rapid and far-reaching that it is not surprising that it has received so much attention from writers and commentators on English rural life. Most of these observations have been elegiac in tone, concerned to document the 'decline of the English village' and enunciate the last rites over any lingering 'community spirit'. As we have seen, whether the rural village has indeed declined as a vigorous community is something of a moot point and one which is ultimately dependent upon the value judgements of the individual concerned: it all depends upon what is meant by 'community'. In this respect the debate about the quality of life in rural England has paralleled the arguments concerning the landscape changes wrought by modern farming methods, where an objective standard of 'beauty' has proved as elusive as that of 'community' and where even quite widely held judgements can be regarded as ultimately a matter of personal aesthetic taste. It has, perhaps, been the very subjective basis of these assessments as much as the intrinsic importance of the issues which has caused so many words to be written about them and which has allowed the arguments for and against these changes to continue for so long and yet be so inconclusive.

A more worrying aspect of this public discussion is that by concentrating on the more subjectively perceived aspects of rural change it has tended to obscure some of the underlying objective realities. For example, although the appreciation of changes in the rural landscape are dependent upon aesthetic judgements, they also have objectively measurable effects in their impact upon the rural ecology. If the removal of a hedgerow or a copse involves the destruction of a unique wildlife habitat, that is something which is objectively calculable: it either is or is not unique; it either will or will not be destroyed. Although the *value* which we place on this destruction is not, of course, an objective matter, at least the precise ecological consequences are. In a similar fashion the long and inconclusive discussion over whether there has or has not been a decline of 'community' in the English village has tended to obscure some of the underlying, objectively assessable changes. This is not to say that the subjective feelings of rural inhabitants are unimportant or should be disregarded; but it is a plea for a little more balance and a good deal more realism in this discussion. For it *is* possible to identify in a reasonably objective manner the important social changes which have occurred in rural England over the last three decades. Indeed the two most important changes are quite obvious, despite not having always been granted the attention which they have deserved. The first concerns the extensive social polarization which has occurred in the rural population since the war, between what is by now an affluent majority (of both newcomers *and*, in many cases, local farmers and landowners) and a poor and *relatively* deprived minority. The second major social change involves the gradual absorption of rural life into the mainstream of English society as a whole. The autonomy and distinctiveness of rural life have gradually but progressively been eclipsed by nationally inspired social, economic and political developments. This has not only narrowed the gap between 'rural' and 'urban' life-styles, but has made it increasingly difficult to understand recent discontinuities in rural life by examining only the indigenous sources of social change.

The social polarization of the countryside has been a slow but inexorable process since the end of the Second World War. Within agriculture the large-scale landowner and farmer has generally benefited at the expense of the small marginal producer and the farm worker. At the same time a stark contrast has arisen in most villages between a comparatively affluent, immigrant, ex-urban middle class and the rump of the former agricultural population tied to the locality by their (low-paid) employment, by old age and by lack of resources enabling a move. The former group lives in the countryside mostly by conscious choice (and this includes the majority of farmers and landowners) and has the resources to overcome the problems of distance and access to essential services. The latter group, by contrast, has become increasingly trapped by a lack of access to alternative employment, housing and the full range of amenities which the remainder of the population takes for granted. While there can be little doubt that the material conditions of the rural poor, the elderly, the disabled and other deprived groups have undergone a considerable improvement in absolute terms since the war (in the sense that they are better fed, better housed, better clothed and better educated), in relative terms they have encountered little improvement and in many cases in recent years an alarming deterioration. Their poverty is often submerged – socially, and even literally, invisible – and there is a danger that, as rural England increasingly becomes middle-class England, their plight will be ignored and their needs overlooked.

In the previous two chapters an outline has been given of this polarization process through a brief examination of planning policies in the areas of housing, employment and land use. A similar process can be observed, however, covering the whole range of social services, especially health services, and even the provision of apparently mundane amenities from shops to sewerage. The affluent sections of the rural population can, of course, overcome any problems which arise by stepping into their cars and driving to the nearest town, whereas the poor, the elderly and the disabled are particularly vulnerable to any decrease in the provision of local public and private services in rural areas, and especially of public transport. It therefore makes little sense any longer to contrast the poverty of rural areas with the prosperity of the towns, for the major divisions lie *within* the rural population between those in need and suffering multiple social deprivation and those who have benefited from living in the countryside in recent years and for whom access to a full range of services and amenities does not present a problem. Numerically it is the latter group which has consistently been in the ascendancy over the last thirty years and which has achieved a firm grasp on the levers of local political power. As a result the deprived section has found it increasingly difficult to obtain recognition of its requirements, let alone feel capable of diverting a larger proportion of resources in its direction. Many rural planning policies concerned with housing and employment have, either deliberately or unintentionally, discriminated against this group. Elsewhere the economics of public service provision have suffered from the fact that the newcomers to the countryside have possessed the means to be self-reliant. As a majority of ratepayers they have demonstrated an understandable reluctance to foot the rapidly rising bill on behalf of their less fortunate neighbours. All too often this is the political reality (and it seems unlikely to change) which underlies the neglect of council housing, public transport and the whole range of social, health and welfare services in rural areas.

During a period of general stringency in public expenditure the pressure to preserve only those services which 'pay' – that is, are self-supporting – has become increasingly strong. In a paper entitled 'Rural Settlement Policy: Problems and Conflicts', John Ayton, a planner with Norfolk County Council, has examined the social implications of these policies for the rural population in his county. Ayton states that:

The opportunities for change in the rural situation are constrained and influenced by the existing physical infrastructure, in terms of the settlement pattern, systems of public utilities and communications networks, and the resources available for modifying it. While it is difficult to anticipate the level of financial resources that will be available, it is clear that they will, for some time, be limited, and planning policies must be framed within the context of what is feasible, or reasonably likely. Those services which are financed from the rates (e.g. education, highways, sewerage, water) will be much more of a constraint than those which are 'self supporting' and budgeted nationally (e.g. electricity, gas, telephones). Investment choices and priorities must be made in those sectors which can influence policy-making in a more restrictive and specific way than the general aim of minimising public expenditure.

This is an interesting comment, albeit presented with a public servant's tact, on local decision-making in a county which is by no means politically atypical for a rural area. What, one wonders, would have happened to rural electrification had it been left in the hands of local ratepayers? Be that as it may, Ayton goes on to discuss the policy options within these constraints and their impact upon individuals and local communities. For the relatively deprived section of the rural population it provides a depressing, though instructive, glimpse of what occurs when their needs are discounted in favour of lower rates. In order to place Ayton's data in some perspective, it is important to realize that 66 per cent of Norfolk villages are below 500 in population and 44 per cent below 300, while at the other extreme only 11 per cent are over 1000. As Ayton points out:

It is the small size of the average village that is critical in terms of the services and facilities that can be expected in each one. Studies carried out by the Planning Department of Norfolk County Council have identified critical thresholds related to various services. For example, at the 300–500 population level, it is estimated that the village can support a shop, a pub and a school with between 30 and 50 pupils. But a primary school with 100 pupils, a fairly economic level, requires a support population of 1000, while a 'middle' school of 240 pupils requires a population of 4000. Each doctor has to have at least 2000 patients and so a practice of three doctors needs a support population of about 6000. A regular surgery seems to be viable only where a village population exceeds 1800. A district nurse is provided for 3000 population and chemists are provided on the basis of a 4000 to 4500 population catchment.

In a rural county like Norfolk this places the location of many of these services at some considerable distance, and therefore cost, from many of those who need them. Although Ayton is simply bowing to economic realities here, it is worth pointing out that, in the case of public services, these 'realities' are in principle (though, one suspects, increasingly rarely in practice) politically negotiable. Within the context of existing rural politics, however, Ayton's conclusions are inevitable: to concentrate service provision in the largest villages, 'backed by programmes to maintain reasonable social services in settlements not selected (e.g. mobile libraries, health visitors, meals-on-wheels and public transport)'. The individual must make an informed choice between 'a small village [and] direct access to services – he cannot get both together'.

To the affluent rural ratepayer, whose opinions carry considerable weight in County Hall, this seems an entirely rational solution. Not only is the cost of service provision held down or even reduced, but by taking advantage of economies of scale it may even be possible to avoid needless underutilization and improve the range of services offered. For the same situation viewed from the perspective of the relatively deprived we can turn to an account of the Suffolk village of Sudbourne, given by the journalist Philip Norman in an article entitled 'Is There Life After Death?' In Sudbourne the nearest shop and post office is two miles away. It has no school and the nearest accident and maternity hospital is in Ipswich, twenty miles away. Norman documents the increasing isolation of those unable to use private transport:

There was a different village here. It exists now only in clues . . . School Road, Hospital Road, lead one blandly, each to a cul-de-sac of distance and forest edge. The school has become a private house, its Gothic class-room windows shortened, its teacher's quarters severed and lately sold to a barrister from London. Hospital Road divulges only four fir trees in a clump, the scene of fire. There was once a shop, they say, at the Red House. Its vanished window haunts it still in a shape of paler bricks. Inside the telephone kiosk a plaque informs the user he is speaking from 'Sudbourne Post Office and Stores'. Looking out, he sees a white housefront, a new double garage, a pale blue, exclusive-looking door.

The Post Office shut down three years ago . . .

The bus timetable, fixed to a wall outside the Chequers, is like a gauge of isolation. It tries to be cheerful, with its promise of money-saving excursions, yet wherever the name Sudbourne occurs in its columns, one might deduce an almost malign wish to keep the village out of step with everywhere. The timetable ordains Woodbridge, 11 miles away, as the nearest town; Saxmundham, Leiston and Aldeburgh, all nearer, are inaccessible from Sudbourne by bus. The morning Ipswich service, calling at Sudbourne just before eight, reaches Woodbridge too late to catch a train. If you take the early evening bus, there is no getting back the same night. The full journey of an hour and threequarters . . . costs almost £1 each way. . . .

For all practical purposes Sudbourne depends on local authority transport, that modern form of charity. School buses take its children to Orford, Butley or Woodbridge. A mobile library calls on alternate Fridays, staying half an hour. Once a fortnight, a County Council minibus takes the elderly to Orford, to collect their pensions and enjoy a half hour's shopping in the metropolitan atmosphere of a Post Office, a sweetshop and Elliott's general store. Not even this conveyance has been able to deliver 83-year-old Mrs Daisy Knights to her house a quarter of a mile from Corner Farm.

Norman's article concentrates on the elderly, who have hardly 'chosen' to live in Sudbourne in any meaningful sense: they have been stranded there by three decades of rural social change and by growing public indifference to their plight. As Norman goes on to point out:

In Sudbourne, or any lonely village, passing some retired couple's bungalow, one can almost envy them their idyll, those faces that float in the big lounge window round a warm blue television screen. Old people, no less than young, seem wonderfully adaptable to the exigencies of life. When their local shops close down they simply go without. When their buses are withdrawn, they somehow struggle on. The world in their eyes is growing madder, more incomprehensible, more dangerous, yet they persistently keep alive, forming no lobbies, no pressure groups, not complaining, only grumbling, in voices they do not expect to be heeded . . . growing ever more disinclined to leave the one safe room, the one small fire, the screen that is their one release. So we abandon them, sentimentally, in semi-dark.

It is not only the elderly who have been abandoned in this way – sentimentally or otherwise. Similarly deprived groups – the poor, the unemployed, the sick and disabled – are also denied access to the services which they need. 'Choice' for them is a meaningless concept.

They lack the resources to convert their needs into demands, yet it is to demand rather than need that most rural public services respond. It is a vicious circle of deprivation which stands in marked contrast to prevailing perceptions of rural life. Indeed at a time when public attention has been focused on the problems of multiple deprivation in inner-city areas, a reminder is needed that on many of the official measures – lack of sanitation, overcrowding, housing waiting lists, etc. – rural areas score equally badly when considered on a *per capita* basis.

It is easy to overlook these problems amidst the general prosperity of contemporary rural England. The appearance of many villages suggests two-car families enjoying a life-style of comfortable affluence in their beautifully restored homes. The other face of rural England is more difficult to seek out since it is now less openly admitted. At least in the past when poverty was the norm the experience of deprivation was one that could be shared by the majority of the village population. But now poverty brings with it a sense of exclusion rather than mutuality. The social polarization of the countryside has enabled a life-style that was once only distantly and fleetingly observed to be encountered at first hand among the new inhabitants of 'their' village. The rural poor find, somewhat disconcertingly, that they and their needs are increasingly regarded as residual – or even unacknowledged. Publicly debated issues have moved on to problems in which they are denied the luxury of participating. They find that more attention seems to be given to the visual appearance of the countryside than to the standard of living of those who are employed in maintaining it; that greater concern is expressed over the effects of pesticides on butterflies than on farm workers. Their new minority status hardly lends itself to making a fuss, however, nor to the expectation that they can achieve any tangible change if they attempted to do so. Consequently their inclination is to 'make do', while the general public is given little reason to alter its image of a cosy and contented countryside.

All of this suggests that any striking improvement in the living standards of the rural poor will in the future, as in the past, be brought about by changes initiated nationally rather than locally. In other words reforms and innovations introduced on a national basis will continue to trickle down into rural areas, enabling their poorer inhabitants to gain twentieth-century comforts regarded as commonplace elsewhere – including among their richer neighbours. A by-product of this process will be the continuing incorporation of everyday life in the countryside into the general life-styles of modern English society and the consequent loss of a distinctive, semi-autonomous 'rural way of life'. This has occurred directly, through the arrival of an ex-urban population with a more cosmo-politan life-style and by the introduction of mass media of communi-cations – newspapers, radio, television – and with them the spread of a modern consumer society. But this slow decline in the unique qualities of rural life has also been created indirectly by the rural population having been towed along in the wake of the general rise in living standards over the past thirty years. Rowland Parker makes this point as the conclusion of his two-thousand-year history of the village of Foxton in Cambridgeshire, *The Common Stream*. Commenting on the post-1945 era, he writes:

Then, gradually at first but with ever-increasing momentum, came the social avalanche which swept away the last traces of 'village life' and transformed life for everybody, everywhere. For the first time in this book I am able to give credit to politicians and planners, and I do it unreservedly – for the 1944 Education Act and subsequent legislation which has brought about a huge expansion in secondary and higher education; for the Social Security plan which did more to abolish poverty in ten years than Poor Laws had done in four hundred years; for Town and Country Planning, Housing Authorities, Health Services, etc. All this, in conjunction with paid holidays, higher wages, cheaper travel, cars by the million, air-travel, television and a host of electrical gadgets in the home, this is what I mean by the avalanche that swept away 'village life'. There is no point whatever in talking any longer about 'village life' and 'town life'. It is just life.

While it is possible to disagree with his assessment of some of these items, his overall point is undoubtedly a valid one. Increasingly the conditions of life in Foxton, or in any other rural village, are not determined there, but nationally and even internationally. Yet this process has also contributed to an important paradox in modern rural life: the absolute improvement in living standards, which Parker indicates, but the relative widening of the gap between rich and poor over the same period.

With the poorer section of the rural population rendered increas-ingly socially invisible, public attention is likely to remain focused, as it has in recent years, upon disputes *within* the affluent majority –

most notably over broadly environmental issues. This is where nationally induced social change, involving increased leisure time and greater personal mobility, has run into conflict with changes in agricultural technology and other conditions of modern food production. As we have seen in the previous chapter, this conflict is not simply an irregular occurrence provoked by daytrippers and holidaymakers, but has been imported permanently into the countryside by the new adventitious village population. Here the political balance, which continues to weigh so heavily against the interests of the rural poor, begins to look rather different. For the first time farmers and landowners, who have traditionally held sway in rural politics, find their hegemony threatened. An articulate and affluent village population, which is dependent upon them for neither employment nor housing, has proved able and willing to voice its opposition to developments in modern agriculture which farmers have long regarded as their private preserve. As the previous chapter indicated, this conflict has manifested itself in a variety of ways, only loosely encompassed by the term 'environmentalism', and while some of these issues are in principle resolvable, given goodwill on both sides, others are not. The problem, despite what some farmers privately hope, will not simply fade away. Indeed the gradual coalescence of a nationally organized environmental lobby suggests that even the established political influence of the NFU and CLA over rural affairs may come under challenge.

At the present time, the most significant test of the relative political strength of the two groups involves attempts to bring agriculture under the control of town and country planning legislation. A number of intersecting influences are at work here. The environmental lobby argues that cherished landscape features in the countryside should be afforded the same protection, and be subject to the same notification procedures, as buildings of historical and architectural interest in towns. In the case of areas of particularly high landscape value environmentalists would wish to see a virtual embargo placed upon any change which will affect the visual aspects of the countryside. This argument is used particularly vigorously in defence of the National Parks, which is why the current test case in Exmoor, referred to in Chapter 6, is so important. The privileged position of agriculture under current planning legislation is strongly influenced by the conditions of wartime England where the drive to maximize home production at almost any cost was a *sine qua non* of national survival. A ubiquitous agriculture clearly made sense. Contemporary conditions are, however, very different. Entry into the EEC has produced a situation of apparently chronic surplus production. The future parameters of agricultural policy are likely to be set by notions of European rather than British self-sufficiency. It now makes sense economically and – bearing in mind the umbrage of consumers – politically to withdraw some marginal land from production, or at least not allow its productivity to be expanded, when the extra production will only be used to further enlarge existing surpluses. In other words, every acre no longer counts. We are no longer digging for victory and some of the marginal land could be released for other uses – including recreation.

Since the majority of the National Parks and other scenically valued areas contain mostly marginal agricultural land, there seems to be a happy coincidence here – and one which has not escaped the notice of a number of environmental organizations. Why they ask, should the taxpayer be asked to contribute to grants for, say, ploughing up Exmoor heathland and pay again for the disposal of the resulting surplus production? The NFU, with its members' livelihoods to protect, not surprisingly takes a different view. It points to the continuing need to expand home production in order to preserve the balance of payments and to preserve a productive potential in indigenous agriculture as a strategic measure. In the final analysis the NFU will demand generous payments for its members, either in the form of compensation for lost income or even redundancy payments. It will also attempt to minimize as far as it possibly can the scope of any resulting planning legislation which may impinge upon the farming industry. Sooner or later surely even the extraordinary lobbying powers of the NFU will meet their match in the combined pressure of environmentalists and consumers. But a fascinating battle will be fought out along the corridors of Whitehall and Brussels in the meantime, a battle on whose outcome will depend the fortunes of rural environmental groups up and down the country.

Such hard-nosed political considerations seem a long way from the idyllic vision of rural England with which we began this book. And yet this is an apt example on which to conclude. Not only has the environmental issue been dominant in the public discussion of rural change in recent years, but it provides an appropriate example through which to observe the complex interplay of attitudes and interests which lie just beneath the surface of contemporary rural life. From the resolution of these many and varied influences emerges the agriculture, the landscape and the type of rural society which exists around us today and which will emerge in the years to come. This, of course, should not prevent the vast majority of us from continuing to regard the English countryside as an artefact of incomparable natural beauty, as a place for rest and contentment, as an escape. Although we try to retain a precious, and increasingly fragile, image of rural England in our minds, in the long run there is little to be gained by falling prey to the fashionable nostalgia which surrounds rural life nor by lapsing into the meretricious clichés about 'natural orders' and 'organic communities'. Eventually our experience of rural England, whether we live in it or only look at it, can only be enriched by a realistic appraisal of the forces underlying change. In this way our enjoyment can be enhanced still further but, equally importantly, we can enter into a more rational discussion about how social change in rural England should be achieved and to which ends it should be directed.

Further reading

1 Rural England: encroachment and disillusion

The most sustained analysis of the countryside in English literature is to be found in Raymond Williams, *The Country and the City* (Chatto and Windus, 1973) which examines this theme in far more depth and subtlety than space has allowed here.

Ideas about landscape and the picturesque in the eighteenth century are examined in the first two chapters of John Barrell, *The Idea of Landscape and the Sense of Place, 1730–1840* (Cambridge University Press, 1972).

The work of landscape gardeners is also discussed in Edward Hyams, *The English Garden* (Thames and Hudson, 1964) and they are placed in a broader context in Edward Hyams, *The Changing Face of Britain* (Paladin, 1977).

However, no discussion of the changing landscape of England is complete without reference to Nan Fairbrother, *New Lives, New Landscapes* (Pelican, 1972).

Punch has long mined a rich vein of humour from our disillusion with rural realities. A representative collection is Alan Coren (ed.), *Punch in the Country* (Hutchinson, 1975) which contains many of Thelwell's acutely observed and marvellously funny cartoons.

The most well-known rural satire remains, however, Stella Gibbons, *Cold Comfort Farm* (Penguin, 1977), but an overlooked, if rather more ambiguous, novel on a related theme is Thomas Hinde, *The Village* (Hodder and Stoughton, 1965).

2 Broad acres

Historical accounts of landownership and landowners are more common than contemporary studies. The most authoritative is F. M. L. Thompson, *English Landed Society in the Nineteenth Century* (Routledge and Kegan Paul, 1963).

There are extended discussions of the gentlemanly ethic in W. L. Burn, *The Age of Equipoise* (Allen and Unwin, 1964), J. F. C. Harrison, *The Early Victorians, 1832–51* (Panther, 1973), and G. Best, *Mid-Victorian England, 1851–75* (Panther, 1973).

The London season is documented in Leonore Davidoff, *The Best Circles* (Croom Helm, 1973).

For a contemporary account of the aristocracy see Roy Perrott, *The Aristocrats* (Weidenfeld and Nicolson, 1968).

In keeping with the general reticence over landownership, recent studies are few and far between. A rare example is D. Sutherland, *The Landowners* (Blond, 1968).

Otherwise consultation of the specialist literature is necessary, such as Alan Harrison (ed.), *Farming, The Land and Changing Capital Taxation* (University of Reading, Department of Agricultural Economics, 1976).

The CLA is described in P. Self and H. Storing, *The State and The Farmer* (Allen and Unwin, 1962).

However, there are no extended accounts of the recent spending spree by the City institutions. This has been too recent to be included in the two companion volumes to this book, although each contains a discussion of land tenure: J. G. S. and F. Donaldson, *Farming in Britain Today* (Pelican, 1972) and Tristram Beresford, *We Plough the Fields* (Pelican, 1975).

Changing patterns of land use are considered in more detail in Chapter 6, but the splendidly iconoclastic work of Robin Best should also be cited here. For example: R. H. Best and F. J. Ward, *The Garden Controversy* (London University, Wye College, 1965); R. H. Best, 'The Changing Land-Use Structure of Britain', *Town and Country Planning*, vol. 44, no. 3, March, 1976; 'The Extent and Growth of Urban Land', *The Planner*, January, 1976; 'Agricultural Land Loss – Myth or Reality?' *The Planner*, January, 1977.

3   The farming industry

This chapter has dealt only briefly and in places superficially with a few major themes. A more comprehensive survey of British agriculture is provided by J. G. S. and F. Donaldson, *Farming in Britain Today* (Pelican, 1972), and A. Edwards and A. Rogers (eds.), *Agricultural Resources* (Faber, 1974).

The politics of agriculture is discussed in detail in Tristram Beresford, *We Plough the Fields* (Pelican, 1975).

Perhaps significantly there are no systematic accounts of agribusiness in Britain, but on the effects of agribusiness in the United States, see R. Merrill (ed.), *Radical Agriculture*, part II (Harper and Row, 1976), and Susan George, *How the Other Half Dies*, ch. 7 (Pelican, 1976).

4 The farm worker

The early history of the farm worker, especially his attempts to unionize, can be found in J. P. D. Dunbabin, *Rural Discontent in Nineteenth Century Britain* (Faber, 1974), E. J. Hobsbawm and G. Rudé, *Captain Swing* (Penguin, 1973), and P. L. R. Horn, *Joseph Arch* (Roundwood Press, 1971).

There is also a swashbuckling account of the trade union struggle in Reg Groves, *Sharpen The Sickle!* (Porcupine Press, 1948).

The most comprehensive studies of the daily life of the farm worker in the days of horses are to be found in the work of George Ewart Evans. For example: G. E. Evans, *Ask The Fellows Who Cut The Hay* (Faber, 1956); *The Horse in the Furrow* (Faber, 1960); *Pattern Under the Plough* (Faber, 1966); *Where Beards Wag All* (Faber, 1970). A vivid fictional account is Melvyn Bragg, *The Hired Man* (Coronet, 1977).

For contemporary appraisals see C. E. Heath and M. C. Whitby, *The Changing Agricultural Labour Force* (University of Newcastle Agricultural Adjustment Unit, 1970), J. E. Bessell, *The Younger Worker in Agriculture: Projections to 1980* (HMSO, 1972), and R. Gasson, *Mobility of Farm Workers* (University of Cambridge, Department of Land Economy, 1974).

The most authoritative survey of agricultural tied cottages is B. Irving and L. Hilgendorf, *Tied Cottages in British Agriculture* (Tavistock Institute, 1975).

5 Change in the village

For the development of the English village in broad historic perspective see W. G. Hoskins, *The Making of the English Landscape* (Penguin, 1970) and W. E. Tate, *The English Village Community* (Gollancz, 1967).

Many descriptions of the English village as an occupational community lose much of their value because they are drowned in a welter of nostalgia. However, the following are both readable and, as far as one can judge, accurate accounts: Flora Thompson, *Lark Rise to Candleford* (Penguin, 1973) and M. K. Ashby, *Joseph Ashby of Tysoe, 1859–1919* (CUP, 1961). See also the work of George Ewart Evans cited in the note to the previous chapter.

On the effects of urbanization see R. E. Pahl, *Urbs in Rure* (Weidenfeld and Nicolson, 1965); R. Crichton, *Commuter Village* (David and Charles, 1964); Clement Harris, *Hennage: A Social Structure in Miniature* (Holt, Rinehart and Winston, 1974); Peter Ambrose, *The Quiet Revolution* (Chatto and Windus, 1974). A more literary portrayal is Ronald Blythe, *Akenfield* (Penguin, 1969).

Useful summaries of the issues surrounding rural planning are to be found in R. J. Green, *Country Planning* (Manchester University Press, 1971) and G. E. Cherry (ed.), *Rural Planning Problems* (Leonard Hill, 1976).

The latter book contains a most useful paper by Alan Rogers on 'Rural Housing' and this problem is investigated further in Marilyn Rawson and Alan Rogers, *Rural Housing and Structure Plans* (London University, Wye College, 1976).

6   Environmentalism and the countryside

There is now a voluminous literature on environmentalism. Useful introductions include A. Warren and F. B. Goldsmith (eds.), *Conservation in Practice* (Wiley, 1974), T. O'Riordan, *Environmentalism* (Pion, 1976), and L. Allison, *Environmental Planning* (Allen and Unwin, 1975).

A lively journalistic account is S. Johnson, *The Politics of the Environment* (Tom Stacey, 1973).

Any consideration of agriculture and ecology must begin with Rachel Carson, *Silent Spring* (Penguin, 1965). A useful update is J. Lenihan and W. W. Fletcher (eds.), *Food, Agriculture and the Environment* (Blackie, 1975).

Recent changes in the rural landscape are considered in Nan Fairbrother, *New Lives, New Landscapes* (Penguin, 1972), and R. Westmacott and T. Worthington, *New Agricultural Landscapes* (HMSO, 1974).

Broader aspects of rural planning, including the gap between theory and practice, are dealt with in two excellent studies: P. Hall *et al.*, *The Containment of Urban England* (Allen and Unwin, 1973), and Joan Davidson and Gerald Wibberley, *Planning and the Rural Environment* (Pergamon, 1977).

The account of the environmental lobby presented in this chapter relies heavily on the work of Philip Lowe, especially P. Lowe, 'The Environmental Lobby', *Built Environment Quarterly*, vol. 1, 1975, pp. 73–6, 158–61, 235–8, and P. Lowe, 'Amenity and Equity: A Review of Local Environmental Pressure Groups in Britain', *Environment and Planning*, vol. 9, 1977, pp. 35–58.

Political aspects of environmentalism are considered in P. J. Smith (ed.), *The Politics of Physical Resources* (Penguin, 1975); R. Gregory, *The Price of Amenity* (Macmillan, 1971); R. Kimber and J. Richardson (eds.), *Campaigning for the Environment* (Routledge and Kegan Paul, 1974); Isabel Emmett, 'The Social Filter in the Leisure Field', *Recreation News Supplement*, July, 1971; Sylvia Law, 'Leisure and Recreation: Problems and Prospects', *Planning Outlook*, Summer, 1974; David Eversley, 'Conservation for the Minority?', *Built Environment Quarterly*, vol. 3, no. 1, 1974, pp. 14–15.

7   English rural society: retrospect and prospect

The broad sweep of agricultural change since the war is best considered in Tristram Beresford, *We Plough the Fields* (Pelican, 1975).

A more academic, and more broad-ranging, treatment is T. E. Josling, 'Agricultural Policies in Developed Countries: An Overview', *Journal of Agricultural Economics*, vol. 25, 1974, pp. 229–63.

John Ayton's paper is to be found in P. J. Drudy (ed.), *Regional and Rural Development: Essays in Theory and Practice* (Alpha Academic, 1976).

The account of Sudbourne is taken from Philip Norman, 'Is There Life After Death?', *Sunday Times Weekly Review*, 29 January, 1978. Some corroboration can be found in Ronald Blythe, *Akenfield* (Penguin, 1969).

An even broader sweep of rural change than has been possible in this book can be found in Rowland Parker, *The Common Stream* (Paladin, 1976).

Index